CLIL in Context
Practical Guidance for Educators

Fred Genesee and **Else Hamayan**

CAMBRIDGE
UNIVERSITY PRESS

CAMBRIDGE
UNIVERSITY PRESS

University Printing House, Cambridge CB2 8BS, United Kingdom

One Liberty Plaza, 20th Floor, New York, NY 10006, USA

477 Williamstown Road, Port Melbourne, VIC 3207, Australia

4843/24, 2nd Floor, Ansari Road, Daryaganj, Delhi – 110002, India

79 Anson Road, #06–04/06, Singapore 079906

Cambridge University Press is part of the University of Cambridge.

It furthers the University's mission by disseminating knowledge in the pursuit of education, learning and research at the highest international levels of excellence.

Information on this title: www.cambridge.org

© Cambridge University Press 2016

First published 2016

20 19 18 17 16 15 14 13 12 11 10 9 8 7 6 5 4 3 2

Printed and bound in Great Britain by CPI Group (UK) Ltd, Croydon CR0 4YY

A catalogue record for this publication is available from the British Library

ISBN 978-1-316-60945-3 Paperback

CONTENTS

Foreword: Peeter Mehisto   vii

Acknowledgements   ix

About the authors   x

ONE   **Introduction**   **1**

Bilingualism in the twenty-first century   2

A new approach to language instruction   5

Educational contexts   6

    Immersion (IMM)   8

    Education for immigrant and indigenous-language students (ILS)   10

    Foreign-language (FL) programmes   13

    International schools (INT)   16

Implementing CLIL in different language contexts   19

    How teachers plan instruction   21

    How teachers teach   24

    How teachers assess   25

Special features of the book   26

Definition of terms   26

TWO   **Key principles of CLIL**   **29**

1.   Additional-language instruction is more effective when integrated with content instruction   31

2.   Explicit and systematic language instruction is important   33

3.   Student engagement is the engine of learning   37

4.   Both languages should have equally high status   41

5.   The first language is a tool for additional-language learning   43

6.   Classroom-based assessment is critical for programme success   46

7.   All children can become bilingual   47

8.   Strong leadership is critical for successful dual-language teaching   50

Summary   54

THREE   **Snapshots of CLIL**   **55**

CLIL in IMM contexts   59

    Overview   59

Rationale   62

Inside an IMM classroom   63

CLIL in ILS contexts   65

Overview   65

Dual-language CLIL for minority-language students   66

Caveat   67

Rationale   68

Inside a DL-CLIL classroom   70

Monolingual CLIL for minority-language students   73

Rationale   73

Inside an ML-CLIL classroom   74

CLIL in FL contexts   76

Rationale   78

Inside an FL-CLIL classroom   78

CLIL in INT contexts   79

Summary   82

FOUR   **Planning for content and language integrated instruction**   **83**

Preparing school staff and the community for a new CLIL programme   84

Organising the curriculum and scheduling   90

CLIL programmes that aim for high levels of bilingualism:
IMM, ILS and INT contexts   94

CLIL programmes that do not aim for high levels of bilingualism:

FL-CLIL programmes   96

Independence of the FL curriculum   96

Pressure from international examinations   96

ILS and INT schools   97

Setting objectives   99

Primary objectives: Content and language   100

Content and language objectives in the four educational contexts   106

Secondary objectives   106

Cross-linguistic objectives   108

Cross-cultural objectives   110

General learning skills objectives   111

Secondary objectives in the four educational contexts   112

Three-phase lesson or unit planning   113

The preview phase   113

The focused-learning phase   114

The extension phase   114

Resources   116

   Human resources: Qualifications of teachers and administrators   116

   Professional development   117

   Material resources   119

Summary   120

FIVE   **Teaching content and language integrated lessons**   **125**

The preview phase   131

   Scaffolding   132

     Building on prior knowledge   133

     Building language   134

       Language use in the four educational contexts   135

     Using concrete referents   139

   Preview-phase activities   139

Focused-learning phase   143

   Paying attention to students' language   144

   Balancing direct instruction with discovery of concepts by students   146

   Useful activities during the focused learning phase   148

Extension phase   154

   Extension-phase activities   156

Materials   158

Summary   161

SIX   **Coordination and integration: The way we work together**   **163**

Coordination involving students   164

Coordination among CLIL staff   166

   Challenges   168

   Strategies for coordination   170

   Coordination across grade levels   173

Coordination between the CLIL programme and the rest of the school   173

Coordination outside of school   176

   How can students' families and their communities contribute to the

     learning process?   176

     The contributions approach   180

     The additive approach   181

       Participation of family and community in the school or classroom   182

     The transformation approach   183

   How can students contribute to their community?   184

     The social action approach   185

Extending activities into the community   185

Activities for extending the unit on renewable energy into the community   186

SEVEN   **Assessment in CLIL classrooms**   **191**

Getting started: Identifying your goals for assessment   192

Effective assessment   196

Unique aspects of assessment in CLIL classrooms   199

Alternative assessment tools   204

1.   Observation   205

2.   Portfolios   210

3.   Conferences   211

4.   Dialogue journals and learning logs   212

Student self-assessment   212

Tests   213

Test formats   216

Summary   219

EIGHT   **Summing up**   **221**

The eight key principles of CLIL: A checklist for implementation   222

Complete CLIL unit planning form: Renewable sources of energy   229

Last words: From CLIL students   236

References   239

Index   247

Foreword

Peeter Mehisto
(University College London, Institute of Education)

Fred Genesee and Else Hamayan call for *context-sensitive* CLIL. It is rare for a book on CLIL to help its readers navigate diverse prototypical contexts whilst also suggesting ways to shape those contexts so they better support student and teacher learning. In addition to helping readers understand the complexity of societal, organisational and professional relations in CLIL contexts, this book situates evidence-based and professionally well-grounded advice on pedagogy – the art of teaching and learning – in those diverse contexts. This is a welcome approach.

Content and Language Integrated Learning may seem like a simple concept but its implementation is far from self-evident. This is the case whether one is seeking to manage and shape CLIL contexts, or whether one is teaching or learning through the L2 in one of those contexts.

From a management perspective, CLIL is always embedded in its societal context, in the community and schools where it is offered, and involves diverse groups that will be affected by or that can affect CLIL delivery. In other words CLIL implementation is, to a greater or lesser extent, always, affected by its stakeholders, and CLIL always also affects its stakeholders. Moreover, the understandings and actions of stakeholders such as CLIL and non-CLIL students, parents, teachers, administrators and politicians always have the potential of interacting in unique ways to create their own constraints and opportunities. This book helps make many of those possible constraints and opportunities visible, and suggests practical steps that can be taken to address those constraints and make the most of the opportunities that CLIL has to offer.

From a pedagogical perspective, teaching and learning in CLIL contexts is not self-evident either. This book offers a rich store of ideas for scaffolding content and language learning, for fostering critical think-ing and conducting assessment with students who have limited language skills, for fostering enquiry-based learning, and for using translanguaging judiciously and making cross-linguistic and cross-cultural connections.

Genesee and Hamayan not only bring both of their particularly rich professional lifetimes of experience to this book but they have drawn in knowledge from diverse CLIL contexts from a substantial number of highly experienced and widely respected practitioners – teachers, pro-gramme and/or school directors, principals, coordinators and vice-prin-cipals, teacher trainers, and researchers. These individuals highlight key knowledge they have used to support CLIL implementation. This also includes sharing diverse challenges such as supporting students in making better use of their L1 in order to learn the L2 and through the L2, as well as the need to raise parental awareness of the valuable role that the L1 can play even when students are learning through an L2 and L3. More importantly, these personal perspectives offer explana-tions of how challenges have been addressed. They also describe some of the rather innovative approaches that have been used in different CLIL contexts (e.g. harnessing the power of drama, creating opportunities to foster the learning of multiple L1s, using self-evaluation to fuel pro-gramme development).

In the same spirit, *CLIL in Context: Practical Guidance for Educators* also provides snapshots from research in the form of short notes that distil key learning from research studies that are relevant to the given point(s) under discussion in the book. Importantly, this book also directs the reader to other resources including articles, books, learn-ing resources, websites, lesson planning tools, a programme evaluation tool, and a major word bank which will help readers access a broad and valuable knowledge base pertaining to CLIL.

Finally, as CLIL programmes are likely to be seen as different from mainstream monolingual education, they will inevitably be called on to navigate the fault lines of that difference. This will be difficult to do if CLIL is taking place behind one or a few closed classroom doors. CLIL calls for a more holistic approach – one that recognises that CLIL programmes exist in symbiosis with their contexts and stakeholders. Sustainable CLIL programmes surpass the capacity of any one teacher or educational institution working alone and, thus, invite cooperation with and learning from others. Welcome to the world of *CLIL in Context: Practical Guidance for Educators*.

Acknowledgements

We would like to thank Naomi Holobow for her very careful review of the manuscript – on several occasions; her assiduous editing has improved the final product greatly. We also owe a note of thanks for Peeter Mehisto for his insightful Foreword and his editorial feedback and Nancy Cloud for her many helpful suggestions. Special thanks to each of the individuals who provided Personal Perspectives on their professional experiences in dual language education and to the students who shared their personal reflections on life as a student learning through a second language; they have enriched the book immensely. Last, but not least, we would like to thank the staff at CUP and especially Paul Sloman for their patience and valuable advice throughout the preparation of this book.

About the authors

Fred Genesee is Professor Emeritus, Department of Psychology, McGill University. He has conducted research on alternative forms of dual-language education for both language-minority and language-majority students. His research has examined the suitability of dual-language forms of education for students who are at-risk for academic difficulty. He has also studied language acquisition in pre-school bilingual children – both typically developing and at-risk children. He has authored numerous publications in scientific journals and has (co-)authored many books for educators and parents.

Else Hamayan is an independent consultant and Director Emeritus of the Illinois Resource Center in Arlington Heights, Illinois. She was born and raised in Lebanon and graduated with a PhD in Psycholinguistics from McGill University. She was Director of the Illinois Resource Center, a professional development center for teachers of linguistically and culturally diverse students before moving to Argentina, where she currently resides. Else provides professional development to teachers and administrators in the US, Latin America and Europe on early childhood bilingualism, English language learners with special needs, cross-cultural learning and dual-language instruction.

1   Introduction

We were motivated to write this book for several reasons. First, there has been a growing interest around the world in providing young learners with opportunities to develop proficiency in more than one language. This has resulted from an unprecedented internationalisation in economic and business spheres of life as well as in educational, cultural, personal and communication domains. Second, there are many school-age students who are learning through an additional language in school. This reflects the growing rate of international migration as people move from their home countries for personal, professional or economic reasons. Third, there have been significant developments in the field of second-language education that are providing schools with new approaches, strategies and tools for teaching additional languages and teaching through additional languages to school-age learners. Many of these approaches focus on teaching language along with authentic content and, in particular, academic content, such as Mathematics. These programmes are commonly referred to as CLIL or Content and Language Integrated Learning.

We wrote this book to provide guidance on these new approaches. It should be of particular interest to teachers who are teaching through students' additional languages, be it in programmes that systematically aim to promote bilingual competence or programmes that teach through only one language but support bilingual development indirectly (such as in the case of immigrant students). We also hope this book will be useful for administrators who are either planning to use these approaches or are already doing so in their schools. We hope that education officials in school districts, policy-makers, teachers in training and teacher educators will also find the book useful.

BILINGUALISM IN THE TWENTY-FIRST CENTURY

Growing interest in developing young learners' proficiency in additional languages is partially due to necessity – many families are emigrating from their homes to countries where a language other than their own is spoken. There are many reasons for the expansion of such immigration, including economic, political and personal. As a result, many children are attending schools with little or no proficiency in the language of instruction. Many of these children are being taught by teachers who have little experience and knowledge of how to ensure that their students acquire full competence in their new language or of how to teach academic content using a language that their students have not yet mastered. Teachers are often at a loss to know how to make abstract concepts in subject areas such as Mathematics and Science comprehensible to their additional-language learners, especially in the higher grades as content gets more and more complex and abstract. They may not even know how to teach these students the additional language skills they need in order to do well in school.

It is not only the children of immigrant or refugee parents who want to learn a second or even third language. There are many regions around the world where more than one language is widely used in the community – for example, in countries such as Canada, Belgium, India, Finland,

RESEARCH NOTE

Increase in immigration around the world

According to the Organisation for Economic Co-operation and Development (2013), approximately 232 million international migrants are living in the world today. Between 1990 and 2013, the number of international migrants in the global North increased by around 53 million (65%), while the migrant population in the global South grew by around 24 million (34%).

Switzerland and South Africa, there is more than one official language and there are advantages in knowing those languages. Parents of children in these countries often seek school programmes where their children can become bi- or multilingual. Even in countries with only one official language, such as Brazil, Colombia and Hungary, there are indigenous or widely used non-official languages. Learning those languages along with the national language is important for day-to-day communication in personal, professional and other contexts.

The surging interest in learning additional languages is also shared by mainstream parents who have a desire to prepare their children for globalisation. In comparison to previous generations, parents and their children now have access to much more information and many more options that are available through modern technology and especially the internet. Globalisation has increased the value of being bi- or multilingual. While English is often the language of choice in these cases, many other languages are also used and useful in the global marketplace or even for personal travel. While some parents are motivated by economic considerations and a desire to give their children more opportunities by learning other languages, other parents are motivated by the belief that graduates in the twenty-first century should be open to, familiar with, and prepared to engage with people with different languages and

RESEARCH NOTE

Popularity of English

One out of four of the world's population speaks English to some level of competence; demand from the other three-quarters is increasing (Crystal, 1997).

cultures. In short, more and more parents in communities around the world want their children not just to acquire minimal proficiency in an additional language (often English), but to reach high levels of bilingual proficiency, and they are looking for innovative educational approaches to achieve this. Knowing other languages will help young people meet the challenges and enjoy the benefits of globalisation so that they can access information on the internet, pursue post-secondary education in an additional language, and compete for jobs in the international job market.

In response to local and global realities, many school districts and national or regional departments of education are requiring that students learn a second or even a third language along with their first. In Europe, for example, students must learn at least one second language until they are 18 years of age, and it is recommended that they learn a third language. The 2012 report from the European Commission highlights the increasing number of pupils learning two languages for at least one year during compulsory education. It notes that, on average, in 2009/10, 60.8% of lower-secondary education students were learning two or more foreign languages – an increase of 14.1% compared to 2004/05. Also, many children grow up in families where more than one language is spoken and their parents want them to become biliterate in the languages used at home. Kazakhstan has embarked on an ambitious project to make trilingual education in Kazakh, Russian and English available to all students in the country.

As well, many international schools (or international-type schools) around the world have sizeable populations of additional-language learners. Some of these students are from the host country in which the school is located and do not speak the primary language of instruction – English in most cases. Yet, other students in many international schools are from other countries and speak neither the language of the school nor the language of the host community. These students are learning through a second, or third, language and can benefit from CLIL approaches to teaching. It is particularly important for these students to develop proficiency in English, the language of instruction, because it may be the only language that is consistently present throughout their childhood and adolescence. A growing number of international schools offer bilingual education or other options that actively support their students becoming bi- or multilingual. For example, the international school in Frankfurt offers some options in German to both host-country German-speaking students who wish to maintain their home language while learning English, the primary language of instruction, and to English-speaking students from around the world who attend their school so that they, too, acquire competence in English and German. In some cases, international schools also offer support for home-language development to students who speak neither the language of the school nor the local community – in accordance with the recommendations of the International Baccalaureate or Cambridge International Examinations (CIE) programmes that they follow. CLIL is relevant to teaching in these schools; we describe why and how in more detail in **Chapter 3**.

Thus, by necessity or choice, the number of young and adolescent additional-language learners around the world is growing at a phenomenal rate. Many parents are looking to schools to make this happen, and many teachers are looking for the most effective ways to develop students' additional-language proficiency.

A NEW APPROACH TO LANGUAGE INSTRUCTION

There has been a dramatic change in the way additional languages are being taught in school. Advances in research in the field of second-language education are providing educators with new approaches for promoting bi- or multilingualism in school and for teaching students through an additional language; but many educators find it challenging to apply these new methods. A primary goal of this book is to assist them with this. Alternative terms have been used to refer to these new approaches. The most common terms are Content and Language Integrated Learning (CLIL) and Content-Based Instruction (CBI). We will use CLIL throughout the book because it is a general term that focuses on both language and content and is widely used today. Both of these ways of referring to CLIL highlight the key innovation of this approach – that is, the integration of content and language instruction drives instructional planning and practice. Moreover, both terms refer to methods that can be used in a variety of contexts.

CLIL can be used not only to teach additional languages as separate subjects (a foreign-language programme), but also to teach significant portions of the academic curriculum in an additional language (an immersion context). They can also be used to teach the required curriculum to non-native speakers of the language of instruction (a main-stream classroom with immigrant students who are learning through the majority language). In a French school, for example, instead of having a class called 'English as a Foreign Language', students may learn music in English. Some schools are going even further and teaching 50% or 90% of the entire curriculum during certain grades in the additional language. In a growing number of mainstream and international schools, there are many students who come to school with limited or no proficiency in the language of instruction – immigrant students or students who speak an indigenous language; CLIL strategies can be useful in these classrooms as well. What all of these schools have in common is that teachers are teaching language and academic content together. Foreign-language instruction has always used some kind of content as a vehicle for teaching language – often the content was the habits, foods and cultures of the groups whose languages were being learned. What is different about this new approach is that the content that is used as a vehicle for teaching the foreign/additional language is the academic subjects that form the prescribed curriculum of study. This novel approach focuses on teaching language that is needed to communicate about and learn academic content.

This approach to teaching additional languages, and through additional languages, has been shown to be more effective than focusing primarily on language in isolation, or on content without paying attention to the language of instruction; the research evidence in support of this approach is discussed in more detail in **Chapters 2** and **3**. This is one of the principal tenets of this book – by integrating instruction in an additional language with instruction of academic subjects or other authentic content that is interesting and relevant to students, students can develop a deeper and wider range of authentic communication skills in the additional language than if the language is taught for its own sake. In the case of majority-language students in immersion, for example, this can be done without jeopardising mastery of academic skills and knowledge or first-language development. In short, it is value-added education. For minority-language students who do not already speak the language of instruction, CLIL strategies can make the academic content more accessible and facilitate acquisition of the majority language.

This brings us to the variety of educational contexts in which CLIL can be effectively put into practice.

EDUCATIONAL CONTEXTS

Children and adolescents learn an additional language, and through an additional language, in a variety of educational contexts in K-12 schools. We discuss four contexts in which CLIL is being or could be used: Immersion (IMM), education for immigrant and indigenous-language students (ILSs), foreign-language (FL) programmes, and international schools (INT); we describe each of these in more detail later. The four types of contexts that we discuss differ according to many instructional variables, including:

- the grade levels when instruction in the additional language is offered – some programmes begin additional-language instruction as early as kindergarten or earlier (in preschool), while others do not start until the last four years of school

- the extent to which instruction in the additional language is integrated into the curriculum – at one end of the spectrum are schools that offer separate classes that focus on additional-language instruction; for example, Italian as a foreign language; and at the other end of the spectrum are schools in which the entire curriculum, or much of it, is taught in an additional language for many years – these are often referred to as 'immersion programmes'.

Most importantly, these programmes also differ in the outcomes that are expected. In some programmes, it is expected that students will acquire knowledge about the language and how to use the language in relatively limited domains – for example, using the target language to describe their neighbourhood. In other programmes, the goal is for students to attain full functional proficiency in the additional language so that they are able to use it in a variety of domains in and outside of school. Despite the fact that different levels of bilingual proficiency might be expected, we use the term CLIL to refer to teaching additional-language learners in these different contexts. Three of the educational contexts that we discuss at length throughout this book can be found in schools where the national or regional language is the primary language of instruction, but students are taught some subjects through an additional or foreign language (see **Figure 1.1**); a fourth context we consider is schools where the primary language of instruction is different from the national or regional language – namely, international schools. Here is a fuller description of all four contexts.

FIGURE 1.1: CLIL instruction in IMM, ILS, and FL contexts in which the language of instruction is the majority language of the community

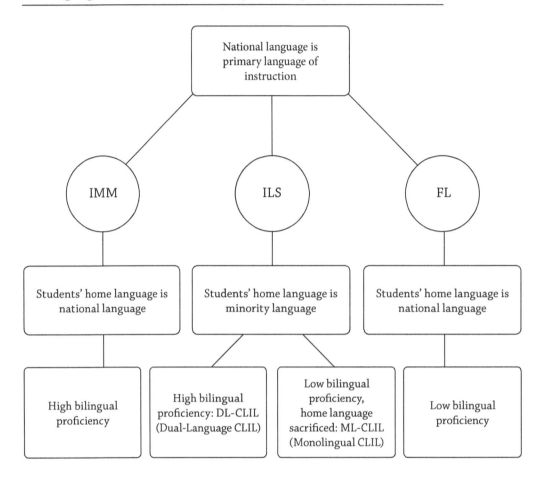

Immersion (IMM)

In these types of programmes, most students are native speakers of the national or majority language. Although schooling for most students in these communities is in the majority language, some students also receive substantial amounts of instruction through an additional language for both academic and social purposes. For example, in a school in Brazil, half of the school day in the elementary grades might take place in Portuguese (the majority language) and the other half in English (an additional language). This means that the students get half of their curriculum instruction, including literacy and other subjects, in Portuguese and the other half in English. In Europe, this type of instructional model is often referred to simply as CLIL; however, we refer to it as 'Immersion' or IMM for short because it is a specific type of CLIL programme – namely, one that provides substantial amounts of curriculum instruction in an additional language. Indeed, many schools throughout the world refer to these types of programme as IMM, after the model that started in Canada in 1965 to teach French to English-speaking students. These programmes might be considered one of the first content-based or CLIL programmes.

RESEARCH NOTE

Summary of St Lambert

> The St Lambert early total immersion programme was inaugurated in 1965 in a community outside Montreal, Canada. The students received all instruction in French, their second language, in kindergarten and in grades 1 and 2; English was not used for instruction until grade 3, for about an hour a day, and then increased to 50% of each day in grades 5 and 6. The pilot students and a follow-up cohort of students participated in research every year until they completed secondary school (see Lambert & Tucker, 1972, for a summary of that research). In brief, the research showed that, in comparison to similar students in all-English programmes, immersion students attained the same levels of proficiency in English starting in grade 3; they also attained the same levels of achievement in academic subjects at all grade levels; and they acquired much higher levels of functional proficiency in French. The results of this research spread around the world and became the basis for many other countries starting their own programmes.

There are a variety of IMM programme models; they can differ from one another along several dimensions. They can differ with respect to the grade level when the additional language is first used as a medium of academic instruction, the number of grades during which the additional language is used for academic instruction, and how intensively the additional language is used to teach academic content. They can also differ in the ways in which they allocate the language of instruction to different content areas. Some programmes teach a specific content area, such as Science, in the same language for several years; some alternate language of instruction for specific school subjects from year to year; yet others switch languages for one content area once a unit is completed. As well, some programmes have different teachers for each language; and others have the same teacher for both languages. In IMM programmes, attaining advanced levels of bilingual competence in both spoken and written forms of the two languages is not only a desired but also a realistic goal. Moreover, students in IMM programmes are assessed on their mastery of academic objectives – in Mathematics and Science, for example, as well as their mastery of the additional language. In **Chapters 2** and **3**, we discuss IMM programmes in more detail from a pedagogical point of view and we review research on how successful they are at achieving their goals.

1.1 PERSONAL PERSPECTIVE
CLIL in indigenous education

Nicole Bruskewitz, Profesora Docente,
Universidad de los Andes, Bogotá, Colombia

In indigenous education contexts, the term CLIL does not carry the same meaning as it does for non-indigenous educators. In Colombia, approximations that would be called CLIL elsewhere are called *ethnoeducation* by the government, and *educación propia* – our education – by the communities. This means that each of the more than 65 indigenous language communities in the country has the right to execute its autonomous education agenda, including choosing culturally appropriate subject matter, selecting teachers and determining the language of instruction. Teaching in the language of the community represents both a right and fight; cultivating linguistic proficiency may mean maintaining or revitalizing a language or culture at risk of dying out. In short, *educación propia* is a politically charged task.

In the communities where I have worked a few noteworthy trends in the practices emerge. First, *educación propia* addresses the goals of content, cognition, communication and culture (the 4 Cs) by teaching of traditional cultural knowledge and skills in the native language. This can range from teaching geometry through weaving of patterns in traditional wool *mochilas*, to learning fishing techniques, to exploring botany and traditional medicines, to oracy through storytelling or singing. All of these practices are related to cultural rituals through which traditional knowledge is passed down. Interestingly, it is often the community members, especially elders, who accompany or replace the traditional classroom teachers. Other schools, like the Achagua school near Puerto Lopez, teach all basic subjects in the endangered language. This includes a literacy block in both Achagua and Spanish.

Many programs struggle to find materials that meet their unique objectives; many schools teaching the national curriculum alongside their autonomous one have created materials in the target language. The Sikuani community in Vichada department is a good example of a group using CLIL to revitalize the local language that has progressively diminished in use due to oppressive language policy and practices in schools. Producing teaching material is part of an attempt to revitalize the language and culture among children and adolescents.

Community leaders do not distinguish between these two things: teaching language is teaching culture and cultural knowledge, and vice versa. Therefore, texts are both language-focused, emphasizing phonetics, and content-focused, centering around oral stories about the *kaliwirinae,* the tree of life from which the world was born. Translanguaging with Sikuani and Spanish and drawing on cultural elements are crucial to reaching content and cognitive goals, which can be challenging due to students' proficiency in Sikuani. Finally, many communities, including the Wayuu, have made huge strides in the creation of digital materials to be used pedagogically.

Education for immigrant and indigenous-language students (ILS)

Many communities around the world have significant numbers of residents who speak a language other than the national language at home.

Children in these families enter school with little or no proficiency in the language of instruction. They must learn the national or majority language in school for the purposes of general education and social integration – an additional-language context. Some of these students are children of immigrants. For example, Turkish-speaking immigrant children in Germany attend schools where German is the language of instruction, or Polish-speaking children in the UK where English is the language of instruction. Some of these children were born in the country in which they are being educated but they have grown up in linguistic enclaves where they heard and used primarily their heritage language and, as a result, have limited competence in the national language. These learners have a triple challenge – they must learn the majority language; they must keep up with academic instruction in the majority language; and often they must also learn how to fit into the culture of the mainstream group.

It is not only immigrant children or children of immigrant parents who are educated in a language that is not spoken at home. This is also the case for students who are native to the country but speak an indigenous language; for example, Peruvian students who enter their community or neighbourhood school speaking Quechua but the language of instruction is Spanish; or Welsh-speaking children in some regions of the UK who speak Welsh at home but must attend English-medium public schools.In many countries, most immigrant and indigenous-language students are taught only through the majority language. This is true in many English-speaking countries, such as the US and Australia, where there are significant numbers of children whose parents came from other countries or are members of indigenous cultural groups and whose children are educated exclusively in English. However, years of evaluation research in some countries has shown us that educating immigrant and indigenous-language students exclusively through their additional language is not always effective. This is true in the US, for example, where it has been found these students often do not reach high levels of proficiency in the majority language, while growth in their home language is stunted. At the same time, they may underachieve in academic domains because instruction is in a language that they do not understand and because teachers do not know how to tailor instruction to meet their specific needs. In contrast, in some countries, such as Canada and the UK, many children of immigrant parents do as well as native-born children. However, because they are being educated exclusively in the national or majority language, they do not develop high levels of proficiency in reading and writing in their first language and they may even lose oral competence in that language.

The US is of particular interest here because it has experimented with alternative forms of dual-language education for such children. These programmes aim to enhance these students' proficiency in English, ensure high levels of academic achievement and support development of the home language along with English. We discuss these alternatives in greater detail in **Chapter 3** along with the rationale for them and the results of research that has evaluated their effectiveness.

RESEARCH NOTE 1.4

For research on minority-language students in the US, see:

Genesee, F. and Lindholm-Leary, K. (2012). The education of English language learners. In K. Harris, S. Graham and T. Urdan et al., (eds), *APA handbook of educational psychology* (pp. 499–526). Washington, DC: APA Books.

For research on minority-language students in Canada and the UK, see:

Aydemir, A., Chen, W. H. and Corak, M. (2008). Intergenerational education mobility among the children of Canadian immigrants. Institute for the Study of Labor (IZA) Discussion Paper 3759. Retrieved from http://ftp.iza.org/dp3759.pdf.

UK Department of Education (2016). Revised GCSE and equivalent results in England, 2014 to 2015. Retrieved from www.gov.uk/government/uploads/system/uploads/attachment_data/file/494073/SFR01_2016.pdf.

Foreign-language (FL) programmes

In this type of programme, students typically are native speakers of the majority language, and they get instruction in an additional language for limited periods of time. The language is usually referred to as a foreign language (FL) since it is typically 'foreign' to the country or community in question. For example, we would refer to a school in China that offers instruction in English or French as having an FL programme. In some cases, a language that can be considered a second language because it plays a vital role in the community is also referred to as a foreign language for social or political reasons. For example, a school in Los Angeles may refer to its Spanish programme for English-speaking students as 'Spanish as a foreign language' despite the fact that many of the neighbourhood's residents are Spanish speakers and Spanish plays a vital role within the community.

Instruction in foreign languages can begin as early as kindergarten (age 5) or later – in secondary school. In many traditional FL programmes, instruction is not content-based but, rather, focuses primarily on teaching grammar and vocabulary, often in isolation. In these more traditional types of FL programmes, the foreign or additional language would be taught as one of the subjects in the curriculum and, usually, as a separate subject, unrelated to other parts of the curriculum. For example, the curriculum in a school in Japan might include English as a foreign language as a subject that is taught twice a week for 40 minutes each time. In FL programmes, full bilingual proficiency is not usually expected; nor is it realistic since students' exposure to the additional language is limited. These programmes can nevertheless benefit from using CLIL approaches by using one or more subject areas as the context for teaching the additional language. This would provide students with functional proficiency in the additional language to a limited extent but certainly more so than in the more traditional approach of teaching primarily grammar and vocabulary in isolation. We include these types of programmes in the book even though they do not aim for high levels of bilingual proficiency because more and more FL programmes are using CLIL approaches, albeit in a limited fashion.

1.2 PERSONAL PERSPECTIVE

Integrating content with language: A student's perspective

Ludmila Nekola, 12th grade student
Instituto Educativo Nuevo Milenio, Unquillo, Cordoba, Argentina

My school offers Italian, English and Portuguese as foreign languages in addition to the primary language Spanish. A custom has been established in my school to mix Italian language classes with a different subject like Music, Art and Theater every year. In my fifth year of secondary school (11th grade) Italian was mixed with Music. The combination of these two subjects lasted the whole school year and it was treated like one subject. We did many activities such as learning the History of Italian music and analyzing operas. We did these activities individually or in small groups. Since we had already studied both subjects separately in past years, we had a base of knowledge so when they combined the two it was more like practicing what we already knew, speaking the language and learning the culture of music.

The benefits of mixing language with other subjects are many: the most important was you get to practice what you have learned throughout the years and to learn the art of speaking. You not only learn about another culture, you learn ways of speaking, you learn to not get scared of making mistakes, you learn to recognize you're not saying something correctly and to keep going, and since you have to make presentations in front of the entire class it helps a lot with shyness and it builds your confidence.

It's also fun learning new words and to discover that the same sounding word in one language means something totally different in another. These similarities sometimes are the key to remember new language and it's fun; it makes you happy when you discover them yourself.

In my opinion it is fundamental to mix subjects with language because language becomes easier to learn and much more fun! It would even be interesting to mix language with subjects such as History or Geography because you can do different types of activities and learn about different parts of the world as you practice other languages.

International schools (INT)

International schools typically promote international education either by adopting a curriculum that adheres to international standards, such as the International Baccalaureate or CIE programmes, or by following a national curriculum different from that of local schools – often this is the curriculum of the US or the UK. Traditionally, these schools have served mostly students who are not nationals of the host country, such as the children of the staff of international businesses and organisations or foreign embassies. The primary language of instruction in many of these schools is English, although not always. We use English in this book to refer to this type of programme; however, our discussions would apply to any international school where the language of instruction differs from the majority language; for example, schools of the Alliance Française or the Colegio Alemán in many Spanish-speaking countries. Increasingly, there are students from the host country who speak the majority language but not the language of the school; for example, German-speaking students attending international schools where English is the primary language of instruction. These schools also serve an increasingly large number of 'international students' – students who come from homes where a language other than English

FIGURE 1.2: CLIL instruction in international school contexts in which the language of instruction is not the majority language of the community

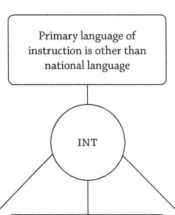

or the language of the host community is spoken. For example, at the International School of Geneva, where English is the primary language of instruction, there are many students from around the world who speak a variety of first languages, such as Vietnamese, Arabic, Japanese and so on. Both students from the host country and those from other countries are taught through English as an additional language (**see Figure 1.2**). These are schools in which teachers need to know how to integrate language and content instruction so that these students can learn English and keep up with academic instruction in English at the same time.

Whether we are talking about immigrant students or indigenous-language students who speak a heritage language at home, or mainstream students who speak the majority language, more and more teachers are called upon to teach both language and academic content to students who have not already acquired the language of instruction. This calls for expertise in content and language-integrated instruction.

IMPLEMENTING CLIL IN DIFFERENT EDUCATIONAL CONTEXTS

CLIL can be successfully implemented in these four educational contexts, but adaptations need to be made in each to maximise its effectiveness. There is not a single way to implement CLIL. Some aspects of CLIL may be easier to implement than others depending on the context. As a general rule, integrating instruction of authentic content with additional-language instruction is an effective route to additional-language proficiency regardless of the type of educational context – evidence of its effectiveness is reviewed in **Chapter 3**. It is important for teachers working in these kinds of school contexts to develop competence in the CLIL approach whether they are teaching in IMM-type programmes that aim for full bilingualism or in FL programmes where there are limited expectations of full proficiency in the additional language. It is equally important that school administrators are familiar and competent with CLIL approaches so that they can provide knowledgeable leadership for the additional-language programmes in their school. Throughout the rest of the book, we discuss topics relevant to successful implementation of CLIL in these four educational contexts; and we identify special issues that may be particularly relevant to one type of programme or another.

1.1 ADDITIONAL RESOURCES

Readings on the four educational contexts

Since we do not intend to discuss at length characteristics of the four educational contexts, we offer this limited bibliography for further reading:

Immersion programmes for majority-language students

Genesee, F. (2004). What do we know about bilingual education for majority language students? In T. K. Bhatia and W. Ritchie, (eds), *Handbook of bilingualism and multiculturalism* (pp. 547–76). Malden, MA: Blackwell.

Genesee, F. and Lindholm-Leary, K. (2013). Two case studies of content-based language education. *Journal of Immersion and Content-Based Language Education,* 1(1), 3–33.

Education for immigrant and indigenous-language students

Genesee, F., Lindholm-Leary, K., Saunders, W. and Christian, D. (2006). *Educating English language learners: A synthesis of research evidence.* New York, NY: Cambridge University Press.

Lindholm-Leary, K. and Genesee, F. (2014). Student outcomes in one-way, two-way and indigenous language immersion programs. *Journal of Immersion and Content-Based Language Education,* 2(2), 196–209.

FL programmes

Curtain, H. and Dahlberg, C. A. (2016). *Languages and learners: Making the match: World language instruction in K-8 classrooms and beyond.* Boston, MA: Pearson.

International schools

Carder, M. (2007). *Bilingualism in international schools: A model for enriching language education.* Clevedon: Multilingual Matters.

Gallagher, E. (2008). *Equal rights to the curriculum: Many languages, one message.* Clevedon: Multilingual Matters.

International School Magazine. This magazine, written by teachers and administrators of international schools, is published three times a year. It offers theoretical and practical discussion of issues pertaining to international schools. Retrieved from www.is-mag.co.uk/.

Shoebottom, P. (2009). Academic success for non-native English speakers in English-medium international schools: The role of the secondary ESL department. Retrieved from http://esl.fis.edu/teachers/support/naldic.pdf.

1.3 PERSONAL PERSPECTIVE

IMM in Japanese and English: Facing some linguistic challenges

Mike Bostwick, Executive Director,
English Immersion/Bilingual Programmes, Katoh Gakuen, Japan

In 1992, Katoh Gakuen introduced the first English immersion program in Japan. Combining English and Japanese, presented a challenge as there was little research on immersion in non-cognate languages at that time. Some decisions we made early on in the program turned out to be pivotal and enabled us to build on our initial success and develop a program that would allow students to go on to post-secondary studies in either language.

We created a two-thirds early partial immersion (66% English/ 33% Japanese) program. The program requires students in grades 1–3 to take four of their six classes a day in the English. The other two classes consist of the Japanese (*Kokugo*) classes that all students in Japan take to learn to read and write Japanese. This guarantees that students progress in Japanese literacy at the same level as the non-immersion Japanese students. Students have thrived in this model.

At the secondary level, our immersion students also complete the International Baccalaureate Middle Years and Diploma Programs in English. It was here that we discovered the importance of moving from a language acquisition focus in the early grades to a more literature-based focus in the upper grades. Initially, our middle years students' language program tended to use texts controlled for vocabulary and with simplified structures. However, we found that this didn't create a rich enough language environment. As a result, we moved to a more literature-based program that resulted in greater interest and motivation as well as higher levels of cognitive processing. Using real literature also required far more extensive scaffolding by teachers in the beginning but ultimately resulted in higher levels of L2 proficiency and enabled students to access better the academically and linguistically demanding International Baccalaureate curriculum in the senior high school. Greater teacher scaffolding, in turn, meant that teachers relied on strategies known to engage students. *(Continued over page)*

Providing professional development for staff has also been a huge challenge. One way we addressed this need was to create regular 'symposiums' in which we could invite experts in the field to our school. Invitations to these symposiums were extended to educators throughout the country and helped to subsidize the program so that the school did not have to commit significant financial resources for our professional development.

Our experience has taught us the importance of understanding the research that may impact on crucial program decisions and student outcomes and how to effectively apply this understanding to the unique context of the school to achieve program goals.

The practical guidance we provide is based first and foremost on research and research-based educational theories, where available. There has been an explosion of research and theory on second-language teaching and learning during the past 30 years that is relevant to teaching additional languages in school settings. We believe that knowledge of this research base and these theories is useful for additional-language educators and any educator working with students who are learning through an additional language. The new knowledge from research and theory that is available is useful for both classroom teachers who work directly with students and for school administrators who oversee existing programmes or who are creating new programmes. It may also be useful for parents who are seeking effective ways for educating their children so that they acquire bilingual competence. However, research does not have all the answers; sound professional opinion and experience also have an important role to play. Thus, we also base our guidance on our own experiences of teaching and collaborating with teachers and administrators who work with additional-language learners in different educational contexts around the world. In **Chapter 2,** we present eight essential research-based principles that any programme must follow in order for CLIL to be effective.

CLIL and its antecedents in CBI, such as immersion in Canada and dual-language education in the US, are changing the way that additional languages are taught in schools. Major changes in instruction and programme design are called for to ensure the success of CLIL. Here are the three major areas where we think change is most significant: 1) the way teachers plan lessons, 2) the way teachers teach and work together, and 3) the way teachers assess teaching and learning. Let's consider each of these briefly now.

How teachers plan instruction

In **Chapter 4,** we discuss in practical terms how teachers and administrators can integrate language and content instruction both to enhance language competence and to make academic concepts accessible to students. We begin by discussing the steps that need to be taken when a school is just beginning to offer CLIL instruction. Taking the time to prepare staff and the community for this new approach to language and content instruction is a key component of the success of a CLIL programme. Most importantly, all teachers, regardless of their specialisation, must see themselves as both language and content teachers. Collaboration among teachers becomes essential as professional boundaries between language and content teachers fade.

We suggest ways of organising the curriculum around content-area themes in ways that are amenable to a CLIL approach. We then describe two types of objectives that can be used to guide lesson planning and instruction: 1) primary objectives – including language and content objectives, and 2) secondary objectives – including cross-linguistic, cross-cultural and general learning-skills objectives. We also propose a three-phase lesson-planning tool that begins with a preview phase that familiarises students with essential language for the lesson and allows teachers to assess what their students already know about the theme of the unit. This is followed by a focused learning phase when the core objectives of the unit are taught intensively and, finally, an expansion phase that expands what students have learned by relating it to other components of the curriculum and to their lives outside school.

Planning instruction in a CLIL programme, like any type of instruction, also requires good resources. This includes human and material resources. With regard to human resources, staff and teachers who teach in CLIL programmes must learn to define their roles as both language and content teachers. This may call for a change in how they define their present role in comparison to the past. If the role that teachers played in school was primarily as language teachers, then they must also pay attention to the fact that additional-language learning is more effective when it is integrated with learning Mathematics, History or other authentic content at the same time. Since students learn additional languages better when they are also engaged in learning meaningful content, it makes sense to incorporate at least some academic subject areas into language lessons and units. If teachers were primarily responsible for teaching specific subjects in the curriculum, such as Science or History, then working in a CLIL programme means they must

1.1 SPECIAL NOTE

Note for CLIL programmes with languages other than English

Although we focus on English as the additional language of instruction in this book, we provide information about resources for other languages whenever possible, sometimes in special notes such as this one, and other times in the text itself. Here are published reports of some CLIL (IMM) programmes in languages other than English:

Basque, Spanish and English

Joaristi, L., Lizasoain, L., Lukas, J. F. and Santiago, K. (2009). Trilingualism (Spanish, English and Basque) in the educational system of the Basque country. *International Journal of Multilingualism*, 6, 105–26.

Hawaiian and English

Slaughter, H. (1997). Indigenous language immersion in Hawai'i: A case study of Kula Kaiapuni Hawai'i. In R. K. Johnson and M. Swain, (eds), *Immersion education: International perspectives* (pp. 105–29). Cambridge: Cambridge University Press.

Finnish and Swedish

Björklund, S. (1998). Immersion in Finland in the 1990s: A state of development and expansion. In J. Cenoz and F. Genesee, (eds), *Beyond bilingualism: Multilingualism and multilingual education* (pp. 85–102). Clevedon: Multilingual Matters.

Mohawk and English

Jacobs, K. and Cross, A. (2001). The seventh generation of Kahnawà:ke: Phoenix or dinosaur. In D. Christian and F. Genesee, (eds), *Bilingual education* (pp. 109–21). Alexandria, VA: TESOL.

Japanese and English

Bostwick, M. (2001). English immersion in a Japanese school. In D. Christian and F. Genesee, (eds), *Bilingual education* (pp. 125–38). Alexandria, VA: TESOL.

Estonian and Russian

Mehisto, P. and Asser, H. (2007). Stakeholder perspectives: CLIL programme management in Estonia. *International Journal of Bilingual Education and Bilingualism*, 10(5), 683–701.

pay attention to the language that students need in order to meet the academic objectives that have been set for them – students studying Science need to learn the language of Science, and the same can be said about each subject in the curriculum.

In addition to discussing teachers' roles in CLIL, we discuss administrators' qualifications and the implications for professional development that give teachers and administrators the skills and knowledge they need to integrate content and language instruction effectively.

It is important to plan ahead to find and adapt the material resources you want to use in CLIL programmes. Because CLIL programmes aim to develop an additional language at the same time as they build students' knowledge and skills in academic subject areas, learning resources – such as books as well as realia and web-based materials – must be given special consideration. Teachers must first make decisions about how the additional language and the home language will be used to teach the curriculum during the day in order to ensure that they have the instructional resources they need in each language and that they align with their objectives. Specific questions about materials include: What materials do we need? Where can we obtain bilingual materials? What criteria do we use for choosing materials?

How teachers teach

In **Chapter 5**, we describe a step-by-step process for creating unit and lesson plans that begins with listing the big ideas of the unit followed by identifying instructional objectives – content and language as the primary objectives, and cross-linguistic, cross-cultural and general learning skills as secondary objectives. Next, the activities for the preview phase are set. These are activities that allow teachers to find out what students already know about the topic before they actually begin teaching it. This phase also allows teachers to familiarise their students with the language that they will need to learn the new concepts and skills that are part of their objectives. These goals can be accomplished through carefully selected concrete activities that involve the students. These activities flow into the focused learning phase when teachers begin to investigate the topic of the unit. This is done through enquiry strategies where students generate questions about the topic and investigate the topic with the teacher's guidance. The lesson ends with the extension phase when learners extend what they have learned into other subject areas. In this phase, students and teachers together also examine the relevance of the new concepts they have learned in the world outside school by connecting what was learned in class with students' daily lives.

When we integrate language and content learning instruction, and when we use themes across different content areas to teach new concepts, it is imperative to make sure that coordination among teachers is efficient and smooth, especially in the higher grades where teachers teach one or two specialised subject areas. Teachers need to work together so that language and content objectives are guiding instruction at all times and so that learning is continuous from subject to subject. Effective coordination among teachers includes not only language and content teachers at each grade level, but also teachers working across grade levels. Cross-grade-level coordination is essential to ensure continuous language development. We need to know what language students have learned in each grade in order to extend their language competence from grade to grade. Coordination among teachers is challenging for many reasons. These challenges and related issues are discussed in **Chapter 6** where we describe what needs to be coordinated and suggest strategies for coordination that allow teachers to work together to make instruction most effective.

Another type of coordination that needs to be considered to ensure that CLIL programmes run smoothly and effectively is social in nature. CLIL programmes should be well integrated into the functioning of the whole school rather than as a separate, stand-alone programme within the school. Integration of the CLIL programme with the community that the school serves also strengthens the programme by drawing on resources in the community and, in turn, by providing resources to the community itself. Strategies for attaining these two types of coordination are also discussed in **Chapter 6**.

How teachers assess

The way we assess teaching and learning must also be reconsidered when a CLIL approach is adopted because students are developing both language and content-area knowledge at the same time. In IMM, ILS and INT contexts where high levels of bilingual proficiency are expected, assessment of content-area knowledge is particularly challenging because students are learning new and abstract concepts in Mathematics,

Social Science and Science in a non-proficient language. This has significant implications for how students are assessed so that we can look at student outcomes that are not biased by incomplete language acquisition. In IMM, ILS and INT contexts, teachers must also be able to assess their students' proficiency in using the additional language for social purposes, not just academic purposes. Administrators also need to ensure that they can describe student performance accurately to interested people, such as parents, policy-makers and board members; and parents, policy-makers and others must learn to consider students' accomplishments in academic domains by taking into account their progress in learning the new language.

Moreover, CLIL is also about teaching language skills that are useful outside school. Therefore, it is important to encourage students' autonomy so that they can monitor, manage and direct their own learning in order to acquire these kinds of language skills. Traditional paper-and-pencil tests are not very good for this purpose. There are other methods of assessment that put students at the centre of assessment and encourage them to take responsibility for their own learning. This is particularly important for students in programmes where the language is used to teach significant parts of the academic curriculum – in IMM, ILS and INT contexts, where the goal is to prepare students to use the additional language outside school – for higher education, professional purposes or personal reasons.

Since all teachers in IMM, ILS and INT contexts are responsible for teaching both language and content objectives, assessment in CLIL programmes requires information about student performance to come from different sources and take different forms. Paper-and-pencil tests can be useful in these ways, but they must be supplemented by alternative forms of assessment. Other useful forms of assessment include portfolios that reflect student progress across a whole unit or year of instruction, learning logs that students keep to monitor their own learning, dialogue journals that are shared with teachers, and observation checklists that teachers can use to monitor students' day-to-day language use. In **Chapter 7,** we discuss how to use alternative methods of assessment so that they are practical and useful in different CLIL contexts.

Chapter 8 provides a checklist that can be used to ensure that you have created a CLIL programme that complies with the eight key principles we discuss in detail in **Chapter 2**. These principles are based on current research findings and our own professional experiences working with educators around the world to create effective CLIL programmes.

SPECIAL FEATURES OF THE BOOK

We include the following special features in the book to point out specific issues or additional information connected to the main text.

- *Additional Resources:* These give additional sources of information and tips for readers so that they can expand their knowledge and find more information regarding the specific topic being discussed.

- *Checklists:* These appear throughout the book and in appendices; they can serve as practical guidelines for planning instruction, selecting resources or assessing progress, for example.

- *Personal Perspectives:* These are short commentaries from teachers and other experts about their experiences in CLIL; they provide first-person accounts of specific issues that are discussed in the text.

- *Research Notes:* Most of these notes are short summaries of important research findings that are relevant to specific practices that we recommend. Putting these brief statements in the margins allows you to see the empirical basis for instructional strategies and classroom activities or programme decisions.

- *Special Notes:* These notes are inserted whenever a special point warrants mention for particular people – such as administrators, parents, teachers at higher or lower grade levels, teachers of students with special needs; or when a remark needs to be made for a specific type of educational context. The notes appear in the margins as 'Note for administrators' or 'Note for programmes for immigrants', for example.

DEFINITION OF TERMS

Before we launch into the remaining chapters, we need to define the terms we use throughout the book. Defining terms is important to minimise confusion that might arise because some of these terms are used with slightly different connotations in the literature.

- **Content and Language Integrated Learning (CLIL)**: CLIL can encompass learning environments with different kinds of learners and very diverse kinds of activities (see Mehisto, Marsh, & Frigols, 2008, for examples). We use *CLIL* to refer to instruction that integrates the development of proficiency in an additional language in school contexts where authentic non-language content (such as Science and Mathematics) serves a vehicles for language teaching and learning. Language itself is also considered a content domain in the curriculum; it includes reading, writing, and literature. We refer to this as Language Arts. To simplify reference to these two kinds of content areas, we use the term *academic content* to refer to the non-language academic content and the terms *language* or *Language Arts* to refer to content that involves language instruction. The outcome of this form of CLIL is development of proficiency in the additional language at the same time as students achieve age- and grade-appropriate levels of achievement in the non-language and language-related areas of the curriculum.

- **Programme**: We use the term *programme* in very general ways to refer to a whole school, the whole curriculum or part of the curriculum. We also use it to refer to a strand within a school when CLIL is offered to a specific group of students. This is typical in schools with immigrant or indigenous-language students, or in international schools where some students are being taught through an additional language.

- **Additional language**: We refer to teaching and learning *additional* languages rather than *second* or *foreign* languages for ease of presentation. We include third or fourth languages under 'additional language', again for the sake of simplicity. If special considerations are needed when third or additional languages are under discussion, we add comments in the margins. Where the distinction between learning a second language and a foreign language has special implications for instruction, we refer to them in special notes in the margin.

- **English**: Since English is the first choice by far for most schools that offer additional-language instruction, we use English as the language of choice in this book, but our discussions and suggestions apply to any language that is added to the students' home language. When special considerations need to be given to other languages – because they use a different orthography for example, we make a special note in the margin and discuss the exception.

- **Majority and minority language**: We use the term *majority language* to refer to the dominant language in the community or country in which the school is located; this is often the official language of the country, although not always. We use the term *minority language* to refer to languages in the community or country that are spoken by a minority of the population or are perceived as having relatively low status and power in the community.

- **Bilingualism and bilingual proficiency**: For our purposes, *bilingualism* refers to advanced functional competence in at least one language and functional competence in spoken or written aspects of an additional language that ranges from relatively low to high. It does not necessarily mean competence that is the same as that of a monolingual native speaker, however. For students to attain native-like competence in an additional language, they need extensive instruction in and through that language and opportunities to use the language outside school with native speakers.

2   Key principles of CLIL

In this chapter we discuss eight principles that are important for effective integration of content and language learning and teaching.
These principles are related to beliefs that can affect the way educators
teach additional languages to school-age learners or the way they plan
a programme where content is learned through an additional language.
Beliefs are important because they affect the decisions we make on a
day-to-day basis and the actions that stem from those decisions. For
example, if you believe that people need extra vitamins to stay healthy,
then you may decide to purchase vitamin pills and take one every day.
In contrast, if you believe that your normal diet provides your body with
all the vitamins it needs, then you will decide to resist all of the ads that
say that vitamin supplements are necessary. Many educational decisions
by policy-makers, curriculum and education specialists, and classroom
teachers are similarly influenced by the beliefs they have about bilingualism, the facility with which young children can learn additional
languages, the ability of students with learning difficulties to acquire
an additional language, and so on. Sometimes, we are not even aware
of these beliefs; we just take them for granted because they have always
been part of our way of thinking. As professionals, it is important to be
aware of your beliefs and how they affect your professional decisions
and actions. In the following sections, we present scientific evidence
along with our own professional advice based on our experiences about
each of the key principles we consider important; and we invite you to
consider your own beliefs regarding these principles.

2.1 SPECIAL NOTE

Self-reflection for professional development

Before you read about these principles, take a few minutes to examine your own beliefs about the topics we are about to discuss. Discuss your answers with a partner and, if applicable, with a group of colleagues.

Check Y (yes) and/or N (no). Do you think that:	Y	N	Why?
1 The best way to teach an additional language is to focus learners' attention on the vocabulary and grammar rules they need in order to speak and read the language correctly.			
2 Without direct instruction of language, learners will have trouble becoming proficient.			
3 It is important to plan instruction so that students are at the centre; i.e. they determine what and how they learn; they learn through activities they do themselves.			
4 It is best to encourage learners to keep their two languages separate when they are learning a new language.			
5 To make learning easier for them, students in CLIL programmes should be allowed to use their first language even when instruction is in the additional language.			
6 Assessment is most useful when it focuses on student achievement.			
7 There are some children who cannot learn an additional language or for whom it is so difficult that it is not worth the effort. Who are these children and why do they have such difficulty acquiring more than one language?			
8 It is important that school leaders – principals/heads of schools and subject-matter heads – be knowledgeable, proactive and committed to dual-language teaching for the programme to work.			

The eight key principles we think are important when planning programmes and instruction for additional-language learners can be seen in the box below.

Key principles of CLIL

1	Additional-language instruction is more effective when integrated with content instruction.
2	Explicit and systematic language instruction is important.
3	Student engagement is the engine of learning.
4	Both languages should have equally high status.
5	The first language can be a useful tool for learning the additional language and new academic knowledge and skills.
6	Classroom-based assessment is critical for programme success.
7	All children can become bilingual.
8	Strong leadership is critical for successful dual-language teaching.

PRINCIPLE 1:
Additional-language instruction is more effective when integrated with content instruction

From a student's point of view, learning a language is radically different in a CLIL classroom in comparison to a classroom with grammar-based instruction. Rather than being expected to memorise new words and grammar rules, and then to use them in repetitive practice activities, students are expected to talk about important events in their communities or personal lives, learn how to do scientific experiments, or to solve mathematical problems – all the time using the additional language. Students are taught the words and grammatical patterns they need in order to communicate. In intensive CLIL programmes, such as IMM, they also learn the language from hearing the teacher use it. It is by using the language that students learn the language. Thus, from the learner's point of view, attention is focused on what is being

RESEARCH NOTE

Effectiveness of CLIL

Part I: CLIL for majority-language students
(from Genesee, 2004; Genesee & Lindholm-Leary, 2013)

a) IMM students achieve the same levels of competence in their first language as similar students in monolingual programmes.

b) IMM students demonstrate the same levels of academic achievement as similar students in monolingual programmes.

c) IMM students achieve advanced levels of functional proficiency in the additional language, significantly more advanced than the levels achieved by students in conventional additional-language programmes.

d) IMM is effective for students with a wide variety of learner characteristics and backgrounds:

  • students with poor first-language skills
  • students with low levels of academic ability
  • students from disadvantaged family backgrounds
  • students from minority cultural groups who already speak the majority language.

e) IMM is equally effective with languages that are similar (English and French) and languages that are very different (English and Japanese).

Part II: CLIL for minority-language students
(from Genesee & Lindholm-Leary, 2012)

Compared to similar minority-language students who are educated entirely in the majority language:

a) Minority-language students in programmes that aim for bilingual proficiency (DL-CLIL) acquire the same or higher levels of proficiency in the majority language.

b) They attain the same levels of competence, or higher, in academic subjects.

c) They achieve higher levels of proficiency in the home language.

d) They have lower failure rates, lower drop-out rates, and greater expectations for continuing on in higher education.

communicated. The teacher's job is to create opportunities in class that will engage students in meaningful communication about interesting and challenging topics, at a level that is appropriate for them cognitively and linguistically. While the teacher is teaching content, he or she is also teaching language that is useful for communication about the content. CLIL teachers use scaffolding strategies to facilitate acquisition of the language and, at the same time, to make the content comprehensible even though it is being taught in an additional language. We talk about how to do that in **Chapters 4** and **5**.

Extensive research carried out over many years has shown that CLIL approaches to additional-language teaching are highly effective – if done well; see **Research Note 2.1**. Moreover, they have been shown to be effective in a wide range of learning contexts, with different languages, and, most importantly, with a wide range of learners – who vary with respect to age, socio-economic background, language-learning ability and academic ability. As we talk about how to implement CLIL effectively, we draw on research on a variety of CLIL classes and programmes from around the world.

PRINCIPLE 2:
Explicit and systematic language instruction is important

Many years of research in CLIL classrooms has taught us that including systematic and explicit language instruction that is linked to students' communicative needs is important in promoting additional-language proficiency even when content is the vehicle for teaching. Additional-language learners are remarkably agile at communicating in an additional language despite the fact that they have not fully mastered the grammar and have limited vocabulary. They develop many strategies for circumventing what they do not know. Indeed, extensive research on the language competence of students in IMM programmes in Canada has shown that even after many years of participation in such programmes there are gaps in their grammatical competence; their vocabulary is limited; and they often lack idiomaticity (Lyster, 2007) if they are not given explicit language instruction in aspects of the language that are difficult to acquire.

Being able to use an additional language correctly and idiomatically is important for students who plan to go on to higher education or to professions where they will use the additional language. Many secondary-level students in countries around the world are learning English with the hope that they will be accepted by an English-language university to pursue their education or because they want jobs in the international job market, where English is often an asset. Although students who are learning an additional language only in school are probably always going to have some gaps in competence, the role of additional-language educators is to fill as many of those gaps as possible. Including systematic and explicit instruction of specific vocabulary, grammar and discourse patterns that are linked to communication in and outside the classroom can help push learners' linguistic competence further and avoid fossilisation of incorrect usage.

2.1 PERSONAL PERSPECTIVE
Intentionally drawing attention to language in meaningful contexts

Roy Lyster, Department of Integrated Studies, McGill University

When I taught grade 8 in a French immersion program in the 1980s, we were advised to neither focus too much on the mechanics of the target language nor give much corrective feedback. It was believed that students would simply 'pick up' the language on their own, thanks to exposure to lots of input provided through subject-matter instruction. We now know that students do indeed 'pick up' lots of language, but not all of it – what often goes unnoticed are non-salient yet important morphological features. Consequently, teachers need to draw their students' attention to these features, but not necessarily through decontextualized language analysis. One of the best ways for teachers to intentionally draw attention to language is in the context of meaningful interaction about content. It is during such teachable moments that students are motivated to use the language and so are well positioned to notice how otherwise hard-to-notice language features play an important role in making meaning.

Teachers have at their disposal at least two ways of intentionally drawing attention to the target language in meaningful contexts. First, they can integrate language with content in seemingly spontaneous ways through a *reactive approach*. Ostensibly unplanned opportunities can take the form of (a) teacher questions intended to increase both the quantity and quality of student output and (b) corrective feedback that serves to negotiate both form and meaning. Second, teachers can adopt a *proactive approach* that requires planning for noticing and awareness activities followed by opportunities for both guided and autonomous practice. Planning for content and language integration in this way involves shifting learners' attention to language in the context of content instruction in cases where they would not otherwise process the language at the same time as the content (see Lyster, 2007).

Explicit language teaching is even more important when the additional language is being used to teach academic subjects, such as Mathematics or Science. Why is this? Increasingly, educators and researchers recognise that the language needed to function effectively in school settings is different from the kind of language people usually use on a day-to-day basis for social communication. School language is often referred to as language for academic purposes; language for day-to-day communication in most situations outside school is referred to as language for social purposes. We provide more detailed discussion of how these two forms of communication differ, and how to plan content lessons to include these kinds of language skills, in **Chapter 4**.

For our purposes here, suffice to say that language used in academic contexts for teaching and learning is more elaborate and complex than the language we use with friends and family members to talk about ordinary things. Language for academic purposes includes words that are seldom used outside school (such as 'meteorological', 'larva', 'asteroids'), grammar that is rare in day-to-day conversations (e.g. complex statements about causality), and discourse/text formats that are unique to talking about academic subjects (e.g. how to structure a science report). As students progress through school, mastery of advanced academic subject matter and cognitive skills that are taught in the higher grades becomes increasingly dependent on the ability to use language in these ways. Moreover, oral language competence is the foundation for competence in reading and writing. Being able to read advanced academic texts or to write complex expository text for Science and History classes requires complex academic language skills. Academic language skills can be difficult to acquire – even students who have been in immersion-type programmes for 12 years often do not master them easily (Lyster, 2007). Teaching academic language skills systematically and explicitly

RESEARCH NOTE

The importance of explicit language instruction in CLIL

a) Strategies for direct instruction are important when teaching literacy to additional-language learners in comparison to implicit or indirect strategies alone (August & Shanahan, 2006; Riches & Genesee, 2006).

b) Corrective feedback when students use incorrect or inappropriate words or grammar can support mastery of the correct forms if done in conjunction with meaningful use of the language (Lyster, 1998, 2007).

c) Recasts, which are a form of implicit correction, are not very effective in North American classrooms; students in those contexts respond more to corrective feedback that is explicit and student-centred. In contrast, recasts are effective in classrooms in other countries where students may be more used to instruction with a focus on correct usage (Lyster, 2007).

d) Oral language proficiency of students in Canadian immersion programmes improves when they are given instruction with explicit language objectives, including a focus on both functional and discrete language skills (Lyster, 2007).

e) Minority-language students' oral language proficiency improves if they are given plenty of opportunities to use new or difficult-to-acquire aspects of the additional language (including discrete grammatical rules and communicative patterns), corrective feedback and appropriate models of correct usage (Saunders & Goldenberg, 2010).

alongside content instruction can enhance the acquisition of these difficult-to-acquire skills and, in turn, makes it easier to process abstract subject-area concepts.

One of the strongest proponents of a balanced approach to language and content integrated instruction is Roy Lyster at McGill University. Lyster has carried out extensive empirical research on instructional strategies that enhance students' competence in their additional language. In his counterbalance approach (Lyster, 2007), he makes a strong case for ensuring that there is an explicit linguistic component to content lesson plans and a content component to language lesson plans. Mehisto (2012) also argues that effective dual-language education makes language and content objectives visible to learners so that they are better able to monitor their own learning. We provide guidance on how to build explicit language instruction into your teaching in **Chapter 4**. In **Research Note 2.2**, we review research evidence to show that explicit language instruction can enhance students' language skills.

PRINCIPLE 3:
Student engagement is the engine of learning

Many additional-language teachers have experienced classrooms full of students who appear to be asleep because they do not want to participate in activities that they find boring and irrelevant. While researchers and linguists are probably interested in language for its own sake, there are very few school-age learners who are interested in learning an additional language for its own sake. Part of the rationale behind CLIL is that using content as a vehicle for additional-language learning engages students in using the language for authentic and deep communication. Certainly, this was the thinking by the educators and researchers in Canada who created the first IMM programmes. They believed that using the additional language to teach core subjects such as Science and Mathematics would engage students in using the additional language in order to do well in school. Grammar-based approaches, while seeking to engage students in make-believe scenarios, often fail because students cannot relate to the situations being depicted in their textbooks and find them phony and uninteresting. Moreover, the make-believe activities of traditional second-language classrooms provide students with little opportunity to use the language beyond individual lessons because use of the language is tied to the textbook or a particular activity. These approaches are also less effective because they use a one-size-fits-all strategy so that all students are expected to be interested in the textbook scenario and to engage in using language in these artificial ways. The key to motivating students to learn an additional language is to select activities that are interesting and engaging and that appeal to individual interests, learning styles and goals. This is especially important when the additional language is a language that is not used normally outside school.

2.2   PERSONAL PERSPECTIVE

Implementing CLIL projects linking English to Environmental Science in a school in Colombia

Edgar A. Garzón Diaz, Biology and Ecology teacher,
INEM Santiago Pérez, Bogotá, Colombia

Educational policies of different countries are often affected by their ethnic and linguistic histories. In Colombia, a Latin American country with more than 60 indigenous languages, surprisingly, educational processes tend to be framed by an English–Spanish duality, in which English is a long-term expectation and Spanish is a long-lasting reality. Additionally, there is an evident gap between the private and public educational sectors, with the former representing privileged cities and socio-economic groups where English is a synonym for high status, and the latter representing regional and ethnic diversity where English learning is a challenge.

An example of the latter is the INEM (in English: National Institute of Middle Vocational Education) Santiago Pérez, a school that was built in order to provide disadvantaged communities with high quality vocational centres. It has students from different regions of the country, some of them displaced by internal conflict and most of them coming from underprivileged backgrounds. However, these conditions do not prevent students from actively participating in a special learning process where knowledge of subject matter (Science) is combined with the use of Spanish and English as vehicular languages.

The process of learning Science mentioned above is character-ised not only by the integration of content and language, but also by the engagement of students through technology-enhanced CLIL-based projects. These projects are set up to raise students' awareness of environmental issues related to their local and global contexts such as: global environmental change, endangered spe-cies, Colombian natural parks, and protected wetlands. They are devised following the 4 Cs framework (Coyle 1999) and are aimed at students' development of critical thinking skills as well as the development of their scientific and citizenship competencies. This learning process is enriched by the use of technology (electronic tablets, virtual platforms such as Edmodo, web quests, and video-making tools) that help students interact in and outside school. It is important to mention that this teaching initiative is finding more support among academic peers who perceive it as a way to bridge the gap between public and private schools in Colombia and eventually to contribute to a more egalitarian educational system.

Embedding additional-language learning in authentic activities that engage students is to teach language as a means to an end rather than as an end in itself. It is important, then, to understand the characteris-tics of activities that actually engage students. John Guthrie (Guthrie, Wigfield & Perencevich, 2004) has done a lot of research on engagement and learning in the context of learning to read. Guthrie has identified four components of engagement that lead to better outcomes: (1) time on task (more time for engagement is better), (2) affect (i.e. enthusiasm and enjoyment promote engagement), (3) depth of cognitive processing (leads to cognitive engagement) and (4) active pursuit of activities that promote learning results in more engagement and better learning. Engaging all students also means that learning activities must be inter-esting and relevant (or authentic) to individual learners.

Learning activities should also be cognitively engaging – during ac-tivities that are cognitively engaging, students are expected not simply to identify the right answer to a question, but to think critically about the topic under discussion. Teaching that engages learners gives stu-dents lots of opportunities to use language. Activities that engage students put more focus on learners and less on teachers. This can be achieved through the use of student-centred activities that give students plenty of time to be involved in discussion and thinking, such as pair work or cooperative learning. A one-size-fits-all approach to teaching does not engage all students because engaging students requires differentiated teaching and learning. This all makes a lot of sense when it comes to learning language. The whole purpose of learning language is

RESEARCH NOTE
The importance of student engagement

a) In a late IMM programme (grade 7) that was student-centred and activity-based, Stevens (1983) found that students acquired speaking and listening comprehension skills in their additional language that were as advanced as those of students in a teacher-fronted IMM programme despite the fact that the activity-based programme provided just over half as much exposure to the additional language as the teacher-fronted programme. Stevens argued that the students in the student-centred programme were highly motivated to learn the language and this offset reduction in exposure to the language.

b) Students in late IMM programmes in schools in which there are many native speakers of the additional language attain higher levels of additional-language proficiency than students in IMM programmes with only additional-language learners. This reflects the importance of engaging in social and academic discourse with native speakers (Genesee, 1987).

c) Student engagement in reading is a significant predictor of reading outcomes, even more powerful than socio-economic background (see PISA results in Organization for Economic Co-operation and Development, 2010).

d) The reading performance of students from families with low income and low education who were 'engaged readers' was superior to that of students from families with higher income and education who were 'less engaged readers' (Guthrie, Wigfield & Perencevich, 2004).

to communicate – if you are not interested in or keen to communicate, there is no motivation to learn the language or become engaged. Talking about local plant life might interest and engage some students, but not others. Talking about how to form the pluperfect subjunctive in English will probably not motivate anyone. **Research Note 2.3** summarises some key findings.

PRINCIPLE 4:
Both languages should have equally high status

In most bilingual contexts, be it in the community at large or in the classroom, one language has more status than the other because it is viewed as the language of power, the 'cool language', or the language that is most useful – we refer to this as the majority language. Even in bilingual families, one language often has more status than the other. This is usually the language that is spoken widely outside the family – English, for example, in English-speaking countries; French in France, and so on. Immigrant children or children in indigenous-language communities are often reluctant or even embarrassed to use their home language because they perceive it to have low prestige in comparison to the majority language. This imbalance in status can create problems in schools and classrooms with a bilingual focus because it disfavours use of one of the languages. Similarly, students' attitudes towards each language can bias them to use what they perceive to be the low-status language (Gaudet & Clement, 2005). Remember that the slogan of CLIL is 'to use language is to learn language'. If students perceive one of the languages to have low prestige, they will be reluctant to use it. This can also affect teachers' language use. Teachers in dual-language programmes who believe that one language has more status than the other risk favouring the language with the high status. This can occur in ways that are subtle but important. Schools can reinforce these perceptions in many ways – by posting notices around the school or sending notes home in the high-status language only, by making announcements over the PA system in the high-prestige or majority language only, by organising fun extracurricular activities in one language only, and so on. Young learners tend to be very pragmatic – if they perceive that one of the languages they are learning is valued in school more than the other, they will be hesitant to use and learn the 'less popular' language.

A critical goal of CLIL educators is to ensure that both languages have equally high status in the school. This is important so that minority-language students see their language being used and respected in the school; so that they feel that they can learn the additional language without sacrificing the home language; and so that students of different language groups develop respect and admiration for one another This might actually mean giving more status to the low-status language in order to level the playing field. Raising the status of a language also means highlighting cultural values and customs of the communities

RESEARCH NOTE

Both languages should have equally high status

a) Students' perception of the status of the language affects their use of that language in class (Gaudet & Clement, 2005).

b) Teachers can unconsciously favour one language over another in dual-language programmes that include minority- and majority-language students. Valdés (1997) found that minority-language students in DL-CLIL classrooms in the US were often called upon by their teacher to provide correct models of the minority language for the benefit of the majority-language students, but they were seldom given enrichment activities to expand their proficiency in that language.

c) An additive bilingual learning environment in which both languages have equally high status supports mastery of both the minority and majority language. Conversely, when one language is favoured over the other, students acquire greater proficiency in the favoured language (de Jong, 2014).

c) Tompkins and Orr (2011) evaluated IMM programmes in English and Mi'kmaq or Maliseet, two indigenous languages found in eastern Canada. They found that Mi'kmaq immersion students' English reading scores were higher overall than those of their non-immersion peers. Although there was no evaluation of students' academic outcomes, researchers reported that graduates of both programmes exhibited high self-esteem, intellectual curiosity, a strong work ethic, and awareness and pride in their ancestral language and culture.

and families who speak that language. Ensuring that both languages have high status and, therefore, are worth learning creates an additive bilingual learning environment – an environment in which learning an additional language does not mean giving up your home language. We discuss how to do this in more detail in **Chapter 5**. **Research Note 2.4** summarises some key findings that reinforce the importance of equalising the status of both languages.

PRINCIPLE 5:

The first language can be a useful tool for learning the additional language and new academic knowledge and skills

For many years, additional-language educators thought that students' use of their first language should be avoided at all costs during classes when the additional language was being taught or used as the language of instruction. Letting students use their first language, it was argued, would become a crutch; so, it was best to ban it from the classroom. As a result, teachers in dual-language programmes usually tried to create monolingual environments in which everyone would use only the additional language during second-language classes and only the first language during time devoted to the first language.

As we discussed in Principle 1, there is some validity to these arguments – if students do not use the additional language, they will not learn it. Letting students use their first language during times when the additional language is the language of instruction makes it harder for them to use the additional language because it is so much easier to use the language they already know. We recommend that CLIL teachers use the additional language as much as possible, but we do not advocate rigid separation of the two languages. Recent research indicates that judicious use of students' first language can be beneficial for learning both the additional language and academic material (see García & Wei, 2014, for a discussion on what they refer to as *translanguaging*). Evidence that using both languages at certain times and for certain purposes can facilitate language development comes from research on many aspects of bilingualism. **Research Note 2.5** summarises research on bilingual codemixing, reading acquisition, and retrieving words from memory, and shows that the two languages of bilinguals are naturally interacting with one another and, therefore, that making connections between the two languages during instruction is a good idea – if done strategically.

However, how much you use the first language during additional-language time, and how you use it, will depend on the status of the two languages. As we indicated under Principle 4, if the first language is a minority language, then it needs more support than if it is a majority language. Let's take two different cases – one from Canada and the other from the US. In Canada, most students speak English, a majority language, at home; and they are learning through French and English in school. Teachers teaching during the French portion of the curriculum in IMM programmes resist using English for fear that their English-speaking students will become lazy and use only English because they 'could get away with it'. This strategy makes sense in this context. Because the first language of Canadian immersion students is a high-status language that is highly valued and widely used outside school, it does not need to be supported very much in school, especially during those times in the day devoted to teaching French. However, in many dual-language programmes in the US, the students speak Spanish as a first language outside school. Despite its status as one of the most widely spoken languages around the world, Spanish is perceived by many native speakers of English and Spanish in the US as having a relatively low status. In this case, encouraging students to use Spanish in order to learn new concepts being taught in English, and to push their proficiency in English forward, would be helpful. By drawing on minority-language students' knowledge of their first language during additional-language class time, you are not only reinforcing students' skills in that language, but also elevating the status of that language to create an additive bilingual learning environment. Similarly, when immigrant children or children who speak an indigenous language are being taught only through the majority language, using the minority home language while teaching in the majority language reinforces their competence and pride in that language. However, it is critical that cross-linguistic teaching be done strategically and purposefully so that students are given plenty of opportunities to use both languages. It should never be used just to make it easier for the students or the teachers.

RESEARCH NOTE

The first language is a tool for additional-language learning

a) Evidence that has examined language processing in bilinguals indicates that they activate both languages no matter what language they are using – although the language in use is more active, the other language is also 'turned on' in the background but 'at a lower volume', metaphorically speaking. Moreover, bilinguals have a common conceptual system that can be used to make sense of either language; for example, when bilinguals search for the meaning of a word 'in their head', meanings from both languages are available (Gullifer, Kroll & Dussias, 2013; Kroll, 2008).

b) When bilinguals codeswitch, they do so in ways that avoid grammatical errors in both languages, indicating that both languages are activated. This has been found even in 3-year-old bilinguals, indicating that it is within the brain's natural capacity to activate both languages at the same time (Genesee, 2002).

c) Successful additional-language readers try to translate the text into their stronger language or they search their mental dictionaries for cognates in the other language when they have difficulty reading in their additional language (Jiminez, Garcia & Pearson, 1996). In contrast, students with weak reading skills in an additional language avoid making connections between their two languages.

d) Phonological awareness, decoding and reading comprehension skills are correlated in first and additional languages. Students who can decode words or comprehend text in their first language learn to read in their additional language more easily than students who lack such skills in their first language (Genesee & Geva, 2006).

e) Literacy instruction that allows students to use both their first and their additional language enhances students' metalinguistic awareness and increases engagement (Lyster, Collins & Ballinger, 2009).

PRINCIPLE 6:
Classroom-based assessment is critical for programme success

Teaching is a complex business and it is made even more complex when you work with students from diverse backgrounds learning through an additional language. However, this is what makes CLIL instruction exciting – you are giving students opportunities to acquire lifelong skills that they would not get in a regular programme. Assessment is critical to guide you in your day-to-day lesson and unit plans and teaching. It is also critical in helping teachers and school administrators to continuously update the curriculum and programme so that it is as good as it can be. We use a broad definition of assessment – the collection of information about teaching and learning that guides teaching and programme development. It is not only about assessing student outcomes; it also includes feedback about the effectiveness of instructional materials and activities; information from students about their preferred learning styles, their interests and their backgrounds; and feedback from students during self-assessment about their accomplishments and ongoing learning needs. To serve all of these goals, teachers need a variety of assessment tools that they can use in a purposeful way continuously to give them the information they need to do a good job. Assessment is doubly important in CLIL programmes because thinking about dual-language teaching and learning is often clouded by myths and misunderstandings that can result in misguided educational decisions (see **Additional Resources 2.1**). By taking charge of their own classroom assessments, and by including students as partners in assessment, CLIL teachers can base decisions on their own evidence.

2.1 ADDITIONAL RESOURCES

Myths and Misunderstandings?

Genesee (2015) discusses some common myths about raising and educating children bilingually. He debunks myths that (a) dual-language learning is more difficult than learning only one language during the preschool years; (b) earlier and more exposure to an additional language in school is always advantageous; (c) children with language impairments are at greater risk if they learn two languages than one; and (d) the best way to understand the accomplishments of dual-language learners is to compare them to monolinguals.

PRINCIPLE 7:
All children can become bilingual

In many communities, it is widely thought that children with learning difficulties, children who struggle and underperform in school for non-clinical reasons, or even older students cannot acquire an additional language easily. Misconceptions about the ability to become proficient in an additional language are most evident when it involves a child who has, or is suspected of having, a language-related impairment, such as specific language impairment or reading impairment. It is also common when thinking about students who might struggle in school for non-clinical reasons – for example, children who speak a non-standard variety of the majority language, children who come from a minority ethnic group, or children from low socio-economic families and communities. Such attitudes can be particularly prevalent in monolingual communities where it is assumed that monolingualism is the norm and, therefore, normal. It is not only parents and educators who believe this, but also some speech and language specialists, child developmental specialists, and medical practitioners. However, to deprive these children of the opportunity to learn more than one language is unfair. It is critical that these kinds of beliefs are subjected to scientific scrutiny.

These beliefs are starting to change as more and more scientific evidence demonstrates that most, if not all, children can become bilingual within the limits of their ability. To start, there is now an impressive body of research from around the world on children who grow up learning more than one language from birth or shortly after birth – what is often referred to as simultaneous bilingualism. This research is important because it shows that young children's ability to learn language is so powerful that even children with serious language-learning difficulties are still able to learn two languages within the limits of their disability – see **Research Note 2.6**, Part I.

What about children who learn another language in dual-language school programmes and who struggle academically? Children with poor first-language skills, or who come from socio-economically disadvantaged families, or are members of linguistic minority groups often, although not always, underperform in school in comparison to other students. It is important to emphasise here that these students do not have developmental disabilities or underlying learning impairments. Any difficulties they have in school reflect external factors, including

a lack of appropriate instructional adaptation in school to accommodate their particular linguistic and cultural backgrounds, inappropriate
assessment procedures, lack of appropriate professional support, and
so on. It is also often thought that beginning additional-language instruction early in school is better than beginning later and that starting late is not as effective. Understanding the success or difficulty of
such diverse students in dual-language programmes can give us a better
understanding of the suitability of dual-language education for learners

2.6 RESEARCH NOTE

All children can become bilingual
(from Paradis, Genesee & Crago, 2011)

Part I: Simultaneous bilingual children

Compared to similar monolingual children:

a) Simultaneous bilingual children with typical development go
through critical milestones in language development at the same
age if they are provided with sufficient input in each language.
Simultaneous bilinguals may differ from monolinguals but
this is usually due to the amount of exposure they have to
each language.

b) Bilingual children often know fewer words in each language but
they know the same number, or more, if both languages are
examined together.

c) Bilingual children score at the same level on standardised
language tests if they are given sufficient input in each
language.

d) The language abilities of children who are raised with two
languages from birth, and who have specific (primary) language
impairment (Paradis, Genesee & Crago, 2011), Down's syndrome
(Kay-Raining Bird et al., 2005) or autism spectrum disorder
(Marinova-Todd & Mirenda, 2016) are comparable to those of
monolingual children with similar impairments and disorders.

Part II: Students with academic difficulties in dual-language programmes

Compared to students with similar characteristics in monolingual programmes:

a) Students with language-learning and academic difficulties can acquire the same levels of first-language proficiency and academic achievement in dual-language programmes. This is true for children with poor first-language skills who may have language impairment (Bruck, 1978, 1982), students with below-average academic abilities (Genesee, 1976), and students with developmental disorders (Myers, 2009).

b) Students with learning challenges who are in dual-language programmes that aim for bilingualism can acquire advanced levels of functional proficiency in two languages (Genesee & Fortune, 2014).

c) Students who struggle in school for the following reasons can acquire the same levels of first-language proficiency and academic achievement in dual-language programmes. This is true for:

   i. children from families with low levels of socio-economic status (Genesee, 1976)

   ii. children from ethnic minority groups who speak the majority language (e.g. students from Mi'kmak backgrounds who speak English in Canada) (Usborne, Peck, Smith & Taylor, 2011)

   iii. children who speak a non-standard variety of the majority language (e.g. African and Hawaiian Americans who speak Black Vernacular and Hawaiian Creole English, respectively) (e.g. see Wilson & Kamanā, 2011, on Hawaiian immersion).

d) Students with these background characteristics can acquire advanced levels of functional bilingualism in dual-language programmes (Genesee, 2007).

e) Students who begin to learn an additional language in late IMM programmes can achieve the same levels of additional-language proficiency as students who begin in early IMM (Genesee, 2014; Muñoz & Singleton, 2011).

with different backgrounds and learning resources. **Research Note 2.6**, Part II, summarises evidence from research that has been carried out on these kinds of students and shows that these beliefs are not supported by scientific evidence.

Results from these studies do not tell us that *all* children will become bilingual easily and completely as a result of dual-language instruction. Adaptations need to be made to create learning environments that allow students who struggle in school to succeed in dual-language programmes. We discuss these adaptations in greater detail later in the book. Dual-language education or enriched additional-language instruction should not be elitist – it should be open to all children.

PRINCIPLE 8:
Strong leadership is critical for successful dual-language teaching

Strong leadership is critical for the success of any school (**see Research Note 2.7**). Strong school leaders are important because they ensure timely, effective and ongoing school-wide planning that supports the work of everyone in the school – teachers, education specialists and students. Strong leadership ensures coherence, continuity and collaboration among all members and components of a programme so that it is maximally effective. For example, we know from many years of research around the world that the benefits of dual-language instruction take time to materialise. This should not be surprising – language is the most complex skill humans acquire and it takes time to become fully proficient in a new language; it does not happen after one school year, or two or three. For students to achieve high levels of additional-language proficiency in school, educators must create rich, developmentally continuous learning environments that are integrated across several grade levels. This requires strong knowledgeable leadership – on the part of the head of the school, heads of departments within the school, and the education specialists who work in the school. This also requires a common vision of the programme, common understanding of the goals of the programme, and shared commitment to work together to achieve those goals. None of this can happen without strong leaders in the school.

It has been our experience that people's thinking about bilingualism and additional-language teaching and learning is often coloured by

RESEARCH NOTE

The importance of strong school leadership

a) Strong school leadership is essential for ensuring a high-quality programme and for guiding decision-making about critical issues in dual-language programmes (e.g. Lindholm-Leary & Borsato, 2006).

b) Successful dual-language programmes engage in extensive and high-level planning and, in particular, they plan for articulation across grade levels (Montecel & Cortez 2002).

c) School-wide planning is critical to ensure: (a) adequate and equitable distribution of school resources; (b) collaboration among dual-language and mainstream teachers in the creation of a coherent and integrated curriculum; (c) the development and implementation of a school-wide curriculum that integrates first- and additional-language instruction with academic instruction at each grade level and across grade levels; (d) equitable instruction and high standards for both language-minority and language-majority students; and (e) appropriate assessment protocols to monitor programme effectiveness (Lindholm-Leary, 2012).

d) Highly qualified teachers are essential in dual-language programmes for minority-language students (August & Shanahan, 2006).

their own experiences as students or by common myths – such as the notion that only high-achieving students can thrive in dual-language programmes. Many of these ideas are not supported by current research and theory, as we just saw. Educators who share these misguided or un-supported ideas run the risk of making decisions that are not in the best interest of their students or the programme. It also takes strong school leadership to make sure that appropriate and timely professional development is provided.

2.3 PERSONAL PERSPECTIVE

Learning vs acquisition: The challenge for a language coordinator

Ian Gulliford, Language Coordinator,
Frankfurt International School (FIS), Frankfurt, Germany

I was hired by the Frankfurt International School as Language Coordinator to design future language programmes and to give shape to existing ones. I was told that teaching was based on proficiency but I soon discovered that 'proficiency' was simply 'what was in the textbook', i.e. learning but not acquisition. Fortunately, over the next few years, the school financed teacher training courses. Proficiency standards and ratings were used each year to assess the progress of our students (grades 2–12) and to plan courses for the following year. The size of the school made it possible to create three intermediate classes (low, mid, high) in ESL, German, French and Spanish. As these standards continued to be applied, we noticed that many students were able to span two to three proficiency levels in one year – e.g. novice low to intermediate low and even mid.

Research has shown that one acquires another language easily if support is given to the mother tongue. FIS students come from 50 countries, 35 languages are spoken and every family wants its language taught! I was appointed Head of a new Language Council and together it formulated a policy that specified a minimum of four students per class for mother tongue support. This allowed additionally for an 'early' immersion German–English stream beginning in pre-primary where art was enjoyed in German. A 'mid' immersion programme was begun in grades 2–3 where topics from the IBPYP's Units of Inquiry were taught in German. Humanities and Science were offered in German in grades 6–8. Bilingual teachers were hired from North America who then in-serviced local native speakers. Parent volunteers were assistants. Most materials in the immersion programme were teacher-produced. Soon we were supporting 12 mother tongue programmes.

My biggest challenges as Language Coordinator were to help teachers modify their teaching methods and to advocate for small class sizes and immersion. The biggest payoff was to see how students' curiosity about the nature of language grew. Formal grammar teaching is sterile before grade 8; however, when explained to learners what proficiency means and how everyone passes through the same stages, even some of the youngest asked, 'Why?' They had become acquirers.

Most schools operate with limited resources – human, financial and physical. Decisions need to be made about how to allocate existing resources and how to obtain new resources. Strong school leaders can do this. Strong school leadership is also needed to advocate on behalf of the school. Dual-language programmes and innovative teaching in general are often criticised by other teachers in the system, by members of the community who do not see the value of other languages, or by parents whose children are not attending the programme. Strong leadership is needed to counteract forces that might destabilise or weaken the programme. Getting the support of leaders in the community is also important because they can elevate the status of a programme and help school leaders advocate on behalf of their programme. Increasingly, business and other members of the community see the value of competent multilingual graduates and many are likely to be keen to support efforts to promote dual-language learning. Business leaders in Indianapolis, Indiana, for example, provided lots of support for the creation of a new multilingual international school with a focus on English and Spanish and English and French. They saw the new school as a way of attracting experts from outside the US to live and work in Indianapolis, home of a number of important international pharmaceutical companies.

For all of these reasons, strong leadership is critical. We discuss what school and community leaders can do to support a dual-language programme throughout the chapters in this book.

2.2 ADDITIONAL RESOURCES

Building bilingual education systems:
Forces, Mechanisms and Counterweights

> *Building Bilingual Education Systems: Forces, Mechanism and Counterweights*
> (Mehisto & Genesee, 2015) is a collection of case studies from around the
> world. Each case study discusses the challenges faced in the development of
> dual-language programmes. Using Mehisto's framework of forces, mechanisms
> and counterweights, the authors highlight the importance of taking a broad
> perspective when planning or maintaining a programme. This involves
> considering factors outside the school that support or challenge the existence
> of the school. The book provides a useful overview of the broad range of factors
> that new programmes should consider.

SUMMARY

It is important to keep these eight principles foremost in your thinking
if you are starting a new CLIL programme and want to establish a strong
foundation based on shared beliefs. If you are working in an existing
programme, you may want to take a step back and reflect on these principles to ensure that the foundation for your programme is aligned with
these eight principles, and, where it is not, that change is called for.
There is no single, magic formula for designing and implementing CLIL
because each school exists in a unique socio-political setting and has a
unique population of learners and teachers with their own strengths
and needs. However, these principles can help anchor the choices you
have to make in important ways that touch on multiple aspects of your
programme. We refer to the eight principles in the remainder of the
book as we provide suggestions on setting up a programme, planning
and providing instruction, cooperating with one another, and assessing
what you do.

3   Snapshots of CLIL

Language teaching has always been shaped in important ways by theory and research. CLIL reflects the culmination of decades of scientific inquiry and educational experimentation into how languages are learned and taught successfully. Prior to the introduction of CLIL, traditional foreign-language teaching focused on explicit and systematic instruction of the components of language –sounds, vocabulary, grammar and formulaic utterances (such as 'Where is the train station?'). These were the pieces of language that it was thought learners needed to learn in order to be able to use the language. These components were often taught in a specific order – present tense first, followed by perhaps simple past tense, then future tense, and then complex conditional tenses. However, there was no evidence that either the particular aspects of language or the order in which they were taught were the right ones; nor were they necessarily useful for all learners. Errors were regarded as breakdowns in learning and were to be avoided for fear that they would become fossilised. The role of the teacher was to provide models of correct language and to provide positive or negative feedback when learners got it right or made an error. Similarly, textbooks provided lots of examples of the correct language forms with many opportunities to repeat them – sometimes by writing the correct answers and sometimes by working with another student to produce a dialogue or take turns changing present tense verbs into past tense, and so on.

This approach began to fall out of favour in the 1960s and 1970s because it was becoming evident that although it could teach students a lot about language, it was not very successful at teaching them how to use language for real communication. However, it is still popular in some foreign-language classrooms. This sparked a shift to what became known as the communicative approach – teaching additional languages so students could communicate in the language outside the classroom. These approaches became popular because the world was becoming increasingly interconnected and schools sought ways of teaching students how to communicate in the second language. For example, the creation of the European Common Market called for citizens who could communicate in one another's languages; and globalisation was becoming more and more evident and was also calling for a bi- and multilingual workforce.

Around the same time, research on first- and second-language learning was indicating that learning language was a dynamic, cognitively engaging and social phenomenon. Research was beginning to indicate that the order in which learners were acquiring the parts of language did not always correspond to the order you could find in textbooks. Moreover, learners made 'mistakes' but the incorrect forms they produced were better seen as attempts to express themselves with whatever knowledge they had at the time in order to communicate something important. For example, students might say *choosed* instead of *chose* because they knew that the past tense of many verbs in English is created by adding *ed* to the verb. Students might be resourceful and use their first language to guess words they did not know in the additional language – a student whose first language is Spanish might say 'library' to refer to a bookstore, transferring the Spanish word *librería*. Research was starting to show that learners actively construct the new language based on what they hear and what they already know in their first language; and errors are an essential part of that construction process.

Out of these studies and insights a new approach emerged, one that put an emphasis on teaching academic content through the additional language so that students would learn functional language skills while they learned about Science, Mathematics and other topics in school. In some CLIL contexts, in fact, the content is as important as the language to be learned – in IMM classrooms, for example. In fact, CLIL can be adapted to many different contexts. Mehisto, Marsh and Frigols (2008, p. 13) identified 13 contexts in which CLIL can be applied, including student exchanges, local projects, family stays, work-study abroad, and others. In this book, we talk about CLIL in schools and how academic skills and knowledge that are part of the school curriculum are integrated with language instruction. CLIL in school contexts has a dual purpose – to teach content and language at the same time. There are several good reasons for implementing CLIL in school – see **Table 3.1**.

TABLE 3.1

Reasons for integrating content and language instruction

- CLIL seeks to draw on the same kinds of language-learning abilities that children use to acquire a first language.

- CLIL exposes learners to authentic forms of language use that integrates reading, writing, speaking and listening. It is artificial to separate these language skills; for example, reading and writing require oral language skills, and speaking skills implicate listening skills.

- CLIL builds on students' interest in learning language for real communication – in CLIL classrooms, students are not just learning language; they are learning Mathematics, Science or other subjects.

- CLIL capitalizes on student motivation by engaging students in cognitively challenging learning activities that provide lots of opportunities to interact using the additional language.

- CLIL ensures that acquisition of the additional language has value outside school because it teaches language skills that are authentic and useful beyond the classroom.

- Using content as a vehicle for learning the additional language promotes negotiation of meaning, which, in turn, enhances language learning.

- In the case of young learners, CLIL integrates additional-language learning with students' social and cognitive development and, thus, is developmentally appropriate and takes advantage of young learners' immense capacity to learn language.

We focus on CLIL in this book in elementary- and secondary-school contexts, but CLIL can also be used with college or university students who want to learn another language (e.g. Edwards, Wesche, Krashen, Clement & Kruidenier, 1984). Because we discuss CLIL in school contexts, we discuss the use of academic subjects, such as Mathematics, Science, Drama, Literature, and so on, as vehicles for teaching and learning additional languages. There are a number of good reasons for using academic subjects as the content in CLIL, listed in **Table 3.2**.

TABLE 3.2

Reasons for using academic content in CLIL classrooms

- Using academic subjects as the vehicle to teach an additional language enhances the value of additional-language learning since the academic curriculum is valued throughout the school.

- Using academic subjects as content also serves to encourage collaboration among language and content-area teachers in the school. A weakness of some other forms of additional-language teaching is that it is the sole responsibility of language teachers and they are often isolated from the activities of the rest of the school. Since all teachers in the school are responsible for achieving the goals of the curriculum, emphasizing teaching languages through prescribed academic subjects includes everyone in the school.

- Using academic content enhances student motivation to learn the additional language insofar as learning the language becomes a means for attaining high levels of academic achievement.

- In a related vein, teaching prescribed academic subjects through an additional language reinforces learning that is taking place during other parts of the school day.

- Using academic content extends and deepens additional-language learning since it is cognitively engaging and challenging.

In **Chapter 1**, we identified four school contexts that we focus on throughout this book, namely: (1) immersion (IMM) programmes; (2) schools with immigrant and indigenous-language learners (ILS); (3) foreign-language contexts (FL), and 4) international schools (INT). In this chapter, we describe the rationale for, and what CLIL might look like in, each of these contexts; in **Chapters 4** to **7** we describe how to make this happen.

CLIL IN IMM CONTEXTS

Overview

We start with a description of CLIL in IMM settings for several reasons. First, IMM programmes provide full-fledged versions of CLIL in academic contexts insofar as the additional language is used to teach substantial sections of the regular curriculum – usually 50% or more for one or more grades. Second, the goals of CLIL in IMM contexts are advanced levels of bilingual competence in reading, writing, speaking and listening. This is a reasonable goal since a lot of time is devoted to teaching in the additional language in IMM over several grades. We describe several models of IMM shortly. In fact, IMM is often the preferred version of CLIL in communities where full competence in both languages is desired because both languages play important roles in the community and are important for students' long-term personal and professional development. For example, parents and school authorities in communities such as Hong Kong or Paris might select immersion in English because English is an important language of business and international development; communities in the Basque Country might choose IMM in Basque or Spanish since both are important local languages. Discussing CLIL in IMM contexts thus allows us to explore the full ramifications of CLIL, and this is useful when we go on to discuss the other contexts. Third, much has been written about IMM, both by researchers and professional educators, so we have a lot of experience and information to draw on.

IMM programmes are intended primarily for students who speak the majority language of the community. This is important because it means that students' development of the home language in oral and written forms is supported by their day-to-day experiences outside school – they see and hear oral and written forms of the language all around them all the time. It also means that they are familiar with the cultural norms and expectations of IMM schools; as we will see later, this is not true for all students (such as immigrant and indigenous-language students; ILS) and, when this is not true, it can create challenges for students. These features of IMM have important implications for the

3.1 PERSONAL PERSPECTIVE
Students' views on integrating language and content

Carolina Bianchini, 4th grade teacher, immersion school, São Paulo, Brazil

When I asked my students to write a paragraph about studying in an immersion school, I was quite sceptical to see if they really understood the meaning of it. Fortunately, their paragraphs really showed me how much they value and understand the importance of learning other languages. Their paragraphs gave me a lot if insight regarding how students make connections between language and content and it definitely helped me to set priorities and make my lessons more meaningful and efficient.

way language is used and students are supported in learning their first language and for how the additional language is used in school, as we will see shortly. There are alternative versions of IMM, some of which have been closely evaluated, so we describe them briefly here. Generally, speaking IMM is defined as use of the additional language to teach between 50% and 100% of the regular school curriculum for one and usually several grades, although there are many variations of IMM that teach somewhat less than 50% of the curriculum. The most widely documented forms of immersion begin in the primary grades (when students are around 5 years of age); but IMM can also begin in higher elementary grades (grade 4, or 8–9 years of age) and even in secondary school (grade 7). Further distinctions are often made between early **total** immersion and early **partial** immersion. In early total IMM, the additional language is used to teach the entire curriculum during the primary grades (from kindergarten to grade 2 or 3). Early partial IMM also begins in kindergarten but only about 50% of the curriculum is taught in the additional language and the remainder is taught in the students' home language (see Genesee, 2004, for more detailed descriptions of these kinds of programmes). Schematic representations of these alternatives are presented in **Figure 3.1**.

FIGURE 3.1: Schematic description of immersion programme models

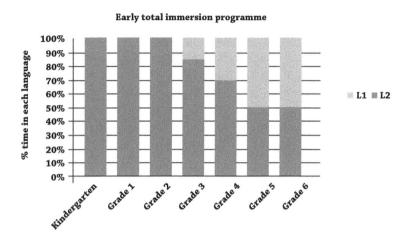

Early total immersion programme

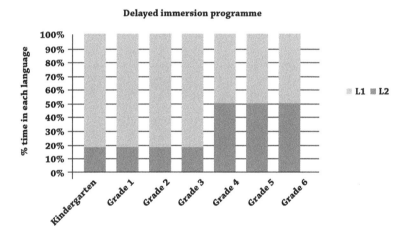

Delayed immersion programme

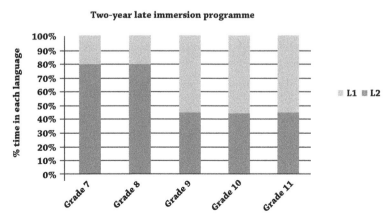

Two-year late immersion programme

Rationale

IMM programmes are based on the assumption that young children are particularly adept at learning a new language if it is used in authentic, interesting, engaging and developmentally appropriate ways; in other words, when language learning is not an end in itself but rather a means to an end – learning to communicate in school. It is also based on the premise that achieving high levels of functional proficiency in an additional language requires extended exposure to the language; it is not something that can be achieved in only 30- or 60-minutes-a-day exposure. Another assumption is that use of the additional language needs to be adapted to reflect the fact that students need lots of scaffolding to acquire the language because they are learning content through that language. In other words, IMM teachers modify the way they use the additional language as they are teaching Mathematics and Science to make sure that the content is comprehensible and that language learning is promoted. Parents and other caregivers adapt the way they use language with young first-language learners for similar reasons.

3.1 SPECIAL NOTE

Misapplying IMM to minority-language students

The success of IMM programmes for majority-language students has been misapplied in US schools to educate minority-language students in English-only programmes. Politicians and some educators in the US argued that because English-speaking students in Canada acquired higher levels of proficiency in French, their second language, students in the US who did not speak English when they started school should be 'immersed' in English-only programmes to ensure that they acquired English quickly. However, the results from French immersion programmes in Canada cannot be generalised to the US situation for two primary reasons: (a) students in Canada speak the majority language while non-English-speaking students in the US belong to minority-language groups, and (b) majority-language students in IMM programmes are in additive bilingual programmes whereas minority-language students in English-only programmes are in subtractive bilingual programmes.

Inside an IMM classroom

What does an IMM classroom actually look and sound like? Here we use early total IMM as the frame of reference since it helps us identify some key features of this form of CLIL. In early total IMM, students are actually allowed to use their home language with the IMM teacher in the beginning, although the IMM teacher uses only the additional language with the students. Students are allowed to use their first language in order to give them time to acclimatise to hearing and learning the new language. IMM students initially use their first language with one another and with the teacher while she speaks to them in the additional language. Students' comprehension of the additional language develops easily and quickly. Often within three or four months of starting school, IMM students comprehend everything the teacher is saying. This is due, in part, to young learners' natural ability to acquire comprehension skills easily when language is used in meaningful ways, and mostly about concrete things. Importantly, however, it is also due to the fact that IMM teachers modify the way they use the language in comparison to how they would use it were all the students native speakers. In particular, IMM teachers use the language in simplified ways with lots of repetition and visual aids, such as gestures, realia, videos and so on, which allow students to figure out what their teachers are saying even if they do not fully understand the language. IMM teachers in the early grades organise teaching around hands-on activities that engage students and give meaning to the language they are using. Classroom activities are often planned as daily routines so that students develop schemas for what is going on and what is coming next; this allows the teacher to repeat sounds, words and sentence patterns over several days and lessons so that students build their language skills over time. Comprehension checks are used frequently to ensure that students understand what the teacher is saying.

Over the first months of the first year, students begin to build their additional language skills by listening to the teacher and by participating in engaging activities. As individual students are ready, they begin to use the additional language – with much encouragement from the teacher. Use of the additional language slowly becomes the norm for all students – usually within the first year. To achieve this, the teacher asks students, when she perceives they are ready, to say what they want to say in the additional language if they have initially used their first language. Most students readily accept that using the additional language is what is expected of them in class, and even outside class, when they are speaking with the IMM teacher. This strategy is adopted quite conscientiously since it is assumed that by using the additional language students will learn it. This way of thinking takes on added significance in the case of IMM for students who speak the majority language. If not encouraged or even required to use the additional language, students from the majority-language group might otherwise favour the majority language because they already know it and because it is the dominant language in their community. Allowing students to use the language they already know reduces their opportunities of learning the new language. A strong bias in favour of the additional language during the primary grades is also important to ensure that students have the advanced-level skills in the additional language they need to cope with academic content in the higher grades, when it becomes increasingly complex and abstract. Making instruction easy in the primary grades by using the home language actually makes instruction and additional-language learning more difficult in later grades. This is not to say that there is no place for the first language in IMM teaching. The same bias is not advisable in ILS contexts where students speak a minority language at home. In **Chapter 5**, we discuss how students' home language can be used in IMM classrooms to promote learning while avoiding overreliance on it to the detriment of additional-language development.

A brief note about errors and error correction. For many years following the inauguration of IMM programmes in Canada in 1965 (Lambert & Tucker, 1972), teachers were discouraged from correcting errors students made when using the additional language. This strategy was adopted because it was felt that this would discourage students from using the additional language and, at the time, there was little empirical evidence when the programmes were inaugurated that error correction was useful. However, research indicates that there are gaps in IMM students' additional-language skills even after many years in the programme (see Lyster, 2007, for a review of this issue). This raises important questions about how language and content instruction are actually integrated in IMM classrooms. In many IMM classrooms, the academic curriculum drives unit and lesson planning and day-to-day instruction, and language objectives are not necessarily included in a systematic way in unit and lesson plans that focus on academic objectives. From a language-teaching point of view, this means that language teaching and, therefore, language learning often occur incidentally during academic instruction. We now know that there is a need for more systematic approaches to language instruction during academic instruction; we discuss how to do this in **Chapters 4** and **5**.

In most IMM contexts, teachers follow the curriculum, in part or in whole, that is prescribed by the district or the state. This is important in order to ensure that IMM students are held to the same high academic standards and achieve the same level of academic competence as students learning through their first language. Modifying the prescribed curriculum to simplify it is both unnecessary and ill-advised. Moreover, research, discussed in **Chapter 2**, has consistently shown that IMM students attain the same levels of achievement in academic domains even in subjects taught through the additional language. However, the curriculum is often adapted in IMM classrooms in order to take into account that students are learning through an additional language. Specifically, the curriculum is rearranged to ensure that academic objectives that are less language-dependent and more amenable to hands-on, experiential learning are taught before objectives that are more abstract and language-dependent; alternatively, objectives that are complex and abstract are taught using experiential, student-centred strategies. By building on students' existing knowledge and skills, and by embedding instruction in hands-on activities, teachers build students' conceptual understanding of the objectives while also building the language skills they need to master those objectives.

CLIL IN ILS CONTEXTS

Overview

ILS contexts are communities with significant numbers of children who at home speak a language other than the majority language. When these children enter school, they often have little or no proficiency in the language of instruction. They must learn the regional or majority language in school for the purposes of general education and social integration. Some of these students are children of immigrants; for example, Turkish-speaking immigrant children in Germany attending schools where German is the language of instruction, or Polish-speaking children in the UK where the language of instruction is English. Some of these children have been born in the country in which they are being educated but they have grown up in linguistic enclaves where they heard and used primarily their heritage language; as a result, they have limited competence in the majority language. ILS contexts are also communities with children who were born in the country where they are being educated and they speak an indigenous language; for example, Peruvian students who enter their community or neighbourhood school speaking Quechua but the language of instruction is Spanish; or Welsh-speaking children in some regions of the UK who speak Welsh at home but attend English-medium public schools. These children often underperform their mainstream peers if there are no special provisions made to accommodate their unique linguistic and cultural backgrounds. While there are undoubtedly multiple and complex reasons why schools are unable to support these students adequately, it is clear that special consideration must be given to improving the quality of instruction for these students.

CLIL is relevant to efforts to improve the education of children with these kinds of backgrounds. There are two ways in which CLIL can improve the education of immigrant and indigenous-language students. In one case, immigrant and indigenous-language students receive instruction in both their heritage language and the majority language. We call this *dual-language CLIL* or DL-CLIL. In the other case, minority-language children are educated by teachers using the majority language but with adaptations based on the principles of CLIL; at the same time, their heritage language is infused into the programme where appropriate and possible. We call this *monolingual CLIL* (ML-CLIL). We start with *dual-language CLIL* (DL-CLIL).

Dual-language CLIL for minority-language students

DL-CLIL programmes provide instruction through students' heritage language along with the majority language for varying amounts of time across the grade levels. The goal of these programmes is to promote achievement in the majority language and in academic domains that is comparable to that of mainstream students who speak the majority language upon school entry. These programmes also aim to maintain and promote full proficiency in students' heritage language. In other words, they aim for full oral and written proficiency in both languages. Educators in the US have experimented extensively with these types of programmes so we focus our discussion on what they have been doing.

There are two main types of DL-CLIL programmes; in the US, these are referred to as *developmental bilingual education* and *two-way immersion programmes* (TWI). In both of these programmes, minority-language students' heritage language along with the majority language are used for literacy and academic instruction beginning in kindergarten and continuing typically through elementary school. The difference between these two models is that whereas developmental bilingual programmes usually include only speakers of the minority language, TWI programmes include speakers of both the majority and a minority language, ideally in equal numbers. This means that students from each language group are interacting with students who speak their second language and, thus, they have same-age models of the languages they are learning and they can learn from one another. This is a distinct advantage when it comes to learning the additional language and providing cross-cultural opportunities for each group to become familiar with and functional in another culture. There are two main variations of each model – these are called: 50:50 and 90:10. In **50:50** programmes, each language (the majority language and the minority language) is used for about 50% of the instructional day from the beginning (in kindergarten) until the end of elementary school (grade 6). In **90:10** programmes, the minority language is used for 90% of the instructional day in kindergarten and grade 1; and more English is added starting in grade 2 until grade 4 or 5, at which time each language is used for about half the instructional day. The most common language combination in these programmes in the US is Spanish and English because Spanish is the most common heritage language spoken in the US.

Caveat

DL-CLIL may not be realistic or feasible in many communities. Minority-language students in many communities may speak too many different heritage languages to make it feasible to offer such programmes, although it may be possible to informally infuse the heritage language of students in classrooms that are otherwise taught in the majority language. There is more discussion of how to do this in a later section of the book (see **Chapter 5**). Even if there were a sufficient number of children who speak a common heritage language, there may be an insufficient number of well-trained teachers or a lack of instructional resources in some languages to support such programmes. There may also be a lack of political or popular support for such options. Nevertheless, we consider DL-CLIL options here because they make sense in some communities, and we know they can be very successful. More importantly, they challenge educators to think in radically new ways about how to educate students who come to school unable to speak the language of schooling, and they highlight the importance of supporting bilingual proficiency, especially among students who already speak an additional language. Failure to support the heritage language of minority-languages students is to squander a resource that these children bring to school. CLIL is an important new way of thinking about how to maintain and develop their linguistic and cultural resources while promoting acquisition of the national language.

Rationale

The rationale for these programmes is based on theory and research from a variety of disciplines, including Education, Linguistics and Cognitive Science (for reviews, see de Jong, 2013, and Genesee & Lindholm-Leary, 2012), and is briefly described here. An important component of the rationale for DL-CLIL is linked to research that has been carried out with students from minority-language backgrounds in the US who are educated in English. There are many such students in the US and research shows that minority-language students who start school with limited proficiency in the language of schooling perform more poorly than native speakers on oral language and reading tests at the outset and that the gap persists in higher grades (Collins, O'Connor, Suárez-Orozco, Nieto-Castañon & Toppelberg, 2014). In fact, minority-language students have a triple challenge – they must acquire a new language; they must keep up with academic instruction presented in that language; and often they must learn how to adapt to a new culture. There are a number of factors besides language that account for these students' academic difficulties, including low socio-economic status, prior incomplete or disrupted schooling, trauma associated with migration in the case of children of immigrant parents, health issues, inadequately trained teachers, inappropriate curriculum, and others. In any case, in order to close the achievement gap with mainstream students, minority-language students must make more academic progress per grade than majority-language students because majority-language students are also advancing in achievement each year. Moreover, they must make accelerated progress for several consecutive grades if they are to eventually close the gap. Minority-language students can make accelerated progress and close the gap in DL-CLIL because they are taught in a language they understand. As a result, academic content and skills that comprise the curriculum are more accessible than they would be were the students taught in their additional language.

In a related vein, use of the heritage language to teach minority-language students can support and even accelerate development in the majority language because the academic language and literacy skills they acquire in the heritage language can transfer to the majority language. There is extensive evidence that strong first-language skills are an important foundation for additional-language development. Specifically related to schooling, acquisition of skills linked to reading and writing, academic oral language skills, and higher-order thinking transfer across languages (see **Research Note 2.5** from **Chapter 2**). Thus, teaching minority-language students using the heritage language for academic and literacy purposes in the primary grades not only permits them to keep up with academic instruction, but also permits them to

3.1 **RESEARCH NOTE**

Cognitive benefits of bilingualism

Cognitive benefits of bilingualism have been found in areas related to cognitive flexibility, attention and cognitive control (Bialystok, 2015). Researchers think that bilinguals have this advantage because, when they learn and use two languages, they must pay careful attention to and process information about context in order to avoid interference between their languages. This results in improved executive control functioning that then enhances performance on both verbal and non-verbal tasks. Even neonates who are exposed to two languages demonstrate such an advantage (Kovács & Mehler, 2009). When bilingual adults age, these cognitive advantages help buffer the onset of the effects of Alzheimer's by as much as four to five years in comparison to monolinguals (Bialystok, Craik, Klein & Viswanathan, 2004).

progress in their development of the majority language. This, in turns, makes it possible for them to benefit from instruction in that language in higher grades, where language is increasingly important for achievement. Indeed, there is growing evidence that minority-language students with advanced proficiency in both languages outperform their peers who have limited proficiency in the heritage language both in English-language proficiency and academic achievement (for reviews, see Lindholm-Leary, 2001; Lindholm-Leary & Howard, 2008).

There are also long-term career benefits for students who are bilingual (Callahan & Gándara, 2014). Finally, providing DL-CLIL options to minority-language students makes sense in light of the growing evidence that childhood bilingualism promotes certain cognitive advantages (see **Research Note 3.1**).

Inside a DL-CLIL classroom

In this section, we describe both the 90:10 and 50:50 models, though the 50:50 model is probably more realistic in most communities outside the US. We start with 90:10 DL-CLIL.

Teachers who teach in **90:10 DL-CLIL** classrooms have native or native-like competence in the minority language and, preferably, have full certification for teaching in that language. Because all or most of the students in the classroom speak the same minority language, teachers in these programmes use that language to teach literacy and academic subjects much as any teacher would teach when working with students who already speak the language of instruction. Teachers follow the curriculum required by the school district or state, using instructional strategies that are student-centred and differentiated to engage students whose backgrounds differ from those of mainstream students. Materials in the heritage language that align with local curricular goals, and that are developmentally appropriate and of high quality, are acquired or created to support instruction. Many minority-language students, although not all, may be recent immigrants or they and their families may be refugees who have fled their home countries for economic or political reasons, and they may have needs that differ from majority-language students. At the same time, immigrant and indigenous-language students participating in these programmes have important language and cultural resources that are assets that they bring to school and that can provide a solid foundation for success in school.

For example, they have a strong attachment to their heritage language and culture; there are strong family attachments; and there is often a rich oral tradition in the heritage language. For these reasons, instruction that is student-centred and differentiated to take into account their cultural backgrounds and linguistic and family resources engages students and makes instruction effective. Ideally, teachers in DL-CLIL classrooms are trained to know how to become familiar with their students' languages, cultures and backgrounds in order to plan differentiated instruction that accommodates all students. In fact, an additional argument for DL-CLIL for minority-language students is that it sensitises teachers, professional-development experts and school administrators to these students' unique strengths and needs.

Minority-language students in 90:10 DL-CLIL classes are taught to read and write in their heritage language during the primary grades. The curriculum also provides for the development of the majority language from the beginning during the 10% of the day that is devoted to the majority language. The focus during instruction in the majority language is often on the development of oral language skills as a basis for later literacy and academic development in that language. As students learn to read and write in their heritage language, beginning in kindergarten, foundational skills for learning to read and write in the majority language are also being laid down. The same is true for oral language development – as students acquire the oral language skills they need for Mathematics and Science – what is referred to as academic language – they are also learning oral language skills that support the development of academic language in the majority language. This means that the time that is devoted to teaching and learning in the minority language does not detract from or jeopardise the students' development of the majority language. To the contrary, it facilitates their development of the majority language while also supporting their academic achievement because they are learning through a language they already know. Of course, there is more facilitation between two languages that are similar, such as Spanish and French, than between languages that are very different from one another, such as Chinese and English.

Beginning in grade 2 or 3, the majority language is used to teach some academic subjects – such as Mathematics or Science. Use of the majority language is increased in higher grades so that approximately equal amounts of instructional time are devoted to each language by grade 4 or 5. The same subjects are not taught in both languages during the same grade. Teachers continue to support students' development in both languages as they continue to teach some school subjects in each language.

In 50:50 DL-CLIL classrooms, both languages play a significant role in teaching in all grades, beginning in kindergarten. In many 50:50 DL-CLIL classrooms, literacy instruction is provided in both languages from the beginning, but adjustments are made to avoid confusion since the same alphabet may be used but different sounds are associated with the letters, and different rules of pronunciation or directionality (right to left instead of left to right) may be involved. It is important for CLIL teachers to determine their students' level of literacy development in each language so that instruction can be tailored to their existing competencies. Usually, academic instruction is divided between the two languages so that the same subject is not taught in both the majority and the minority language in the same grade. The decision as to which subjects should be taught in each language may be made on very practical terms – for example, does the minority-language teacher have the competence and confidence to teach certain subjects in the minority language? – or decisions may be made more systematically by, for example, teaching each subject in each language for only one or two years and then shifting languages of instruction to ensure that each subject is taught in each language equally often. In some countries, certain subjects such as History, Geography or other topics of unique national interest are always taught in the national language while other subjects, such as Mathematics, Science or Physical Education, may be taught through the minority language.

Coordination of the teachers who use the minority language and teachers who use the majority language is particularly important in 50:50 DL-CLIL classrooms to ensure that each avoids redundancy in their teaching and that they capitalise on cross-linguistic and cross-disciplinary linkages. For example, returning to the case of reading, if the minority-language teacher ascertains that some of her students already have beginning-level decoding skills in the minority language, she would pass this information on to the majority-language teacher so that she can build on, rather than re-teach, what the students already know.

As we saw in **Chapter 2**, DL-CLIL for minority-language students is very effective – if it is implemented well. What is important here is that, contrary to what might be thought to be common sense, minority-language students who are in programmes that devote instructional time to the home language do not experience setbacks in the development of the majority language. Similarly, minority-language students who receive instruction in academic subjects, such as Mathematics and Science, in the heritage language do not fall behind in Mathematics and Science in the majority language – what they learn in the heritage language is accessible through the national language.

Monolingual CLIL for minority-language students

We prefer DL-CLIL approaches for educating minority-language students because they aim for full bilingual proficiency and provide a solid basis for their educational development and future careers. However, we realise that it is not always feasible and some parent and educator groups may not be prepared to take on such programmes. An alternative approach that takes advantage of CLIL principles is to include immigrant and indigenous-language students in mainstream classrooms where the majority language is the language of instruction and teachers use principles of CLIL to plan instruction in that language. To be maximally effective, these programmes also infuse the minority language in the classroom – we discuss how this can be done in **Chapter 5**.

Rationale

If a monolingual education is the most realistic route to take with minority-language and indigenous-language students, then it is important to provide them with a strong ML-CLIL programme because use of CLIL strategies will facilitate their acquisition of the majority language and their academic achievement. Teachers who are trained to use CLIL strategies, even in a monolingual programme, are more aware of their minority-language students' language needs in content areas. CLIL strategies make it easier for students who are still acquiring the language of instruction to process abstract concepts and acquire new cognitive skills because teachers know how to make these concepts and skills accessible in the students' additional language; we show how this can be done in **Chapters 4** and **5**. Teachers in a good ML-CLIL programme also show respect for their minority-language students' home languages and cultures – in this way, they create an additive bilingual context. This is important because minority speakers need to see that their language is valued and that they can use it to help them learn the additional language and academic subjects.

Inside an ML-CLIL classroom

ML-CLIL classrooms include students who speak the majority language of the community along with students who speak another language only or primarily at home. Some minority-language students may be children of parents who are recent immigrants or refugees to the country; some have been raised during the preschool years in the country where they are now being schooled; and yet others are members of indigenous ethnolinguistic groups who have been resident in the country long before the current majority group was there. In short, the language, cultural and immigration status of the children in these classrooms is heterogeneous. Likewise, their parents are heterogeneous with respect to immigration, prior educational and professional background, current employment, economic status, and so on.

The classroom teachers in an ML-CLIL classroom are usually native monolingual speakers of the majority language. Ideally, they have had prior professional development experiences that have prepared them for working with such a diverse group. They use the majority language exclusively for all instruction since that is the only language they know; however, they have learned how to adapt their language use and their materials to engage minority-language students and accelerate their learning and social integration in the school. ML-CLIL teachers also know how to draw on the students' home language so that they can make links between it and the majority language and so they feel valued in this otherwise monolingual classroom. Teachers start the year off by doing informal but systematic assessments of their students' current levels of oral and written proficiency in the majority language. This is a common and useful practice for all teachers but is particularly important for CLIL teachers because their students are so diverse. In **Chapter 7**, we describe how to do this. They also do this in a more limited way whenever they begin a new unit of study to see if there are particular words, grammatical constructions or background knowledge that the students do not know. Although the teachers are monolingual, they have developed strategies for assessing what their minority-language students can do and might know in their heritage languages – see **Chapter 7** for suggestions on how to do this.

Once teachers have gained a sense of each student's level of language proficiency, they engage students in pre-learning activities to find out what they already know about what is going to be taught. Teachers then re-examine the units of instruction they have planned to see what adjustments might be needed to make them more accessible for the minority-language students whose proficiency in the language of instruction is basic or minimal; and they identify instructional materials they can use to make the content accessible and culturally meaningful to the students. They have learned to focus their unit and lesson plans on concepts and skills that can be taught easily using hands-on or experiential activities; they also identify language linked to the objectives that they think the minority-language students might have difficulty with so that they can provide additional support to enhance their understanding. They notice that many of the vocabulary items and grammatical patterns that could cause problems for the minority-language students might also cause problems for many of their majority-language students. For example, in a Science unit on density, the teacher could realise that talking about conditional situations – 'If I put the grape and the apple in the bucket of water, which will float? Why do you think this is so?' The majority-language students will likely know the words 'grape' and 'apple' while the minority-language students might not; in contrast, both groups might have difficulty with complex conditional sentence constructions using *if*. Therefore, a strategy is planned for making this comprehensible. One strategy the teacher has developed over time is to get students who speak the same heritage language to work together to discuss the answer and then to prepare a response to the whole class in the majority language.

As teachers prepare units and daily lessons, they also think about ways in which they can include the students' heritage languages – teachers have found that minority-language students are very proud when they can 'show off' what they know in their own language and it also engages them so that they feel a real part of the lesson. It is also good for mainstream students because they learn that different languages do things differently – for example, Arabic is written from right to left instead of left to right; and Spanish puts question marks at the beginning and end of a sentence, not just at the end as in English. Engaging all students in these kind of cross-linguistic 'games' enhances their metalinguistic awareness. It also enhances their appreciation for one another.

In particular, mainstream students see that their minority-language peers know things they do not know.

CLIL IN FL CONTEXTS

CLIL methods can also be used in foreign-language contexts where students are taught an additional language for designated and relatively limited periods of time – two to three times per week, for example. In many FL classrooms, the additional language is taught separately and independently from other content areas. The instructional materials that are typically used in FL classrooms usually have little relation to the rest of the curriculum, and typically spotlight the daily life of young adults or adolescents in a country where that language is spoken. Students follow Pierre and Janine or Edward and Nancy as they go to the supermarket or the movies and have somewhat stilted conversations with each other about everyday events. Lessons concentrate mostly on the structure of language, highlighting specific grammar points and vocabulary.

This traditional approach to teaching an additional language often results in students learning about the language but not being able to use the language functionally even after several years of instruction. By taking an approach that makes use of CLIL strategies, teachers can nurture and promote acquisition of the additional language that includes the ability to use it for real communicative purposes. Despite the fact that language-learning expectations are much more modest in FL contexts than in other forms of CLIL, integrating content into the instruction of an additional language can be tremendously beneficial in FL contexts.

3.2 PERSONAL PERSPECTIVE

Integrating foreign-language lessons with Arts, Music and Drama

Gabriela Tribaudino, elementary- and secondary-school Italian teacher, Instituto Educativo Nuevo Milenio, Unquillo, Cordoba, Argentina

The idea of teaching Italian through another subject area came to me probably because of my previous career, *Licenciatura en Artes,* which gave me flexibility to work with other disciplines. I tried it first with an 11th grade class of 25 students, in collaboration with the Music teacher. The Music teacher and I planned activities together, such as asking students to talk in Italian about their favourite songs: why they liked it, when they listened to it for the first time, or the meaning of the text. With the Music teacher, students learned about musical features in the main language of instruction, Spanish. We also listened to and analysed contemporary Italian songs. We studied Opera: students, in groups, were given different operas and they searched for information about plot, music, composer and historical background. They then chose one scene and acted it out either in a video or through a live performance in Italian. We evaluated students on both the content (what they learned in Music) and linguistic accuracy (Italian).

When the principal saw students' high motivation, she asked if I could extend this approach to other grade levels. We integrated Arts in 10th grade since there is such a rich Italian artistic heritage and also because students were going to travel to Italy the following year. So, teaching Arts in Italian was a natural combination! The students made PowerPoint presentations of major artistic movements of the 20th century and the work of artists such as Michelangelo and Leonardo.

The most interesting experience was the integration with Drama in 12th grade. In the first three months, I used short films in Italian to expand comprehension and production. In the following three months, we read short stories in Italian, and, finally, students, in groups, wrote their own stories in Italian. The class voted and chose one of these stories and the whole class produced a video of that story, as part of their Drama and Media classes. We obtained remarkable results; students forgot they were learning a second language because of the enthusiasm the experience awoke in them.

It took flexibility and a collaborative spirit to plan, teach and assess with four different teachers. But ultimately, the experience was remarkably worthwhile because of students' motivation, which, for High School foreign language teachers, is always a big challenge.

Rationale

Even in minimal FL instructional contexts, use of content and activities drawn from the school curriculum can enhance competence in an additional language because it promotes communication and interaction among learners and teachers about authentic content; at the same time, it can enhance learning in the rest of the curriculum. In contrast to IMM and other CLIL contexts, in FL-CLIL contexts, the primary focus is on language, and content is chosen that promotes second-language learning. Thus, the content area serves as the context for moving language forward. Unit and lesson plans are shaped by both language and content considerations. Evaluation of the effectiveness of teaching in FL-CLIL contexts is based primarily on students' acquisition of the language and secondarily on content mastery. Typically, the FL teacher works closely with the teacher of the chosen content area to evaluate students' progress collaboratively. By choosing content or themes from the curriculum, FL instruction also builds on skills and knowledge that students are learning in other subjects. Moreover, students will have acquired background knowledge for learning content through the additional language. The strongest rationale for a CLIL approach to teaching FL is student engagement. Teachers who use CLIL strategies in their FL classrooms see students motivated to learn and use the additional language in a way that is never seen in traditional FL lessons where students are conjugating verbs and memorising vocabulary lists.

Inside an FL-CLIL classroom

In FL classrooms that use CLIL strategies, teachers work from a language curriculum and choose content from the academic curriculum that lines up with those language objectives. The content may be chosen from one subject in the curriculum, but content can also be chosen from several subjects depending on the FL objectives. Integration can also be achieved by using activities from the rest of the curriculum. Activities related to the academic content or theme that has been selected to teach the additional language must be chosen carefully to introduce students to language skills that they are expected to learn and to give them opportunities to use the language while engaged in the activity. For example, in an FL class for 5th graders learning to talk about time in the additional language, students might write down the times of day they eat, sleep, read, do sports, watch TV and so on. They would then calculate the percentage of time during a 24-hour day that they spend on each of those activities (M. Met, personal communication, 26 January 2016). Activities can be chosen that are the same as, or related to, activities they have already experienced in their other lessons – in this case, students can map new language onto familiar actions or themes, or activities that are specifically suited to the FL class being compatible with something students have done in another subject. An FL unit for primary-level students might focus on the theme 'home' and could draw on several content areas in the curriculum, such as Natural Science (the habitats of animals in the forest), History (habitats of past and present-day people), and Social Studies (homes of people in different regions of the world). In FL contexts, the content area or areas, as well as the activities that are chosen to teach the additional-language lesson, are chosen because they allow the teacher to teach the language that students are expected to learn and because they provide students with opportunities to learn and practise those language skills. While students perform the activity, teachers can observe carefully how they use the additional language to identify what they have learned and what they need additional support with. While getting the right answer is important, it is secondary to the use of the language, especially if the FL teacher is taking the lead in the lesson.

CLIL IN INT CONTEXTS

INT schools often have students with very heterogeneous backgrounds. For purposes of simplicity, we discuss INT schools in which English is the language of instruction. Many students in INT schools are children of English-speaking parents who are working outside their home countries; international schools provide continuity in their children's education. Increasingly, students from the host country who do not speak English are also attending INT schools; they may or may not have acquired proficiency in English. Finally, there may be 'third-language' students from other countries who speak neither English nor the host-country language; they too may or may not have acquired proficiency in English. Since many students in INT schools do not speak the language of instruction at all or fluently, they will be learning through an additional language; therefore, CLIL is relevant to teaching them. Different CLIL models that we have already discussed apply to these students because of their diversity and the diverse goals the school might have with respect to teaching additional languages – see **Figure 1.2** in **Chapter 1** for a summary.

3.3 PERSONAL PERSPECTIVE

Celebrating multilingualism

Eugenia Papadaki, Founder and Director,
The Bilingual School of Monza, Monza, Italy

The majority of our students (85%) come from primarily mono-lingual Italian-speaking families, and 15% from 'international' or mixed marriage families, representing 14 languages. Instruction is through English and Italian, and Spanish is introduced in Grade 1. The value of home-language maintenance and development is embedded in our school philosophy as we are committed to multi-lingualism and view linguistic and cultural diversity as a resource and an opportunity for enrichment!

Thus, home languages are carefully interwoven into our daily practices following Gallagher's (2008) interlingual teaching and learning approach. This includes the following:

- Classroom, school displays and the Welcome message on our school website, are multilingual.
- The staff are committed to learning a few words in the different languages of our students in order to be able to greet students in their home languages.
- Early Years section parents are invited to share their language and culture with the students and teachers. These events are documented for staff professional development and parent education.
- Students are encouraged to make connections between the languages of instruction and their home language, thus developing their metalinguistic awareness.
- The school and classroom libraries have a fair selection of books in the students' home languages.
- Students may use their home language during small group work.
- Home language use is included in many of our assessment practices.
- Students who are literate in their home language produce dual language texts, often involving parents' support.

We also work closely with our parents. Our parent education program includes a home language maintenance module. Parents meet monthly with a coach who provides guidance on supporting home language literacy outside school. These meetings also serve as a forum where parents share their experiences, discuss matters of interest and seek advice. Teachers encourage students to share their home language learning experiences with the class.

Embracing multilingualism has been empowering for the whole school community. We believe that all languages deserve equal respect and appreciation. We want all our students, staff and parents alike to feel proud of who they are. By including students' home languages in our day-to-day practices and offering them opportunities to use these languages while they are acquiring the new language/s, students feel empowered in their learning journey.

First of all, third-language students in INT contexts are like ILS students. They do not speak English as a native language, and their home languages may not be highly valued by the school community and are generally not used very much; however, they must learn English for academic and social purposes within the school. These students are often labelled as 'ESL kids', a label that may carry some stigma within the school and among parents. The ML-CLIL model we discussed in the preceding section is relevant to teaching these students – that is, teaching in English using CLIL methods for the benefit of students who are learning through English as an additional language. Second, if the same school taught part of the curriculum through English and through the host-country language, then DL-CLIL is also relevant since minority-language students in the school would be learning the curriculum through two languages.

Third, IMM models are also relevant in INT schools that offer a dual-language option for students who speak the language of the school – English in our example. This can take different forms. For example, Frankfurt International School, where the primary language of instruction is English, offers a partial German IMM option for English-speaking students so that they can acquire advanced levels of proficiency in the host-country language, German. The British Vietnam International

School in Saigon offers a Vietnamese–English IMM option for its students, all of whom speak Vietnamese as a first language.

Finally, even the FL version of CLIL, discussed in the preceding section, is relevant in INT schools that teach an additional language to all students regardless of whether they speak the language of the school or not. For example, the International School of Geneva teaches French to all of its students.

SUMMARY

As you can see from these snapshots of CLIL, where additional languages are being taught in different contexts, the principles behind CLIL are largely the same. What differs is the extent to which CLIL is used, how it is used, and how much it is linked to the academic curriculum or content related to the curriculum. As Met (1999) has pointed out, you can think of CLIL instruction as falling along a continuum – from programmes that are content-driven (e.g. IMM for students who speak the majority language) to language-driven (such as FL-CLIL) to models in between where language and content are equally important (such as CLIL for immigrant and indigenous-language students). You might want to revisit the diagrams in **Chapter 1** – **Figures 1.1** and **1.2** that summarise the diverse contexts and learner groups we refer to throughout this book. The focus of evaluation also differs depending on the focus of the programme. In some cases, evaluation of language learning will be of primary importance – FL contexts; in other cases, evaluation of content knowledge will be relatively more important, although language outcomes are not ignored – IMM contexts; and in some cases, both language and content are evaluated with equal focus – ML-CLIL and DL-CLIL for ILS students. We discuss assessment methods that work well in CLIL contexts in **Chapter 7**.

4   Planning for content and language integrated instruction

As with any other instructional programme, CLIL requires careful planning. Planning for CLIL involves the steps that are usually taken in any K-12 educational setting. However, all levels and aspects of planning a CLIL programme and instruction must take into account a critical additional factor: students are learning new concepts through a new language and perhaps in an unfamiliar cultural context. This applies to all educational CLIL contexts – even FL contexts where the integration of language and content instruction is limited.

Instruction with a CLIL focus has to be planned and prepared in such a way that lack of proficiency in the language of instruction does not stand in the way of students understanding new concepts that are being taught. Conversely, and as importantly, units and lessons must be planned so that the process of understanding and mastering new concepts helps to move language development forward. In addition, you must plan for assessment to provide information about how well students are learning the subject matter content objectives as well as, and independently of, students' proficiency in the two languages.

Planning for CLIL is not limited to the classroom or the teacher. Planning at the programmatic level is also crucial for creating or maintaining a successful CLIL programme. In other words, it is important that the whole school is organised in a way that maximises students' ability to learn an additional language while learning academic subjects at the same time. Planning also extends to matters that are beyond the school itself – you need to plan how to work with parents and the communities that students live in. Extending efforts into the home and community ensures that whatever students learn at school is connected and relevant to their daily lives. By taking this holistic approach to planning CLIL, you make it more likely that students will learn efficiently and attain both academic and linguistic competence.

Schools that are just beginning to consider CLIL as an instructional framework need to prepare staff and families for the change that will take place. We begin this chapter by addressing issues that are particular to starting a new CLIL programme. Then we consider planning four aspects of CLIL that apply to both new and existing programmes: 1) setting curriculum and scheduling; 2) setting objectives; 3) using a three-phase instructional planning tool; and 4) human and material resources. In each of these, we discuss implications at both the classroom and school or district-wide levels.

PREPARING SCHOOL STAFF AND THE COMMUNITY FOR A NEW CLIL PROGRAMME

The decision to start using CLIL strategies across the curriculum, or even in only some parts of the curriculum, entails a change in many aspects of what you do:

- the way the curriculum is organised
- the choice of language of instruction in some content areas, or, in the case of FL-CLIL, in some units of study
- the way lessons are organised and taught
- recruitment of teachers, especially in the more extensive CLIL contexts (IMM and ILS) that aim for high levels of bilingual proficiency
- the choice and acquisition of instructional materials
- the way students are assessed.

Most importantly, CLIL instruction requires teachers who are confident that they know how to integrate language and content instruction. To begin, teachers and other school staff need to understand the reasons for choosing CLIL as an instructional model and the research that supports it. **Research Note 2.1** in **Chapter 2** summarises research on the effectiveness of CLIL and can be used as material for professional development or in information packets for teachers and other staff. In CLIL programmes aiming for high levels of bilingual proficiency, teachers who are proficient in the additional language must be hired, and those who are not experienced in CLIL must have extensive professional development. All teachers who will be teaching academic subjects through students' additional language will need to acquire skills and strategies in integrating language instruction with content instruction. Teachers who know how to teach academic content need to become familiar with strategies that support language learning. They need to be skilled in providing strong scaffolding to help students learn new concepts through a language that they may not be fully proficient in. Similarly, language teachers need to become skilled in supporting content learning (Mehisto, 2008). Aspects of professional development that can be offered to new and experienced teachers are described at the end of this chapter in the section on human resources.

The decision to adopt CLIL in a school calls for an ethos of collaboration and sharing of responsibility among all school personnel – teachers, administrators, specialists and support staff. Teachers who are responsible for a specific content area cannot implement CLIL effectively without collaborating and planning with the Language Arts teachers and other content-area teachers as well. Such collaboration requires a time commitment that teachers need to make. However, and more importantly, it is an aspect of daily school life that must be supported and made possible by administrators (see Principle 8 in **Chapter 2**). When the goal of the CLIL programme is for students to learn academic content and develop proficiency in an additional language simultaneously, all teachers must begin to see themselves as teachers of both content and language, regardless of their area of specialisation. This can be a big challenge for many teachers. The main barrier in accepting this challenge lies in teachers' identities as language-only or content-only teachers.

Elementary school teachers are more likely to accept the integration of language and content instruction naturally. In contrast, middle- and secondary-school content teachers often draw on their area of specialisation to form their professional identity and, as a result, they may have difficulty seeing themselves as 'language teachers' (Genesee, 2008). Language teachers in FL programmes who generally teach language independently of the rest of the curriculum may experience this challenge even more acutely. Even in IMM programmes, content teachers may be concerned that time and attention spent on language will detract from content learning (Fortune, Tedick & Walker, 2008); they may need to be reassured that CLIL does not mean that either language or academic competence is compromised.

4.1 PERSONAL PERSPECTIVE

Changing from a second language to a CLIL program

Rola AbuSaqer, Development and Curriculum Program Director, Dhahran Ahliyya Schools, Dhahran, Saudi Arabia

The Dhahran Ahliyya Schools (DAS) have historically been Arabic language schools and most subjects have been taught in Arabic along with a strong English-as-a-second-language program. At the beginning of the 2009–10 school year, DAS introduced its new dual-language International Program. This program aims to ensure that DAS graduates can learn, work and think effectively in both English and Arabic. An additional benefit of the program is that students are able to make use of up-to-date resources, methodologies and technology in both languages throughout their school career.

Since the start of the program, we faced many challenges. Teachers and students were resistant to the idea since it would require more effort. Teachers were worried that teaching and learning difficult subjects, such as Science, are not easy even in the mother tongue and would be even more challenging in English. To solve this dilemma, DAS administration provided extensive professional development in teaching content through an additional language for Science and Maths teachers. Teachers were shown how to incorporate scientific discourse into conversations with students so that they would have multiple opportunities to practise new vocabulary and content. Students not only learn Science, but they also find ways to investigate and experiment, which will make learning in a new language an easier process. In addition, DAS requested teachers to analyze the language that students will be reading, writing, listening to and producing while planning their lessons. Also, teachers have to think about key vocabulary that students will be exposed to during the lesson, and to teach the terms that make the academic vocabulary accessible and easier to learn.

As students started the program, lessons were becoming more enjoyable and students were learning not just Science, but English and Science. The more students were exploring science in a new language, the better they became at learning both the subject area and the language at the same time.

Along with students, teachers have also become engaged and interactive in teaching Science in English especially with all the professional and supporting material that is now available in English.

The barrier that is created by teachers' perceptions of themselves as specialists needs to be overcome since the more comfortable they feel about their new roles, the more likely it is that the programme will succeed. Overcoming this barrier requires extensive sharing of information about CLIL as well as professional development. In CLIL programmes that aim for high levels of bilingual proficiency (IMM, some ILS and some INT programmes), teachers who are not proficient in the additional language of instruction may feel threatened. They need to be reassured that they will continue to play an important role in the school. Self-reflection by both teachers and administrators will encourage instructors to step outside their traditional comfort zones and cross professional boundaries in order to explore the multiple factors that make CLIL successful (Mehisto, 2008).

The community that is served by the school also needs to be prepared for the change from a traditional way of teaching to CLIL. Parents of students in the programme will initially see changes that may elicit

RESEARCH NOTE

Challenge for teachers

Mehisto (2008) concludes that implementation of CLIL often causes a tension between educators' current way of teaching and the new approach. As many teachers may find it difficult to apply a dual focus on content and language instruction, Mehisto (2012) argues for ongoing professional development in this area.

anxiety. They need to be reassured that in the long term their children will not lag behind in academic content or language learning because they are learning through a language that they are still acquiring. Parents who are not proficient in the new language need to be reassured that a support network will be created to help students do their homework and resolve any questions they have. They must also be convinced that they are a vital part of the school community and that their opinions are welcome despite that fact that they cannot communicate in one of the languages of instruction.

4.2 PERSONAL PERSPECTIVE

Empowering emergent bi/plurilingual learners through collaborative community learning

Andrea S. Young, University of Strasbourg,
School of Education (ESPE), Strasbourg, France

Working in the Alsace border region of France where French/German bilingualism is high on both the education and the political agenda, it strikes me as a paradox that although school bilingualism in these two languages is heavily supported through various programmes (bilingual schooling, CLIL classes, dual certification for final school leaving examination), family bilingualism in languages other than German and French is frequently viewed as a handicap to learning. How can it be that some forms of bilingualism are regarded as extra strings to a learner's bow, whereas others are outlawed and shamed?

When visiting schools, I have observed that children for whom the language of schooling is not their first language are often ignored, excluded and silenced in the classroom. The youngest are unable to communicate in French, yet all too frequently are forbidden to use their home language. The older ones struggle to keep up with their fluent-in-French contemporaries as they try to comprehend new concepts and procedures through a second language, often with little or no scaffolding.

I collaborate with teachers and colleagues who are keen to redress this balance and to refuse what Skutnabb-Kangas (1988) refers to as linguicism and linguistic discrimination. We have observed how emergent bi/plurilingual pupils can be empowered when their bi/plurilingualism is viewed as a resource rather than as a problem. To do this we lean heavily on Cummins's (2000) theory of the Common Underlying Proficiency, notions of investment in identity and engagement in literacy. We have documented and discussed positive multilingual pedagogies such as those practised in the primary school in Didenheim (Hélot & Young, 2006) where parents and teachers co-constructed lessons which helped children to understand some of the complexities of what it means to be bilingual and bicultural. The wealth of stories, songs and cultural practices which the children were exposed to opened a window onto a world of shared resources, experiences and identities.

We are currently analysing and reporting on practised language policies observed in pre-primary, where educators create safe spaces in which parents, children and staff use translanguaging as a pedagogical tool to help the children make sense of their multilingual worlds. When interacting with storybooks, for example, both children and adults authorise themselves to use any of the languages in their linguistic repertoires. This pooling of resources, supported by facial expressions, gestures, pointing to pictures, questioning, naming, repetition and commenting, simultaneously supports mutual learning and collaborative meaning-making.

It is particularly important to convince the community of the benefits of CLIL when an additional language is being introduced for the first time, especially if the community does not value bilingualism. Sometimes, even when bilingualism is valued by native speakers of the dominant language, it may be seen as unnecessary or even detrimental to the community and to minority students if they are learning their heritage languages in school (Hélot, 2006). This is the case for many ILS schools as well as some INT schools where little or no attention is paid to the host-country language or to the home languages of students from non-English speaking backgrounds.

Making sure that the school and the community in which the school is located are ready for the change to CLIL is equally important for IMM as well as ILS and INT contexts, all of which aim for high levels of bilingual proficiency. It can also be a good idea to go through these preparatory steps even in new FL programmes that plan to offer only a few instructional units from one or two content areas in the additional language.

Regardless of how accepting the school and parent community are of CLIL, new CLIL programmes need to start slowly and small. New programmes that aim for high levels of bilingual proficiency must resist the temptation to start the programme too soon or at too many different grade levels. It is not uncommon for schools to decide to establish a CLIL programme during one school year and expect to have it in place by the following year. It may be possible to plan a new FL-CLIL programme relatively quickly because this form of CLIL typically involves minimal integration of content and language instruction. As a result, the amount of coordination and planning is similarly limited.

4.1 SPECIAL NOTE

Note for ILS and INT programmes

Schools that serve families who speak diverse languages should try to provide information packets in at least the major languages represented in the school if the parents speak neither of the two instructional languages.

Regardless of the type of educational context, it is advisable to create a planning team that is representative of various sectors of the school and community to assume responsibility for ensuring that the necessary steps are in place to implement the new programme. The checklist at the end of this chapter identifies the various steps that need to be taken before a new CLIL programme is ready to be launched. Administrators, teachers and ancillary staff can participate in this team. Having an oversight team is useful even for existing CLIL programmes so that key facets of the programme can be revisited, newly emerging needs identified and changes planned systematically. Next, we discuss issues that need to be considered by both new and running CLIL programmes.

ORGANISING THE CURRICULUM AND SCHEDULING

We suggest using academic content-area themes as the skeleton or frame around which instruction is built in any type of CLIL programme –

whether you aim for high levels of bilingual proficiency, to use the majority language to teach the core curriculum to non-native speakers, or to apply CLIL methodology in FL contexts. Thus, a Language Arts lesson on genres can use the theme of weather borrowed from the Science part of the curriculum for teaching the concept of genres. For teachers who identify themselves as 'language teachers', this may be a bit of a challenge. For some teachers, especially teachers in FL programmes, who are identified by their colleagues as 'the French teacher' or 'the Italian teacher', it may even feel as a slight to their professional status if they perceive that language is taking a secondary role to other subject areas. However, any sense of loss of professional pride that Language Arts and additional- or foreign-language teachers might feel can be offset by the realisation that they will be advising content-area teachers on what language skills students need in specific content areas and how best to teach those skills during content instruction. After all, it is FL teachers who are specialists in teaching language directly.

Shifting the focus of the Language Arts class or the additional-language curriculum more generally to include a consideration of academic content as a basis for teaching not only reinforces students' mastery of academic subjects but also promotes their acquisition of the additional language (see our discussion of Principle 1 in **Chapter 2**). In all CLIL contexts, all language teachers also begin to see themselves as teachers of Science, Mathematics, Social Studies, Art and Music. In turn, content teachers in CLIL programmes can benefit from the assistance of the 'language experts' in the school as they plan the language objectives of their units and lessons. As a result, the teachers who teach non-language academic content, such as Science, may also begin to think of themselves as teachers of language. They may better see the value of using language-teaching strategies in their lessons.

The pivotal role that academic content plays in planning instruction in CLIL programmes that teach a considerable portion of the curriculum through the additional language should not detract from the importance of teaching language. Just as language teachers need to use content-area topics as the basis for advancing language proficiency, content-area teachers need to see their texts and their discourse during content instruction as opportunities for promoting language development. The use of themes that cut across domains of the curriculum makes it easier to link units of study in one subject area to other subject areas. This also makes it possible to provide students with a tight and well-supported language-learning continuum that includes different academic domains (Hamayan, Genesee & Cloud, 2013). When studying nineteenth-century European history, for example, students can investigate the significant scientific discoveries in that same era in their Science class; literature of that century can be studied in Language Arts class, and so on. Consequently, students can hear and use aspects of the additional language while learning about a general theme that permeates different domains of the curriculum.

4.1 ADDITIONAL RESOURCES

Ways to integrate across content areas
(adapted from Fogarty, 1991)

- **Connected**: Within each subject area, topics and concepts are connected, with attention paid to the language of these concepts, making cross-linguistic connections along the way.

- **Nested**: Within each subject area, multiple skills are targeted: a social skill, a thinking skill, a content-specific skill. The language needed for these skills is highlighted. If different subjects are taught in different languages, cross-linguistic connections are made.

- **Sequenced**: Units of study from different subject areas are sequenced to coincide with one another. The overlap in language used for the units reinforces new-language acquisition.

- **Shared**: Organising elements such as reporting strategies or data-gathering techniques that students have to learn for both Science and Mathematics are taught together. The overlap in the language used helps move proficiency forward. When different subjects are taught in different languages, cross-linguistic comparisons can be easily made.

- **Webbed**: A general theme is webbed into various subject areas. This provides an opportunity for extending language.

- **Threaded**: Thinking, social, study and technology skills are threaded in different subject areas. Common language is reinforced.

The use of themes that cross different domains of the curriculum also allows students to build knowledge that is part of an integrated system that reflects real human experience (Goodlad, 1984) and not simply a conglomeration of disparate segments. The division of the school day or week into subjects that are taught in separate periods encourages a segmented rather than integrated view of knowledge. This not only makes it more difficult to retain information and to understand new concepts; it also gives students the sense that what is learned at school is artificial, cut off from their everyday experiences. Integration across the curriculum can take many forms (see **Additional Resources 4.1**), some of which will be more appropriate for your specific educational context. The oversight team suggested earlier in this chapter can consider the list in the resources box below and start a discussion as to how integration can be best attained.

In the section on setting objectives later in this chapter, you will see that setting both content and language objectives is essential for units and lessons that are primarily focused on academic content as well as those that focus on Language Arts. In this way, content teaching and learning are integrated into language classes and language teaching and learning are integrated into content classes. For all these reasons, we recommend that curriculum and thematic-unit plans be developed by instructional and administrative staff collaboration so that a common array of themes can be taught by all teachers of the same grade level.

It is critical to make time available to coordinate instructional planning during the academic year. This is when administrative support becomes crucial (Principle 8). Teachers need to be given time during the school day to plan lessons and units together. Establishing virtual networks and email groups can help alleviate the time for face-to-face meetings but cannot replace them completely.

The use of academic subjects as the skeleton around which instruction is built applies to all four educational contexts we describe in this book. It is themes linked to the academic subjects in the curriculum that determine what Coyle (2008) calls *the learning path* for all the content areas where an additional language is used as the language of instruction. Nevertheless, as discussed in **Chapter 1**, there are significant differences in the social and pedagogical frameworks for the three CLIL contexts that aim for high levels of bilingual proficiency – IMM, DL-CLIL in ILS contexts and DL-CLIL in INT contexts, in comparison to traditional FL contexts that can only achieve relatively low levels of bilingual proficiency. Schools with students who do not speak the language of instruction, such as immigrant or indigenous-language students in ILS contexts, and students in INT schools who do not speak the language of schooling, must plan their programme carefully to make the best out of a pedagogical scheme that has not been shown to yield the best results.

Since planning the curriculum has different implications for each of these types of CLIL contexts, we now consider significant issues in curriculum planning for each separately.

CLIL PROGRAMMES THAT AIM FOR HIGH LEVELS OF BILINGUALISM

IMM, ILS and INT contexts

IMM programmes provide an excellent setting for a rich and coherent application of CLIL, as do ILS and INT programmes that aim for high levels of bilingual proficiency and use a dual-language education model. In IMM and dual-language ILS and INT programmes, instruction is usually provided in an additional language anywhere from 50% to 90% of the time. A CLIL approach is essential in these cases. Teachers must be aware of students' need to learn language at the same time as they learn new concepts. Once the interconnecting themes from the subject areas have been identified for each year of the programme, decisions about how to allocate the language of instruction to the various content areas can be made. An explicit and formal plan is needed to show who teaches what content area in what language over what period of time. In addition, decisions must be made about the way the two languages will be used in the classroom by teachers and students – whether the teacher uses only the language of instruction, to what extent students use their two languages, and how the teacher responds to students who use the non-instructional language (Hilliard & Hamayan, 2012).

Teachers and administrators must also decide how often the language of instruction is switched for each subject area. Schools differ greatly in their language-allocation choices: some schools switch the language of instruction for the same content area weekly or even daily, while others make the switch only at the end of a grade. In the first example, History would be taught in one language for a week or day and then either the same teacher or another one continues instruction in History in the other language. In the second example, History would be taught in one language for one whole grade, and the following year it would be taught in the other language.

RESEARCH NOTE

Effectiveness of different language-allocation models

The limited research available on this topic suggests that 'massed learning' – that is, learning that is concentrated in time, is more effective than distributed learning – learning that takes place during shorter and more widely distributed intervals (Collins & White, 2012; Muñoz, 2012). We favour using the same language for teaching a given subject for more extended periods of time rather than for only a week or day at a time. Using each language for more extended periods of time makes it easier for teachers to build students' skills in that language and it makes it easier for students to consolidate skills in each language. Changing the language of instruction only after each grade makes it easier to identify and construct materials and activities, since few switches occur.

The choice of one plan over another often depends on the availability of materials and teachers who can teach the various content areas in each language as well as how well a specific language-allocation plan fits with the rest of the school schedule. While the availability of human and material resources is a crucial factor, it should never be the sole determining factor in structuring a programme. Rather, the programme should be structured on the basis of what makes sense from the perspective of the learners and what we know about the most effective ways children and adolescents learn through two languages. Obtaining materials and other resources is discussed in a later section of this chapter. Whatever plan is chosen, it is the quality of instruction that results in successful content and language learning.

In programmes where the two languages do not enjoy equal status, it is important to establish strategies within the classroom as well as in the school at large to raise the status and value of the lower-status language (Principle 4). This is particularly critical in ILS and INT contexts, where the primary language of instruction is often seen as the only important language in the curriculum. Schools with immigrant and indigenous-language students are particularly prone to this inequality, with the larger society viewing these students as 'at risk' of failure because they speak a low-status language and come from a low-status cultural group.

CLIL PROGRAMMES THAT DO NOT AIM FOR HIGH BILINGUALISM

FL-CLIL programmes

Two factors – one positive and one negative – can have a significant impact on using CLIL in an FL context. The first, positive, is the independence that the FL curriculum has within the school. The second, negative, is the influence of international language tests on the FL curriculum.

Independence of the FL curriculum

FL instruction typically has little to do with the rest of the curriculum. This provides an opportunity to pick and choose content-area themes that the FL teacher feels are most conducive to developing proficiency in the additional language. Content areas that are less dependent on language and that involve concrete activities, such as Biology, Chemistry, Physical Education, Art and Music are good candidates for use as the basis of FL-CLIL lessons. An added advantage of this is that themes that are most interesting to students can be integrated into the FL class, thus increasing the learning quotient (see Principle 3). At the same time, it can be a challenge for FL teachers to coordinate with content-area teachers to make sure that they use themes from the academic curriculum at the same time they are being taught by the content teacher. This requires common planning time for teachers during the school day.

Pressure from international examinations

This factor limits rather than expands the choice of themes that can be used from the content domains in the FL class. It also runs counter to the very premise of CLIL that languages are learned most effectively when they are useful for authentic and meaningful communication. Our personal experience with FL programmes in many countries around the world points to the tremendous power that international language exams can have on the FL curriculum. They put pressure on the school, parents and students to pass tests that focus mostly on the structure and form of language rather than communicative uses of the language. This, in turn, narrows down the choice of what is taught and expands how much explicit focus there is on teaching the structure and grammar of the language. FL lessons can end up concentrating, sometimes solely, on grammar, vocabulary and phraseology in isolation. As a result, it is not uncommon to find adolescents who have taken years of FL classes, who score quite well on international language tests but can only carry on very limited conversations in that language and cannot even read extended texts, such as novels or non-fiction books.

There is no reason to eliminate explicit instruction of the structure and grammar of language altogether. In fact, it is advisable to provide some explicit instruction on the grammar of the language explicitly (see Principle 2), especially when it involves aspects of the language that are difficult to learn. However, when providing explicit instruction, we recommend that you use authentic materials and situations taken from the school curriculum to do so. Doing this can achieve two important goals. First, it makes explicit focus on language structure meaningful to students and, therefore, is more likely to be learned. Second, it exposes students to authentic language as it is used in actual communicative contexts, thus making it more likely for students to develop functional proficiency in the language while reinforcing concepts being taught in another academic subject area (see Principle 1). In other words, even in a situation where there is a focus on explicit language instruction, using CLIL strategies can enhance learning by emphasising authentic, meaningful communication. This is bound to be more effective than expecting students to learn parts of the additional language for the sake of passing an international exam.

ILS and INT schools

Schools that have immigrant and indigenous-language students may not be able to aim for high levels of bilingual proficiency in those home languages if a large number of languages are represented at each grade level. In classrooms with 10 or 15 home languages, it is difficult to teach academic content through all of these languages. However, it is essential that all home languages are supported and valued in informal but visible ways in the classroom and throughout the school (Principle 4).

References to the languages represented can be inserted into lessons, and the curriculum should reflect the multilingualism in the school. See the suggestions in **Additional Resources 4.2**, as well as Eugenia Papadaki's personal perspective in **Chapter 3**.

4.2 ADDITIONAL RESOURCES

Reflecting multilingualism in the school

- Ensure that the school and classroom libraries acquire books in the languages spoken by students in the school and display them prominently.

- Place multilingual signs and posters in the different languages of the students along the hallways.

- Make some public announcements in the various languages, with speakers of those languages acting as interpreters for those who do not understand.

- Dedicate a section of the weekly or monthly newsletter to the languages spoken in the school.

- Urge parents to talk about school work in the home language.

- Provide workshops to parents on how to support the home language.

Many ILS and INT schools have students with primarily one home language that is different from the main language of instruction. It is realistic to think that these schools could provide students with CLIL instruction that aims for high levels of bilingualism in their home language and the language of instruction. For example, an INT school could provide dual-language education for students in the school who already speak the language of instruction, or, if there is a large group of students, they could provide dual-language instruction to students who do not speak the language of instruction but speak the host language of the community. ILS schools with a large number of students who speak the same minority language could provide dual-language education in that language and the majority language. However, many schools do not offer full-fledged bilingual instruction to these students despite extensive research that shows dual-language education is the best option not only for developing bilingual proficiency but also for optimal academic achievement. If these schools choose not to offer bilingual instruction, they must recognise that students are not being given the best option available to them. In this case, using CLIL strategies in the majority language is still critical to ensure that students who are not already proficient in the language of instruction develop high levels of proficiency in that language and master the academic curriculum.

In any school context with students who do not speak the language of instruction, the school should take steps to make the students' home languages visible in the curriculum, and throughout the school, even if no formal instruction is provided in and through that language. Providing students with opportunities to make cross-linguistic connections is one way of doing this. Students can be called upon to ask how they would say something or express an idea in their home language, or to indicate how their language differs from the language of instruction. Making minority-language students' home languages part of their learning process in these ways, as well as others described in more detail in **Chapter 5**, can alleviate some of the negative effects of a monolingual approach. You can ensure that cross-linguistic connections are made by including cross-linguistic objectives in every lesson and unit.

The following section describes the primary and secondary objectives that play an important role in CLIL instruction.

SETTING OBJECTIVES

Once the themes are set for the year, teachers can begin to set objectives for their lessons or thematic units. Five types of objectives can help guide a CLIL lesson and assessment regardless of which language is being used to teach. Writing five different types of objectives for each lesson or unit is daunting for most of us; so it may be helpful to distinguish between primary and secondary objectives so that you are not overwhelmed and can set priorities for your units and for specific lessons. We consider content and language objectives to be of primary importance, and cross-linguistic, cultural and general learning-skills objectives to be secondary, but still important.

Primary objectives: Content and language

We discuss content and language objectives together because, in a CLIL unit or lesson plan, you can rarely pay attention to one without the other. Because students are learning new concepts through a language in which they are not fully proficient, it is necessary to make sure that they are familiar with the language that is needed to learn about academic content topics or themes. Content objectives tell us what the students will learn about a topic. Content-obligatory language objectives tell us what aspects of language students need in order to learn and demonstrate their mastery of specific content, whether it be through listening, reading, speaking or writing (Echevarria, Vogt & Short, 2013). Many teachers think that language objectives can be found in the Language Arts part of the curriculum. In fact, the Language Arts teacher has an important role to play in CLIL by aligning her language objectives with the topics and themes the students are studying in their other subjects. For example, when students are studying a topic related to climate in Science, the Language Arts teacher can compare and analyse genres by using a piece of fiction, a newspaper report or a scientific explanation of hurricanes. This is really a case of cross-curricular integration. Language Arts is a subject just like Science, Social Studies or Mathematics. In CLIL classrooms, Language Arts calls for the development of content objectives along with language objectives (see the example in **Table 4.1**).

In addition, in CLIL classrooms, you need to plan for language development at all times when you are teaching content through an additional language. Language that is required to understand and to express knowledge about a concept in any content area must be learned as soon as the topic is introduced. Thus, by setting language objectives in a timely fashion, you can ensure access to the curriculum for students who are still developing proficiency in the language of instruction. This is true whether you are teaching in dual-language or monolingual programmes.

TABLE 4.1

Academic Language (adapted from Cloud, Genesee & Hamayan, 2009)

ACADEMIC LANGUAGE OF SCIENCE

Text/talk features

- complex sentence structures made up of multiple embedded clauses
- highly specific vocabulary that conveys scientific concepts and understandings
- if/then sentences
- use of the conditional tense (what could/might happen)
- active explanations and descriptions of phenomena
- use of metaphors – 'a comet is like a …'; 'think of a comet as a …'
- high level of visual support – diagrams, photographs, illustrations

Major text/talk structures

Definition, description, cause/effect, chronological/sequential, comparison/contrast, problem/solution

Subject-matter-specific vocabulary

e.g. omnivore, vertebrae, lava, mineral, thorax, molecule, carbohydrate, precipitation

Words used in new ways

e.g. cell, space, crust, matter, property

Phrases and lexical bundles: words that often co-occur

e.g. food chain; water cycle; cloud formation; wind generator; the nature of …; in the form of …; as a result of …; as shown in Figure X

Common transition words and connectors

Unless, although, finally, because, also, consequently, therefore

Common communicative functions

Name, classify/categorise, ask and answer questions, report, describe, explain, predict, hypothesise

(Continued over page)

ACADEMIC LANGUAGE OF SOCIAL STUDIES

Text/talk features

- complex sentences with independent and dependent clauses; descriptions of related events; causes and effects
- verb plus infinitive (refused to obey, offered to write)
- time references; temporal phrases
- third-person pronouns that refer to actors previously named in the passage (he, she, they)
- causative words

Text/talk structures

compare and contrast; generalisation/example; enumerative; cause and effect; sequential/chronological; problem/solution

Subject-matter-specific vocabulary

e.g. continent, landform, goods, services, raw material, consumption, patriotism, rebel, boycott, taxes, delegates

Words used in new ways

e.g. party, capital, assembly, press (as noun), lobby

Phrases and lexical bundles: words that often co-occur

e.g. at the same time, had the right to, became known as, one of the most, as a result of, the fact that

Common transition words and connectors

from that time forward, furthermore, as a result, finally, so, never before

Common communicative functions

Explain, describe, define, justify, give examples, sequence, compare, answer questions

ACADEMIC LANGUAGE OF MATHEMATICS

Text/talk features

- conceptually packed
- high density of unique words with specific meanings
- great deal of technical language with precise meanings
- requires multiple readings
- requires a reading-rate adjustment because text must be read more slowly than natural-language texts
- uses numerous symbols
- many charts and graphs

Text/talk structures

cause and effect, comparisons, logical or chronological sequence

Subject-matter-specific vocabulary

e.g. divisor, denominator, integer, quotient, coefficient, equation, protractor, place value, proper/improper fraction

Words used in new ways

e.g. table, column, variable, carry, irrational/rational, mean, factor, term, expression, odd, set

Multiple ways of saying the same thing

e.g. add, plus, combine, and, sum, increased by, total; subtract from, decreased by, less, minus, differ, less than, have left

Phrases and lexical bundles: words that often co-occur

e.g. least common multiple, standard deviation, square root, a quarter of, divided by vs divided into, as much as, common factor, the size of the, greater than or equal to, not more than

Common transition words and connectors

If, then, if and only if, because, that is, for example, such that, consequently, either

Common communicative functions

following directions in a sequence, show, tell, ask and answer factual questions, predict, explain, justify, hypothesise

Since we are using academic content as the basis for organising the curriculum, content objectives have to be set first. Once the content objectives have been set, you can extract specific aspects of language that students need to learn in order to attain those objectives. You need to think through the unit and each lesson and identify the specific language skills that will be used. It is tempting to identify only terminology (words) that may be unfamiliar to students. However, language that is necessary to process a new concept goes beyond the word level. Mastery of academic content and skills also requires acquisition of certain grammatical forms, or phrases, lexical bundles, connectives and transition words that are typical of a particular academic domain; it may also require certain kinds of common text structures and talk features (see **Additional Resources 4.3** for examples of academic language).

4.3 ADDITIONAL RESOURCES

Examples of academic language

The following web site contains academic vocabulary lists of English that are based on 120 million words of academic texts in the Corpus of Contemporary American English (COCA): **www.academicwords.info/**

Some of the language that requires attention will be specific to the particular content and the concept(s) being learned. For example, knowing the meaning of the term *precipitation* is key to understanding a lesson on the water cycle. Understanding the phrase *A causes B to C* (e.g. *cool temperature causes vapour to condense*) is also critical for this lesson. We call this type of language *content-obligatory language*; it has also been referred to in the literature as academic language (Anstrom et al., 2010; Cummins, 2012; Scarcella, 2003). Other aspects of content-obligatory language are more generic. In the example above, *steam* is a common word that most native speakers will have learned by the grade level when the water cycle is typically taught. A second-language learner may not have come across that word and this can lead to difficulty with the lesson. We call this more generic language *content-compatible language* (Snow, Met & Genesee, 1989). Content-compatible language tends to be language that native speakers would have picked up or learned but that second-language learners may not have. Examples of specific content and both types of language objectives can be seen in **Table 4.2** for Science, Mathematics and Language Arts.

TABLE 4.2

Sample content and language objectives
(adapted from Cloud, Genesee & Hamayan, 2013)

Content objectives	Language objectives
Science: To describe the transformative life cycle in insects	**Content-obligatory:** To list the names of common insects that undergo metamorphosis To recite the names of stages in the life cycle of insects **Content-compatible:** To use the present tense accurately
Mathematics: To count forward and backward using cardinal numbers	**Content-obligatory:** To call out the name of numerals from 1 to 20 shown to them in random order **Content-compatible:** To demonstrate understanding of the terms forward and backward by following oral instructions to walk in those two directions
Language Arts (a lesson based on the topic of hurricanes): To identify characteristics that personal, factual and analytic genres share and that are different	**Content-obligatory:** To point to the appropriate texts when the teacher calls out the names of the three genres **Content-compatible:** To point to the appropriate parts of a Venn diagram from an earlier lesson when the teacher uses the phrases: *characteristics that are different* and *characteristics that are shared*

Content and language objectives in the four educational contexts

The importance of these two primary objectives – content and language – is the same regardless of educational context and regardless of whether the programme aims for high levels of bilingualism or not. Whenever CLIL instruction is provided because students are learning through a new language, whether it is in IMM, ILS, FL or INT contexts, then it is essential that content and language objectives guide unit and lesson planning. The amount of planning that is needed to coordinate language and content instruction, however, will vary depending on how much content is taught through an additional language and whether that content is a primary focus of instruction. In an INT school with many students who spend most of their time learning through an additional language, lessons need to have both content and language objectives to make sure that students' lack of full proficiency in the language of instruction does not stand in the way of learning. In an FL context, where academic themes are used to teach the additional language, the amount of coordination required between the FL teacher and the content-area teacher(s) whose subject is being used as a vehicle for teaching the additional language is far less than in the previous example.

The checklist on the facing page (**Checklist 4.1**) shows a possible sequence of steps for setting and using content and language objectives.

Secondary objectives

Secondary objectives are not as critical in lesson and unit planning as content and language objectives, Nevertheless, it is important to include them in every unit and lesson plan in order to ensure that students:

a) make connections between their two languages (cross-linguistic objectives)

b) focus their attention on cultural issues (cross-cultural objectives)

c) are supported by being provided with strategies that they can use for learning (general learning-skills objectives).

We refer to them as secondary objectives because they depend on content and language objectives, which must be determined first. Like the primary objectives, the secondary objectives need to be identified ahead of time so that they can fit into the unit and each lesson, and so that they

4.1 CHECKLIST: SETTING AND USING CONTENT AND LANGUAGE OBJECTIVES ✔			
	Programmes that aim for high bilingual proficiency	**Programmes that aim for low bilingual proficiency**	**Who's responsible?**
☐	Thematic units are set for each grade level for all teachers to use	Thematic units that will be taught through the additional language are determined	Teacher(s) and administrator
☐	Content and language objectives are set for each unit that is to be taught through the additional language		Content and language teacher(s)
☐	Time is set aside (at least one hour a week) solely for the purpose of content-language and cross-content coordination		Administrator
☐	Content and language teachers plan the introduction of the new language so that, if possible, it precedes the introduction of new content-area concepts		Content and language teacher(s)
☐	As the unit progresses, teachers get together on a regular basis to monitor how and when the objectives are attained		Content and language teacher(s) with support from administrator
☐	Content-language coordination is adjusted for necessary revisions as units are completed		Content and language teacher(s)
☐	Lockstep planning continues for subsequent units		Content and language teacher(s)

can support the primary objectives set for content and language learning. However, teachers should be prepared to seize 'teachable moments' during their lessons when they can include secondary objectives that were not foreseen. The following is an example of a teacher making a cross-linguistic connection that arose unexpectedly:

T: *Hey! This reminds me of something we looked at last week. Remember how we analysed the newspaper article about the hurricane in Miami in English and Spanish?*

Ss: *Yeah. Yeah. Longer in Spanish. More excited.*

T: *Yes, exactly. The reporter in Spanish wrote more about emotions and feelings of people who lived close to where the hurricane landed, no? Look at this piece here [a science report]: do you notice how there are so many verbs where you don't have to say who did what? Instead of saying the doctors did this and that, you can say 'it was done'. This is the passive voice where you don't even say who did what! Well, you sort of do, but it's more objective. It makes it more ... not so personal. Can you find some examples of that?*

S: *'When the acid is placed in the beaker', right?*

T: *Yes. Now how would you say that in Spanish? Can you use the same kind of construction? Ariel?*

S: *Yes, yes, you can ... 'El ácido se puso en el tubo de ensayo.'*

Ss: *No, no! That sounds funny. It sounds like when Mr Hubbard speaks Spanish.*

Cross-linguistic objectives

Setting cross-linguistic objectives gives students the opportunity to explicitly make connections between their two languages. This, in turn, encourages students who are developing proficiency in more than one language to take advantage of all the resources they have accumulated in all their languages (see Principles 4 and 5 in **Chapter 2**). This has been shown to be effective and helpful for both general learning and the development of bilingual proficiency (see **Research Note 4.3** for a summary of findings on the positive outcomes of making cross-linguistic connections).

However, you need to think about how to use cross-linguistic connections carefully in order to promote learning and not simply make things easy for students. Of particular importance, how, and the extent to which, you make cross-linguistic connections depends on the particular CLIL context of your programme. Research on the importance

RESEARCH NOTE

Pedagogical reasons for making cross-linguistic connections (from Cummins, 2007; García & Wei, 2014; Genesee & Geva, 2006; Hornberger & Link, 2012)

- Cross-linguistic connections create meaning.

- Learning in and about one language supports learning in and about another language.

- Making the two languages an integral part of lessons reflects the value and high status of both languages.

- Discussing concepts in more than one language helps to better encode knowledge in the brain for later use.

of cross-linguistic connections and, in particular, discussions of translanguaging (García & Wei, 2014) have focused primarily on students from minority-language and cultural backgrounds who are learning the more powerful majority language of the community at large. Many studies that discuss translanguaging involve immigrant students in the United States whose home languages are not highly regarded. Moreover, in many of the settings where this research has been conducted, bilingualism is an exception rather than the norm, and these students are seen as a challenge rather than an asset to the school. For our purposes, this would apply to immigrant and indigenous minority-language students in ILS programmes in countries around the world and students who speak languages other than the main language of instruction in INT schools.

Highlighting the importance of minority-language students' home languages in your classroom and throughout the school is critical when these students' home languages are seen as having relatively low status. As we noted in **Chapter 2**, for CLIL to be maximally effective, both languages should enjoy equal status (Principle 4). Minority languages in CLIL classrooms are often less valued and, thus, need to be elevated and reinforced so that students' motivation to learn the language remains high (see Principle 3); this is equally true for minority-language students themselves as for majority-language students. In contrast, students from the mainstream group who speak the majority or high-status language as a first language do not need additional support for their home language since it occupies a prevalent position in society and its status and continued existence are not questioned. These students need to see the value of the other language and to have significant exposure to it if it is not valued or used widely in the wider community. When the majority or high-status language is highlighted during a lesson when the low-status language is being used for instruction, you have to be careful that it does not come to dominate language preferences in the classroom. For these reasons, cross-linguistic connections need to be planned carefully ahead of time, as much as possible. For example, if you encourage majority-language students to use resources in their language, you need to carefully monitor that the majority language does not come to be used as a crutch and as the preferred language of interaction among all students in the classroom.

With these cautions in mind, let us examine what cross-linguistic objectives look like. Making cross-linguistic connections can take two forms.

- Drawing students' attention to similarities and differences between the two languages. For example, *using a text that has just been read in a History lesson in English in a French school – compare the use of morphemes in English and French to indicate 'the opposite', such as disappear/ disparaître, disrespectful/irrespectueux, disable/désactiver, and so on.*

- Encouraging students to unravel the meaning of the unfamiliar language by drawing on resources from their other language. For example, *in a lesson in Science taught in English to Spanish-speaking students, guess the meaning of a conditional phrase in English by relating it to the conditional in Spanish.*

Cross-cultural objectives

Learning through an additional language is a great opportunity to expand cultural horizons. By incorporating cross-cultural objectives into CLIL units and lessons, you can give students the opportunity to learn about customs, norms and values of other families and communities so that they become more aware of their own norms and values. Making cross-cultural connections also provides a pathway for examining prejudices and stereotypes and for valuing diversity. Although these aspects of learning are hardly ever included in tests or evaluations of the success of a school, they are a fundamental responsibility of any school – the formation of world citizens who can live in harmony with people from different backgrounds. By considering cross-cultural comparisons, students can become mindful of their interdependence and the connection they have with others as part of a larger global community.

Here are some examples of cross-cultural objectives and how you can build them into your lessons:

- To develop a sense of different approaches to daily life, norms and values.

  How to: have students compare and contrast the structure of a typical family in their community with that in a story they just read, and identify values that are reflected in these differences/similarities.

- To learn about the contributions of writers, scientists and philosophers from different cultural communities to the academic domains they are studying in school.

  How to: in an Italian FL lesson when students are studying nuclear power in Physics, have students describe the accomplishment of Enrico Fermi that led to his being awarded the Nobel prize in Physics.

- To explore how beliefs and values are reflected in our language.

  How to: in a Spanish–English IMM programme, after studying different types of writing in Language Arts in English, have students list 3 or 4 'dichos' (adages or sayings) in English and Spanish and describe the values that they reflect.

Cross-cultural objectives are also an excellent opportunity to make links between school and home by incorporating resources from students' families. We examine these opportunities in greater detail in Chapter 6.

General learning-skills objectives

Learning can improve when we explicitly teach students general learning skills; that is, how to learn more efficiently. This includes learning how to:

- take notes from an oral presentation
- take notes when reading a text
- make diagrams to represent information
- search for information on the web

- form an idea about written text by skimming and focusing on titles and headings
- ask questions
- form visual links to new words so as to remember them more easily
- create an individual dictionary
- summarise a sequentially organised text
- read maps, charts, graphs and diagrams
- work with a partner
- use a table of contents and an index
- organise completion of an activity.

General learning skills can be pulled out of any lesson in any content area. Teaching learning skills explicitly is more effective if done in the context of a content-area lesson because students can see its usefulness immediately. As with cross-linguistic and cross-cultural objectives, opportunities may arise unexpectedly for you to teach general learning skills and you should be prepared for these moments – e.g. explaining a strategy that students can use to help them do something as they are doing it.

Secondary objectives in the four educational contexts

There are two ways in which secondary objectives have a more prominent role in ILS and INT contexts that do not aim for high levels of bilingualism. First, many students in these programmes are often accorded low status by mainstream students and teachers in these schools. Consequently, their home languages and cultures are often not given the importance they deserve. By incorporating cross-linguistic and cross-cultural objectives into your teaching, you are acknowledging the value of the rich linguistic and cultural backgrounds that these students bring with them to school. Building in these kinds of objectives also makes it possible for these students to make use of all the resources they have in their home language as well as their home culture. This can compensate, at least partially, for the fact that they are not otherwise able to draw on the funds of knowledge they have because they are being taught through a non-native language.

Second, many students in ML-CLIL programmes in ILS and INT contexts have general learning skills that differ from those that are valued or prominent in the school environment. They may need help to learn how to use general learning strategies that are better suited to the norms and customs of the school and the textbooks they are using. For example, students from some cultural backgrounds may follow time constraints only loosely; they need to learn the importance of following the more rigid time guidelines of the school. Or students who are familiar with a different text organisation, such as the table of contents appearing in the back of a book rather than in the front, can be shown how to navigate through textbooks more efficiently. In all of these cases, it is a matter of focusing on general learning-skills objectives that can help students become more effective learners.

THREE-PHASE LESSON OR UNIT PLANNING

With your primary and secondary objectives in place, you are now ready to plan the unit. Because coordination and co-planning by teachers is so important in CLIL classrooms, we highly recommend the use of a common lesson- or unit-planning tool across grade levels. Using a common planning tool makes it easier to see which aspects of instruction can be integrated across domains – for example, what part of a lesson in Mathematics in English can be coordinated with a lesson in Social Studies in the additional language. With a common lesson-planning tool, unnecessary overlap can be avoided, and gaps can be filled so that teaching by two teachers (or even two classes in different content areas taught by the same teacher) are conducted in a seamless manner. We suggest a three-phase unit-planning tool that begins with a preview activity, followed by a focused-learning phase, and ending with an extension activity. A copy of the planning tool we use can be found in **Appendix 4.A**.

The preview phase

The purpose of the preview phase is to reveal knowledge that students already have about the topic or theme of the unit. This is also the time to familiarise students with the language that they will need in order to understand and learn new concepts and skills, and that will be introduced in the focused-learning phase. During this phase, you can build word and phrase knowledge for both content-obligatory and content-compatible language, preferably through a concrete activity with the students. This can be done by offering scripts and giving students opportunities to learn chunks of new useful language. This can also be done by asking specific questions that refer to concrete aspects of the activity; for example, after visiting a wind farm for a unit on renewable energy, you can ask: *What was the energy from the wind turbines used for? Why was the wind farm built in that particular place? What factors do we have to consider when planning to establish a wind farm?* By observing students' responses carefully, you can determine what content-obligatory language skills they have and which ones need attention (Principle 6). The preview phase needs to be clearly linked to the concepts to be taught and to be as concrete and experience-based as possible so that students can relate what they already know to what they are going to learn – for example, going on a field trip, playing a game, building or taking apart an object, watching a video, reading a well-illustrated book. In **Chapter 5**, we focus explicitly and in more detail on what happens during this phase; a sample lesson plan is used to illustrate this.

The focused-learning phase

Once the new concept has been introduced in a concrete manner and content-obligatory and content-compatible language have been developed during the preview phase, it is time to focus explicitly on the new concept to be learned. This phase is most effective if the onus of learning is shared by students and the teacher. The inquiry approach, which takes a hands-on and research-based disposition to learning and teaching, is well equipped to do that. Based on explicit and direct instruction by the teacher (Principle 2), students are led to discover aspects of the concept under study. This approach increases student engagement, fosters understanding and gives concrete opportunities for students to construct knowledge under the guidance of the teacher, all of which benefit students who are learning through a non-proficient language. During this phase, it makes most sense to also bring to students' attention the general learning skills that will help them retain or search for new information and to master new concepts.

The extension phase

Students often do not get the chance to see how what they learn in school relates to the world outside. The third phase of a unit allows students to apply what they have learned in school to a real-life situation. This not only reinforces the new concepts but also gives students a chance to engage with and influence the community in which they live.

4.2	**CHECKLIST: SECTIONS NEEDED IN A CLIL UNIT-PLANNING TOOL** Check these sections against the lesson-planning tool you currently use; if any of the sections below are missing from the existing tool, add them. ✓

☐ Theme or topic

☐ Big ideas:
'Students will learn that ...' or 'Students will learn how ...'

☐ Time frame

Objectives:

☐ Content

☐ Content-obligatory language

☐ Content-compatible language

☐ Cross-linguistic

☐ Cross-cultural

☐ General learning skills

Major teaching activities:

☐ Preview phase

☐ Focused-learning phase

☐ Extension phase

☐ Background knowledge needed

☐ Materials

☐ Extensions to other subject areas

☐ Extension to students' lives outside of school

Assessment:

☐ Formative

☐ Summative

The students can partner with a local business or organisation, or they can do a project that applies what they have just learned and contribute something positive to their community. Outreach and connections to the community and family are discussed further in **Chapter 6**. The extension phase is also the time for students to see how what they have learned in one content area relates to another. As well, this phase of the unit provides teachers with an opportunity to make any cross-linguistic or cross-cultural connections that had been set as objectives but were not attended to earlier.

Regardless of the particular planning tool you use, and regardless of the type of educational context you are in, your planning tool should include the sections listed in the checklist on page 115. If the tool that is being used does not include any of the sections in this checklist, then you may want to simply add them to your existing lesson-plan framework.

RESOURCES

Qualified staff and high-quality material resources are key for the success of CLIL, even in an FL context where only some aspects of the academic curriculum are integrated into language teaching. In the first section below, we focus on qualifications of teachers and administrators as well as issues of professional development.

Human resources: Qualifications of teachers and administrators

It is challenging for schools that offer extensive forms of CLIL to find qualified teachers. Many schools resort to hiring teachers on a short-term basis from other countries where the additional language is spoken. At times, teachers are recruited through outreach programmes supported by foreign governments. Teachers are also often recruited through programmes supported by foreign ministries of education (Mehisto, 2008). Effective and efficient integration of content and language instruction can be provided by the following types of teachers. We begin with the most limited form of CLIL (FL contexts) and then move on to consider the most extensive (IMM and DL-CLIL in ILS and INT) contexts:

FL programmes:

- FL teachers who can work in close collaboration with content-area teachers to offer a unit taken from the content-area curriculum in the additional language.
- Content-area teachers who understand the value of CLIL and are happy to collaborate and work as a team with the FL teacher.

ILS and INT programmes that do not aim for high levels of bilingual proficiency; that is, ML-CLIL:

- Content-area teachers with skills in teaching in the additional language and who are willing to accept help from additional-language teachers.
- Additional-language teachers qualified in some content areas.
- Additional-language teachers who provide additional support to classroom teachers by teaming up with them in or outside of the classroom.

IMM, ILS and INT programmes that aim for high levels of bilingual proficiency:

- Teachers qualified in both the content area and in teaching an additional language.
- Teachers skilled in CLIL strategies.

It is also recommended that all schools implementing CLIL have special-needs teachers who can provide support to students who might face extra challenges. Since we believe that any student, regardless of cognitive, linguistic, general learning or academic abilities, should be given the opportunity to develop proficiency in two languages (see Principle 7), we must give these students the support they need. Specialist teachers who can provide this support in both languages or, at least, who are familiar with issues relating to additional-language learning, are essential in any CLIL programme.

Professional development

The dearth of qualified CLIL teachers makes it imperative to have a solid ongoing professional-development plan. Perhaps the most challenging aspect of professional development in CLIL is the one we mentioned at the beginning of this chapter – teachers' perception of their roles and identities. As we have noted before, content-area teachers often resist thinking of themselves as language teachers and, similarly, language teachers usually do not see the development of content-area concepts as part of their responsibility. Crossing these specialisation boundaries is a crucial first step in the development of CLIL teachers. Mehisto (2008) and many others (Clark, 1995; Dewey, 1933; Hole & McEntee, 1999; Osterman & Kottamp, 2004) identify reflection as a valuable professional-development tool that can help break down these artificial boundaries. Analysing and articulating one's attitudes and beliefs about one's professional roles and responsibilities are fundamental departure points for improving teaching.

Mehisto (2008) suggests that professional reflection is important not only with respect to one's identity as a teacher but also with respect to one's openness to collaborating with other professional educators in order to learn and to change – what Dweck (2006) has called a growth mindset. Reflection can also help professionals become aware of the theoretical basis and belief system on which their practice is based and why they make certain critical decisions about teaching. Reflection helps teachers identify their strengths and weaknesses, and the latter can then become the focus for professional development. Espousing education as a lifelong process, trying new techniques and strategies in the classroom, evaluating one's own teaching critically, and thinking creatively can improve teaching and student outcomes. Moreover, when teachers engage in this type of professional development, they serve as models for their students, in whom they try to instil these same characteristics.

The following is a list of possible topics for professional development in CLIL:

- What is CLIL? Core features of content and language integrated teaching.
- What are the goals of our CLIL programme?
- On what pedagogical principles is CLIL based?
- How can integration be achieved in the classroom?
- How can teachers collaborate and to what end?
- How do children and adolescents become bilingual and biliterate?
- How can we make cross-linguistic connections between the two languages of instruction?
- What strategies for previewing, teaching and extending a lesson can we use?
- How can students be grouped for different types of activities?
- How do we promote cross-cultural development?
- How do we assess student progress in academic domains in their additional language?

• How do we evaluate instruction?

Effective professional development is a sustained and collaborative process (Sparks, 2002). Follow-up to a single professional-development event is essential. Coaching, study groups, teacher inquiry or research groups, ongoing collaboration with colleagues to develop learning outcomes and unit and lesson plans, and team teaching are all long-term approaches to growing professionally as CLIL teachers (Crandall, 2012). Professional development in a CLIL school should not be limited to teaching staff. Lack of interest in and knowledge about CLIL instruction in any sector of a school are counterproductive. This can be alleviated by offering non-CLIL teachers as well as non-teaching staff opportunities for professional development as well. Offering monolingual teachers classes in the additional language of instruction is also highly recommended.

Material resources

Some programmes make the mistake of letting learning materials form the basis of decisions about the curriculum and scheduling. This can happen because of past practices, availability, cost or the fact that materials were chosen before important decisions about the curriculum and scheduling were made. It is important to remember that materials support the curriculum rather than the other way around. Only once plans for the CLIL programme are made, including the steps that we have discussed so far in this chapter, should the search for materials begin. Materials include primarily textbooks and other kinds of texts and visuals that would be used in the preview and extension phases. For early-grade levels and for students with low proficiency in the languages of instruction, realia and manipulatives are also needed. If textbooks in the additional language are not available in the country where the school is located, they can often be obtained from the countries where that language is the official language of instruction. In that case, the texts need to be aligned with the curriculum at each grade level and with the culture of the community. Embassies can also be a source of support for obtaining textbooks as well as auxiliary materials. Auxiliary materials – such as games, songs, videos, newspaper articles and blogs – can be found on the web in most languages.

Quality learning materials guide teachers in making critical decisions that make textbooks fit the specific needs of their particular group of students. Quality learning materials do not just present information for students to memorise; rather, they push students to ask critical questions, to figure out what additional information they need in order to learn, and to reflect on their own learning (Mehisto, 2012). Quality materials also encourage collaboration among students and lead them to reflect on how what they have learned relates to their daily lives, their families and their communities. For an exhaustive analysis of criteria for producing CLIL materials, see Mehisto (2012). The checklist below can be used to evaluate materials for inclusion in your CLIL programme.

4.3	CHECKLIST: EVALUATING CLIL MATERIALS (adapted from Mehisto, 2012)	✓
☐	Big ideas regarding the content area are easily identifiable; that is, you can easily identify what it is that students will be learning.	
☐	Academic language (content-obligatory) that will be needed for learning the concepts is easy to identify.	
☐	It is easy to identify the content-compatible language that students will be taught.	
☐	It is easy to break down lesson(s) to avoid cognitive and linguistic overload.	
☐	New concepts are introduced step-by-step through scaffolding.	
☐	Language flows smoothly and naturally and sounds authentic for the context.	
☐	The materials make it easy to form cooperative groups.	
☐	The materials foster active student participation.	
☐	Students are consistently encouraged to take responsibility for their own learning by doing independent work.	
☐	Students are challenged to think creatively and critically.	
☐	The materials involve the students in peer and self-assessment.	
☐	New concepts can easily be extended into students' daily lives.	
☐	Connections to various cultures and communities are made on a regular basis.	
☐	A diversity of perspectives, people and social contexts are represented in a dignified and stereotype-free manner.	

SUMMARY

The checklist below can help you to monitor the planning that needs to be completed in order for the school and the classroom to be ready for instruction.

| 4.4 | CHECKLIST: PLANNING INSTRUCTION | ✔ |

In new CLIL programmes

☐ A team has been formed to oversee the planning of the CLIL programme.

☐ A brief statement regarding the goals of the programme has been prepared.

☐ A brief summary of the research supporting CLIL instruction has been prepared in terms that are clear to educators and non-educators alike.

☐ An outside advisor who can give ongoing support has been identified and enlisted.

☐ A plan is in place for letting everyone in the school know about CLIL (meetings, information packets, videos).

☐ Professional-development sessions are planned for all school staff and specifically for teachers who will be using CLIL.

☐ An informational packet that addresses parent and community issues regarding the programme has been prepared.

In existing CLIL programmes

☐ There is consensus regarding the goals of the programme and, in particular, the importance of integrating language and academic content instruction.

☐ If the curriculum that was in place before CLIL, or in the monolingual part of the school, is not adequate for the CLIL programme, a revised curriculum has been established.

☐ The scope of CLIL has been determined: how many content areas will be taught in the additional language and to what extent?

☐ A language-allocation plan for each subject area is in place for at least five or six years.

☐ Teachers and other staff have been contracted.

☐ A unit/lesson-planning tool that will be used consistently by all teachers across the programme has been chosen.

☐ A schedule has been developed.

☐ Teachers have started to collaborate in order to develop content and language objectives for their lessons.

☐ Assessment methods and schedules have been determined.

☐ Professional development has been planned collaboratively by teachers and administrators for all CLIL teachers and others in the school.

☐ Materials have been ordered for the content areas to be taught through the additional language.

☐ A plan to evaluate the programme has been developed, and any necessary base data have been obtained.

APPENDIX 4:A   UNIT-PLANNING TOOL

Topic:	
Big ideas:	
Time frame:	
Content objectives:	**Content-compatible language objectives:**
	Content-obligatory language objectives:
Cross-linguistic objectives:	
Cross-cultural objectives:	
General learning-skills objectives:	
Background knowledge needed: **Assessment:**	

PREVIEW PHASE:	
Teaching activities:	Grouping arrangements:
Assessment:	
FOCUSED-LEARNING PHASE:	
Teaching activities:	Grouping arrangements:
Assessment:	
EXTENSION PHASE:	
Teaching activities:	Grouping arrangements:
Assessment:	
Materials:	
Assessment at the end of lesson:	

5   Teaching content and language integrated lessons

As reviewed in **Chapter 3**, a significant body of research has shown that students in CLIL programmes develop higher levels of proficiency in the additional language while attaining the same high levels of academic achievement as their peers who are not in CLIL classrooms. However, as is the case with any other pedagogical trend, embracing the CLIL name without strictly adhering to its principles does not automatically lead to effective instruction or successful learning. As Mehisto (2015) emphasises, it is the quality of instruction that is critical for building successful dual-language programmes. So, what is quality instruction in a CLIL classroom? In **Chapter 4** we set up a plan for instruction that includes:

- a curriculum that is thematically organised (Principle 1)
- content and language objectives for each lesson (Principle 2)
- cross-linguistic, cross-cultural and general learning-skills objectives throughout a whole unit (Principles 3, 4, 5)
- regularly planned meetings for teachers to coordinate instruction with each other (Principle 8)
- a three-phase progression of lessons beginning with a preview phase, followed by a focused-learning phase, and ending with extensions into other subject areas and into the students' daily lives (Principle 3).

To help you choose the activities and strategies that support this plan, we turn to a significant body of research and a substantial amount of practical experience of teachers with whom we have worked that point to 1) the value of a three-phase lesson plan and 2) effective ways of teaching in a CLIL lesson.

As we describe these three phases one at a time, we will build a sample unit to illustrate how this planning template can be useful. We have written the sample unit as it would be implemented in a CLIL classroom where students have at least minimal proficiency in the additional language. In general, it is safe to say that the pedagogical strategies that are used in any CLIL classroom, whether in IMM, ILS, FL or INT contexts, and regardless of whether the programme aims for high or low levels of bilingual proficiency, do not differ significantly from one another. The main difference lies in the amount of preparation devoted to planning for and delivering language instruction – that is, the scaffolding you provide before and during the in-depth teaching of new concepts. Thus, it is most likely that the preview phase will look a little different in programmes that do not aim for high levels of proficiency in the additional language – such as FL contexts and ILS and INT contexts that aim primarily or solely for proficiency in the main language of instruction without much value given to the student's other language. CLIL units in an FL context are also likely to be different from units in the other three contexts in the choice of content. Since the primary reason for CLIL in an FL programme is developing functional proficiency in an additional language, teachers are not limited to specific content subjects; rather, they can choose content that is less complex and abstract and more concrete and experiential in nature to make it more suitable for students with relatively low levels of proficiency in the additional language. For this reason, Music, Art and Science would be better choices than History or Mathematics (see the personal perspective by Gabriela Tribaudino in **Chapter 3**). In our description of each section of the unit plan, and of the activities and strategies we use, we point out how the implementation of CLIL would differ in contexts that aim for higher levels of proficiency than this FL context.

5.1   PERSONAL PERSPECTIVE

Integrating language and content learning through a three-phase approach

Elisa Rivera, grade 2 dual-language teacher,
Veterans Memorial Elementary School, Central Falls, Rhode Island, USA

In my second grade classroom, English and Spanish language instruction is allocated by content area. One of the principles set during my district's development of the Dual Language programme was to maintain a strict separation of languages. The native language of all of our students is Spanish; however, some of them have native-like proficiency in English. We noticed students became discouraged when they couldn't verbalize their prior knowledge in the target language. In order to truly assess the content area knowledge students possess, we knew we had to encourage students to express themselves in the language they felt most comfortable with, all while the teacher remained in the target language. As a result, there was an increase in student participation.

This practice is particularly crucial to the preview phase of the units I teach. For example, one of the Science units I teach is on matter. I have students draw and/or write what they know about matter. On a KWL chart [see p. 133], I record what they know about the topic in the language of their choice. This allows me to pre-assess content area knowledge and misconceptions. I note students' language use of English or Spanish. This helps me determine the vocabulary and language structures I need to focus on and teach, and helps me to provide students with multiple opportunities for interacting in the target language during the focused learning phase.

To help support students during the focused learning phase, I partner students heterogeneously by language proficiency. This way, students serve as language models for each other. Students complete a hands-on activity such as sorting and categorizing solid objects based on their properties. I create anchor charts using the unit's vocabulary for students to reference. This ensures that their product is in the target language.

The extension phase includes a home-school activity. Parents help their children label pictures of solids. We discuss the different terms families used to name objects. For example, a 'drinking straw' was labelled 'pajilla' 'popote' and 'sorbeto'. This activity increases students' Spanish vocabulary, as they're exposed to language variations. We also compare and contrast the unit's vocabulary and phrases in English and Spanish to determine cognates and analyze the surface structures of both languages. Teaching language through content in this three-phase approach not only deepens students' content area knowledge; it also helps students' proficiency in both languages to grow.

The lesson-plan template we use in this book is an adaptation of one we have used in another publication (Hamayan, Genesee & Cloud, 2013). However, you can use whatever lesson-planning tool your school has already adopted. Just make sure that your template allows you to plan for preview, focused instruction and extension phases where you can apply what students have learned to other areas of the curriculum and outside of the school context. A blank template can be seen in the Appendix at the end of **Chapter 4**. Remember, as we mentioned in the previous chapter, integration is easier when all teachers are using the same lesson-planning tool. This is true even in an FL context.

If this is not the case in your school, you may want to form a working group that can look into unifying the various lesson-plan formats or perhaps adopt an entirely new one (see sources for templates in **Additional Resources 5.1**).

5.1 ADDITIONAL RESOURCES

Unit/lesson-plan templates

There are many ways and forms that can be used to plan a lesson or unit. Pick one and adapt it to your specific needs. Just make sure that you are incorporating the three-phase system that gives students the chance to build their content-obligatory language in ways that facilitates their understanding and mastery of the new concepts in a lesson or unit. The following websites offer different templates for lesson planning:

www.teachthought.com/uncategorized/10-teacher-resources-lesson-planning-templates-tools/:
  Brief descriptions of ten websites that offer lesson-plan templates.

www.educatorstechnology.com/2012/07/3-excellent-tools-to-easily-create.html:
  Reviews three tools for planning lessons.

www.edutopia.org/blog/five-free-web-2.0-tools-lisa-dabbs:
  Shows five general web-based tools for teaching.

www.commoncurriculum.com/:
  Allows for real-time collaborative lesson planning.

www.cal.org/twi/TWIOP.pdf:
  Describes elements of a lesson plan and gives examples of lessons in IMM settings.

FIGURE 5.1: Unit-planning template: topic and objectives

Topic: Renewable energy

Big ideas: (These can be identified by the teacher prior to beginning the unit; however, final big ideas will be an amalgamation of your initial ideas and big ideas that emerge from students' questions during the focused-learning phase.)

We will learn that some sources of energy are renewable while others are not.

We will learn which sources are renewable and how they function.

We will learn why renewable sources of energy are becoming more important instead of, or in addition to, non-renewable sources.

Time frame: 2–3 weeks (this time frame was determined arbitrarily for this example; it will depend on how much this unit is extended into other subject areas and who teaches what part of the lesson).

Content objectives:

- To describe the difference between renewable and non-renewable sources of energy.
- To list five types of renewable energy: hydropower, wind power, solar energy, geothermal energy and bio energy.
- To explain in general terms how any two of these types of energy function.
- To give three reasons why we need to use renewable energy.

Content-obligatory language objectives:

- To write or say the names of the five types of renewable energy using words such as *provide*, *system*, *result*, *use*.
- To use appropriately the phrase *X does Y by Z-ing* (e.g. wind produces energy by turning a propeller), or *X does Y in order to Z* (e.g. solar panels convert the sun's power in order to produce electricity).
- To use appropriately the phrase *X does Y; therefore …* (e.g. coal contaminates the air; therefore, we should use it for producing energy as little as possible) or *because X, we can Y* (e.g. because renewable-energy sources never run out, we can use them for a long time).

Content-compatible language objectives:

- To demonstrate what *light bulb*, *wind* and *waste* mean.
- To define, give examples or show what energy is.
- To define, give examples or show what *renewable* means.
- To use the future tense appropriately.

(Continued over page)

Cross-linguistic objectives:

- To see if there are cognates for important words in the texts we read.
- To compare the use of the negative affix *non-* in English with the way negatives are formed in the other language.
- To compare how questions are formed in the two languages.
- To compare where adverbs are placed in the two languages.
- To compare the text used in class with a similar text of the same genre in the other language (younger students can compare concrete aspects, such as length and use of expressions, while older students can compare the tone of the piece and the way words are used to convey social values and attitudes).

Cross-cultural objectives:

- To compare the level of renewable-energy use in our country to that of its neighbours and other countries around the world.
- To compare the symbolic meaning that the sun, water and earth have in different communities as evidenced in myths, legends, sayings.
- (For older students) To analyse the reasons for differences in the levels of renewable-energy use in different countries.

General learning-skills objectives:

Choose any of the skills listed in the section on general learning skills in Chapter 4 that can be brought out during the lesson, e.g. how to scan a text for key ideas; how to keep track of key ideas brought up in discussion groups.

The theme we have chosen for our sample unit is *renewable energy*, a topic that can appear in the curriculum anywhere from grade 5 to grade 12. The lesson is to be taught in English as an additional language, but can be adapted to other languages quite easily. The activities in our lesson are aimed at the lower grade levels but can be adapted for higher grade levels. **Figure 5.1** above shows the first part of the unit-planning template that includes the topic, big ideas and the objectives that fit into this lesson.

With this basic information about the lesson, we can now turn to the instructional activities that we want to use to introduce, teach and reinforce concepts regarding renewable energy, beginning with the preview phase.

THE PREVIEW PHASE

This first phase of a lesson is crucial for building the language that students will need in order to understand, process and master the new concepts during the focused-learning phase of the unit. This is a critical basic step for ensuring that the integration of content and language instruction goes smoothly. Infante, Benvenuto and Lastrucci (2009) have found that this is still an area that many CLIL teachers find challenging. In the first step of any unit, you can familiarise students and find ways of having them actively use content-obligatory language necessary for learning a new concept; this will help comprehension of the new content. You can also make new content comprehensible in the additional language by introducing it in concrete and experiential ways that actively engage learners. This first phase of a lesson is also the time to discover what students already know about the topic.

The following are key components of the preview phase:

1. investigating students' prior knowledge about the topic (Principles 5 and 6)

2. familiarising students with the language that is necessary for the unit (Principle 2)

3. introducing the concepts and language that they are about to learn in concrete ways, preferably through a student-centred activity (Principles 1 and 3)

5.1 SPECIAL NOTE
For IMM, as well as DL-CLIL ILS and DL-CLIL INT contexts

Students who have been in a programme that aims for high bilingual proficiency for at least five years should have reached a high enough level of proficiency in both languages to be able to learn new concepts without a lot of language preparation or scaffolding, although some such support is always needed because there is always new content and, therefore, new language to be learned. Moreover, these students should already have enough content-compatible language to manage the lesson. However, it is advisable to list content-obligatory and content-compatible language objectives anyway and check familiarity before getting too far into the lesson.

4. motivating students so that they are excited about the unit and become more invested in it (Principle 3).

These four components feed into one another naturally – when students are engaged in a concrete activity and contributing information that they already have about the topic, they are immersed and surrounded by language that is likely to be essential for learning the concept. These four components, which are so vital in the preview phase, are part of what is called scaffolding, an essential aspect of CLIL instruction (Van Lier, 1996). They can also be part of informal assessment that you undertake to ascertain how much your students already know about the topic – it is a matter of observing students carefully and making notes about what they appear to know and, importantly, what they do not know – see **Chapter 7** for more details about how to do this in the actual lesson.

Here are some important themes to think about as you plan the preview phase.

Scaffolding

Scaffolding is an important component of the preview phase of teaching. It has been defined as breaking up learning into chunks and providing support, or structure, that makes each chunk more manageable and learnable (Gibbons, 2002). In a CLIL classroom, you must be sure to support both language as well as concept learning (Principle 1). Scaffolding should be prominent not only in the preview phase of a unit, but also throughout the unit. It can include the following strategies:

- showing or doing while telling
- pre-teaching language explicitly
- pointing out key words and phrases
- organising words and phrases into categories
- having students practise words, phrases or discourse patterns before doing an oral or written presentation
- making language more comprehensible by using short sentences and paragraphs
- tapping into prior knowledge

- giving time for students to process

- pausing, asking questions, pausing again, reviewing

- repeating nouns instead of using pronouns.

Building on prior knowledge

It is best to gather information about students' knowledge of the topic early on in the unit. Prior knowledge is not limited to what students know about the topic; it is also about knowledge of the language that is pertinent to the topic in the students' home language. You can familiarise yourself with students' prior knowledge in a focused and explicit way by dedicating time to assessing the language they already have that is relevant to the topic before doing anything else; and you can also gather information about their existing language skills indirectly as you complete preview activities. We discuss informal methods of assessment that let you do this in **Chapter 7**. For the first option, the following strategies can be used: oral surveys of what students know, short essays that students can write on the topic, teacher-led questioning about the topic, brainstorming about what students know and want to learn about the topic – what Ogle (1986) calls 'KWL', anticipation guides and peer interviews, during which they talk with one another about the topic. Since your purpose is to find out as much as you can about students' prior knowledge, you can encourage them to use either or both languages. For the more indirect option, you need a way to record your observations either orally, on a hand-held device or using anecdotal records (to be described in more detail in **Chapter 7**) as you engage students in preview activities. Sheets of adhesive labels can also be used to make notes about what students know, and these can be attached later to the class list or individual student folders that you keep during the school year. **Figure 5.2** shows the section of the unit-plan template that lists the background knowledge that students need to have for this lesson.

Determining students' background knowledge during this phase is important because it is knowledge that will help students understand the new concepts when you move into the focused-learning phase. Therefore, it is important to write down what you think is critical background knowledge in the preview phase of the lesson plan to ensure that your attention is focused on these precursors of learning as you observe them during preview activities. By examining students' pre-existing knowledge in the preview phase, you can better gauge how much foundational work needs to be done before the new concepts are taught intensively.

FIGURE 5.2: Unit-planning template: Background knowledge needed

Background knowledge needed:

Awareness of the fact that we use different sources of energy.

Awareness of what energy is used for.

Assessment:

Brainstorming and developing a KWL chart that we add to as the lesson proceeds (to be described in greater detail in Chapter 7).

Teacher observations with anecdotal records of what students know and do not know about the language related to the topic and the topic itself.

Entries in journals, learning logs.

Building language

If your preview activity takes place in the classroom, or if you have a board or flip chart easily available, you can highlight the language that students need to know by writing words, phrases and grammatical structures for them to see as the preview activities unfold. If you have gone on a field trip as part of the preview phase, make sure to jot down content-obligatory and content-compatible language you observe students using during the activity that they will need during the focused-learning phase; later, post known and unknown language on the classroom wall when you return to school. This will serve both as a reminder to students of what was important about the field trip and as a resource they can use if they need to look up a word or a phrase to complete an activity. The display of terminology, words or phrases can be made more cognitively complex and interesting if a semantic web is built as the words appear during conversation or oral presentations about the preview activities. **Figure 5.3** shows an example of such a web for our sample unit. The semantic web can be displayed in two languages and this would address the first two cross-linguistic objectives we listed in the beginning of the lesson-planning tool (**Figure 5.1**).

FIGURE 5.3: Example of a semantic web built during the preview phase

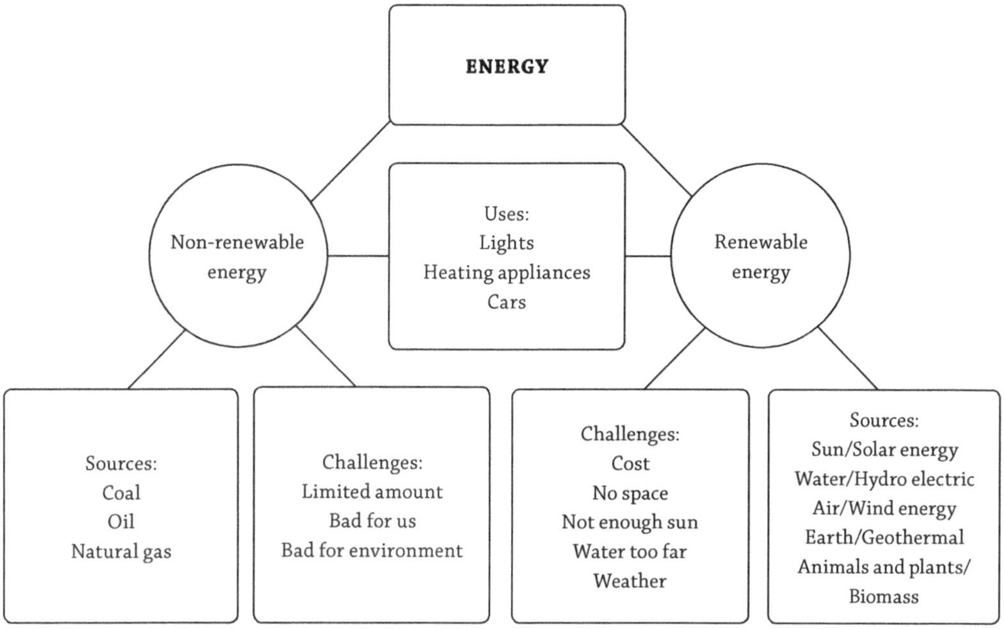

Language use in the four educational contexts:

Research shows that encouraging students to use all the resources they have in their two (or three) languages not only helps with the attainment of new concepts but also enhances the development of language for academic purpose (Cummins, 2007; García, 2009, 2011). However, we must differentiate between students for whom the additional language is a minority language and students who come from a minority-home-language background and are learning the majority language as an additional language. With Spanish-speaking students in Argentina, learning English as an additional language, for example, encouraging the use of Spanish during English class extensively may be counterproductive. These students need to practise and spend as much time as possible learning their additional language (English). Their home language, Spanish, is not under threat – it has high status in and outside school, and it plays a vital role in all aspects of people's lives. This does not mean banishing Spanish from the classroom; judicious use of cross-linguistic connections will help these students remember words, learn new phraseology, and learn new content in English.

In contrast, Korean-speaking students in an international school in Europe or in a public school in North America where English is the main language of instruction, for example, should be encouraged to use their home language to help them process new concepts and understand and master English. The difference in these two cases lies in the fact that the Korean students are surrounded by English, the language of power and high status in the school. In this case, the school needs to support the use of Korean as there may be limited support for the language in or outside school. The cross-linguistic connections these students make by using Korean along with English is a useful way of not only developing their proficiency in English but also advancing their academic achievement. Moreover, if CLIL teachers can call on these students to use Korean in the classroom, this will raise the value of the minority language and will enrich the majority students' funds of knowledge about language: they will learn to 1) value other languages (Principle 4), 2) see the complexities of languages other than their own (Principle 2), and 3) value other ways of seeing the world around them (Principle 5).

5.2   PERSONAL PERSPECTIVE

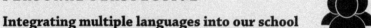

Integrating multiple languages into our school

John Deighan and Jana Schubert, Mother Tongue Coordinators; Duff Gyr, Principal; Marcia Banks, Vice Principal; Primary School, La Grande Boissière Campus, International School of Geneva

We decided to offer classes in various mother tongues (MT) in our schools because there was a demand and because we know that sound knowledge of one's MT facilitates learning other languages. Offering support in MT became part of the language policy of our school as it helps preserve and promote MT languages and cultures. After all, we are an international school! We pick our languages based on demand from parents and by looking at the number of students speaking each language. We offer classes in 16 to 20 MT languages each year.

We reach out to the community in many ways to get the parents in and show that we are genuinely interested in their cultures and languages. We used to send out flyers at the beginning of the year but now the communication is done mainly via email, telephone, meetings and our school website. Teachers also play an important role in communicating to parents the opportunities for MT instruction.

Our MT coordinators liaise with the Office of Admissions to learn of parents who may be interested in enrolling their child in MT classes. The primary school principal meets with all the MT teachers at the beginning of the year to ensure that there is no conflict in the timing of the introduction of formal literacy instruction in MT classes with the introduction of formal literacy skills at the primary school.

We have faced some challenges:

1. Getting the parents to see that their language and cultural heritage are just as important as English or French.

2. Cost – given that the parents pay high school fees, the additional fees, which are expensive, may be prohibitive.

3. Some parents are ambitious and want their children to start too early.

4. Some MT teachers want to teach to their national curriculum and we ask them to hold off introducing the written language as long as possible.

5. Children who are struggling with the demands of the curriculum resist taking on more lessons after school hours.

6. Finding space when we have many other after-school activities.

Despite these challenges, we feel privileged having many nationalities and mother tongues in the school. Some communities, like the Chinese, are very active and even organize trips for students, or, like the Arabic parents, organize events like an Arabic evening. We have 'a poem in your pocket day' where children are proud to share a poem of their choice in their MT.

By offering these classes, we enable quite a number of students to take their mother tongue for IB requirements. This is what an international school means for us: keeping your mother tongue while excelling in the language of instruction.

5.2 SPECIAL NOTE

For third-language students

Just as it is important for emergent bilinguals to use all the resources they have in their two languages, third-language students whose home language is different from the two languages of instruction can benefit from being given opportunities to use all three of their languages in school. Trilingual students need to see that: 1) their home language is highly valued, 2) they can use their home language to support learning academic content that is taught in another language, 3) their home language is useful for promoting proficiency in the other two languages, and 4) it is important to develop the home language to high levels of proficiency. In order to accomplish this, we recommend that you encourage and show parents how to support the growth of their child's home language.

5.2 ADDITIONAL RESOURCES

Ideas for a unit on renewable energy

See excellent lesson plans for various grade levels at www.leics.gov.uk/index/leisure_tourism/museums/ open_museum/resource_box/energykits/energykits_ teaching.htm.

For links to videos, pictures, vocabulary games, quizzes and puzzles on renewable energy, see www.neok12.com/ Energy-Sources.htm.

Find a variety of resources for renewable-energy lessons at https://www.tes.com/teaching-resources/ search/?q=renewable+energy.

See https://www.teachingenglish.org.uk/article/green-energy for ideas for lessons on renewable energy.

For younger students, see www.TouchstoneEnergyKids. com and www.kidsenergyzone.com/images/ data/files/Teacher%20Lesson%20Plans/ RenewableEnergyLessonPlan.pdf.

Using concrete referents

Here are suggestions for activities that prepare students for this unit on renewable energy in concrete ways that are engaging and provide opportunities for language learning: watching a video about renewable energy, going to a wind farm, visiting a factory that produces solar panels, showing pictures of different kinds or sources of energy, visiting a house or a business that uses renewable energy, making a solar oven, cooking something in a solar oven (and sharing it with others at the school), showing solar panels or parts of a small wind turbine, and, if you have access to a photovoltaic kit, making a light bulb work with a simple circuit fed by a solar panel.

Preview-phase activities

For our sample unit plan, we begin by distributing pictures related to energy sources and energy use to individual or pairs of students and ask them to guess what they think the topic of the lesson is going to be. First, the students find other students who have pictures that go together; for example, the sun, solar panels and electrical outlets would form a group; wood, fire and cooking would form another group, and so on. Once groups with related pictures are formed, they call out what they think their pictures represent. Next, you build a semantic web on the board using words that the students used to describe their pictures. You continue by writing a short text describing the activity that you just completed. This can be done as a whole group with one student or the teacher writing a description of the activity as other students call out ideas and sentences. Alternately, students in IMM, ILS and INT contexts that aim for high levels of bilingual proficiency can work in small groups to write their own texts since these students have probably acquired enough proficiency in the additional language to do this. Older students can focus on 'what we learned' instead of the more concrete 'what we did'. Students can be allowed to use the non-instructional language during either of these activities, but you must make sure that majority-language students do not overuse their language at the expense of using the additional language. Depending on the status of the students' home language, the teacher may reinforce students' use of that language before adding to the semantic web or story using the language of instruction. The following is an example of how you could respond differently to students' use of the other languages in different settings.

Scenario 1

A Spanish-speaking student (majority language) in an English FL class in Chile:

T: *Who wants to start? What did we do first?*

S1: *We ... umm ... together ... empiezamos a buscar fotos como el nuestro, que andaban junto con nuestra foto.*

T: *Very good, Sebastian.*

T: *Can someone help Sebastian say that in English?*

S2: *We start looking for pictures that are same as our pictures and then put together photographs that go together.*

T: *Excellent, Daniela. Let's write that on the board. Sebastian, why don't we do that together? I'll help you.*

With the teacher's help Sebastian writes the sentence in English in the column on the right-hand side on the board under the label *English*.

Scenario 2

A Spanish-speaking student (minority language) in a Science class in English in Australia:

T: *Who wants to start? What did we do first?*

S1: *We ... umm ... together ... empiezamos a buscar fotos como el nuestro, que andaban junto con nuestra foto.*

T: *Muy bien, Sebastian. Please write it on the board where it says 'Spanish'.*

(If the teacher has some Spanish, she might say *Muy bien, Sebastian. Escríbelo por favor en el pizarrón donde dice Español* – she asks Sebastian to write his sentence on the board under the label Spanish.)

S writes the sentence in Spanish in the left-hand-side column on the board.

T: *Can someone help Sebastian say that in English?*

S2: We start looking for pictures that are same as our pictures and then put together photographs that go together.

T: Excellent, Daniela. Let's write that on the board. Sebastian, why don't we do that together? I'll help you.

With the teacher's help, Sebastian writes the sentence in English in the column on the right-hand side on the board under the label *English*. The teacher stops to focus on the past tense and asks students if they should change *start* to *started*, and asks if there are other words or phrases that she chooses to modify. She asks about the cognates *foto* and *photograph* and the group discusses the use of *ph* in spelling in English in contrast to *f* in Spanish. A student brings up the fact that *pharmacy* and *farmacia* show the same phenomenon. The teacher decides to start a side-by-side chart showing words that begin with *f* in Spanish and *ph* in English.

Then, you watch a short video of about five to ten minutes about energy sources. This could add to students' motivation to learn more about the topic and show them why they should care about it and how it matters to them and their communities. Remember that for students with low proficiency the rate of speech in the video may be challenging. Many videos available on the web allow you to slow down the presentation, and, if not, you can stop frequently to allow students to catch up and ask clarification questions. After watching the video, students decide whether they want to change the composition of their groups in any way; for example, the group that called themselves *The Sun Powers* may decide that they need something representing electrical power and look for someone who has a picture about electricity to join their group. During the activity, the teacher walks around, observes students and makes notes of any evidence of prior knowledge and relevant language that students reveal while engaged with one another.

When the small groups are finalised, introduce the notion of renewable versus non-renewable energy by showing a picture of something cooking on a stove and a picture of something cooking on a wood fire. Get the students to determine the difference between the two methods of cooking. Introduce the labels *renewable* and *non-renewable* using the root term *new*, the prefix *re-* and the use of the negative affix *non-* to describe the two types of energy resources. A brief detour to discuss the use of the affix *non-* in the two languages would help reveal the meaning that you are trying to get across. Elicit suggestions from students about the topic that you are going to study. This can be done in the small groups with the whole class reaching a consensus as to the best name for the topic.

The topic is then written down on an evolving lesson-plan chart on the wall. One reason for doing this is for students to see where they are going during the unit as it transpires. This, of course, helps them plan their own learning. It also shows students that they are, at least partially, responsible for what they learn, and even how they learn. Having this evolving lesson plan is also invaluable for enabling the teacher to see the differences between her originally planned lesson and the way it actually happened.

Figure 5.4 shows the preview phase on the unit-plan template.

FIGURE 5.4: Unit-planning template: preview phase

Preview phase	
Sample teaching activities:	**Grouping arrangements:**
1. Distribute energy pictures.	1. Individual or pairs
2. Students guess topic.	2. Whole class
3. Students form groups that belong together and produce a label for their group.	3. Small groups
4. Call out label for group.	4. Groups
5. Write a text describing activity or, for older and more advanced students, what we learned.	5. Whole class
6. Build a semantic web as lesson unfolds.	6. Whole class
7. Watch video.	7. Whole class
8. Groups can reorganise as a result of what they saw on the video if they wish.	8. Groups
9. Show pictures for renewable and non-renewable energy. For students with low proficiency in the language of instruction, show examples of *new* and *renew*.	9. Whole class
10. Elicit topic and write down on an evolving lesson-plan chart.	10. Small groups and whole class
Assessment: *(To be described in Chapter 7)*	

FOCUSED-LEARNING PHASE

The focused-learning phase is when you teach new concepts directly and in depth. Although many of the activities suggested in the preview phase would also be quite appropriate to use now, this is the time to use direct instruction activities. However, teacher-directed instruction is not limited, by any means, to the teacher talking at the students; it includes modelling, scaffolding and creating the right environment for bringing out the students' natural curiosity to discover and to learn (Principle 3). It also means creating a classroom environment where students are led to discover features and elements of new concepts – what has been referred to as the discovery or enquiry approach (Bruner,

RESEARCH NOTE

Effectiveness of activity/enquiry-based instruction

- Students in an activity-based programme where only 50% of the time was spent in the additional language did as well or better than their counterparts in a teacher-centred classroom where instruction was given through the additional language 80% of the time (Stevens, 1983).

- Enquiry-based instruction stimulates collaboration and communication among students about the concept of study and its relevance to applications outside school (Thompson, 2006).

- In an extensive meta-analysis, Hattie (2009) concluded that a variety of instructional strategies including, but not limited to, enquiry-based instruction can maximise student achievement.

- Effective enquiry-based learning involves hypothesising, investigating, observing and evaluating (Banerjee, 2010).

- Marshall and Horton (2011) found a relationship between enquiry-based instruction and higher-order thinking in students.

- Teachers who are trained and encouraged to employ enquiry-based teaching approaches demonstrate greater and more sustained commitment to students' development of critical-thinking strategies (Ortlieb and Lu, 2011).

1961; Hmelo-Silver, 2004), and it fits well with activity-centred lessons. This approach is ideal for CLIL contexts where attention must be paid to both language proficiency and concept attainment.

In the discovery or enquiry approach to learning, which is also sometimes referred to as learner-directed, student-centred or activity-centred instruction, concept attainment is embedded in interesting and engaging activities in which language is used for authentic purposes. In more traditional instructional approaches, students memorise information given to them by the teacher and in textbooks. Lessons are characterised by a group-centred approach where all students study the same topics according to the same timeline. In contrast, in a discovery-based classroom, students are typically given projects or tasks that lead them to discover aspects or characteristics of the concept under study; student engagement is a core feature of this approach (Principle 3). Often, students are given choices about what they would study within the general context of the lesson and how they would attain an understanding of the big ideas. Students are led to ask questions about new concepts and to do research that would help them get answers. Groups of students may be working on different aspects of the lesson, which then are shared with the rest of the class.

Paying attention to students' language

In CLIL contexts where proficiency in the additional language is still developing and may even be in the early stages of development, providing students with opportunities to use language is vital. Students need to be provided with the time and the context that pushes them to talk to one another as well as to the teacher, while the teacher remains silent and listens instead of doing the talking most of the time. A likely consequence of encouraging student talk in the additional language, especially during the early stages of development, is a lot of inaccurate or inappropriate language because students still lack proficiency in the language. By observing how students use the language, you are able to gauge what they are learning well and what they need more support to learn (Principle 6). In particular, it is quite likely that they will need support learning content-obligatory language that is specific to the academic domain you are focusing on. For example, in our lesson on energy, they will need to learn new terms (hydro-electricity) as well as new phrases – 'energy is renewable if it can be replenished'.

Of course, there is also a place for informal social language with all of its jargon and idiomatic expressions, and you need to ensure that students get the opportunity to develop those aspects of language as well. This is especially important when the additional language is a majority

---

5.3 SPECIAL NOTE

Formulaic language in FL programmes

Teachers in traditional (non-CLIL) FL programmes, in which content instruction is secondary to language instruction, often claim that students produce a lot of language in their FL classes. However, we have observed that much of what they produce is rote chanting or repetition of memorised chunks of language in a context that has little to do with reality or with authentic communication. The most common of these unreasonable expectations can be seen in the introductory lessons of many FL classes where, in answer to the questions *What's your name?* or *How old are you?* students are expected to say, *My name is Juan* and *I'm 13 years* old instead of the more appropriate response of just *Juan* and just *13*. As well, because a 'correct' standard is being modelled and memorised, many teachers come to expect perfect renditions of language and they tend to correct deviations from the standard, sometimes leading to students' reluctance to take any risks using the non-proficient language.

---

language. Students in ILS and INT programmes, and who are members of a minority group in either the larger society or within the school community, would fall in this category; for example, Arabic-speaking students in French schools (ILS) or Korean-speaking students in an international school in Germany (INT). When students' home languages are not highly valued either by the larger society or within the school, or when their status as additional-language learners is held in low esteem, fitting in with peers and being able to 'sound cool' is critical. Learning how to use the new language for social interactions with their peers is important for these students, and CLIL teachers can help them do that.

When social language is used inappropriately, teachable moments arise (Principle 2); you can draw students' attention to what makes it inappropriate, when it would be appropriate, with whom it can be used, how it is different from more formal uses of language, and so on. This can take place in a lesson that is focused on language (like Language Arts) or it can take place as a mini-lesson within the focused-learning phase of your unit plan. Focusing on language as students need it helps push their proficiency forward because they are learning something they need right away; it can also develop their metalinguistic awareness (see Research Notes for Principle 5 in **Chapter 2**) and students' content-compatible language.

Students who are learning through a non-proficient additional language are very good at avoiding the use of complex grammar, phrases and vocabulary if they are likely to make mistakes – students might use *level* instead of *shelf*, or *glass* instead of *beaker*. If you see students using improvised forms in this way, you need to push them to reach beyond their comfort zone. As Lyster (2004, 2007) has pointed out, when errors and inaccuracies in language use persist, and when we notice avoidance strategies being used often, we need to provide students with form-focused instruction and corrective feedback (see Principle 2). How much to correct, what to correct, and how much to focus on the form of language is a delicate balance that must be kept with each student and with the awareness that too little will stop language from improving and too much may inhibit students from using new forms in the additional language (see the personal perspective by Roy Lyster in **Chapter 2**). Systematic and specific corrective feedback from the teacher is important for advancing students' language competence (Meyer, 2010). In order to create an environment in which students are enthusiastically engaged in learning new concepts and skills and, at the same time, learning to use the new language correctly, you need to strike a balance between teacher-directed and learner-centred activities.

Balancing direct instruction with discovery of concepts by students

The question still remains as to how much learning should come from direct teacher instruction and how much should come from student-initiated learning. Although minimally guided instructional approaches have gained popularity, there is evidence that learning is more effective when teachers actively guide students within their zone of proximal development, to use Vygotsky's terminology (Vygotsky, 1978, p. 86). Just how much to intervene is a decision that each teacher must make

RESEARCH NOTE

Guidance during enquiry-based instruction is important

Although unguided or minimally guided instructional approaches are very popular and intuitively appealing, these approaches ignore important scientific evidence about how we learn. Evidence from empirical studies over the past half-century consistently indicates that a balance between teachers' guidance and student exploration of new topics and concepts is needed. Teachers do not need to provide the same level of guidance if students have a lot of prior knowledge about the topic and the concepts they are about to learn. This prior knowledge will support students as they begin to investigate more information about the topic (Kirschner, Sweller & Clark, 2006).

continually during a lesson and throughout a unit. The goal is to maintain momentum and, at the same time, to stay on track. Remember that letting students take a lead in investigating and perhaps even in deciding how they are going to learn the big ideas does not mean letting go of the class. The teacher is still the conductor of this student orchestra. Informal assessment of students during classroom activities has an important role to play in helping you decide when to intervene and when to let students' take the initiative (Principle 6) – discussed in more detail in **Chapter 7**.

One way of creating this balance is to be a learner right alongside your students. As Hawley (2015) suggests, teachers must stop teaching as if they have all the answers. A powerful way to apply an enquiry-based approach is to design ways in which you, the teacher, can become a true learner of some aspect of the concept under study. To do this, we recommend that you devise one or two questions to which you do not know the answers. In this way, you can contribute to students' learning, and students can contribute to your learning. As a result, a genuine community of learners is created in the classroom. This strategy moves teachers away from lecturing and simply talking about isolated pieces of information that students are expected to memorise and repeat in response to closed-ended teacher questions.

Useful activities during the focused-learning phase

The start of the focused-learning phase is simply a continuation of the preview phase. There should be a smooth transition with no visible break between these two phases. To achieve this smooth transition, the first thing that you can do, once the preview phase has been completed and everyone agrees on the topic of the lesson, is to ask students if they have more questions about the topic. Remember, you as the teacher also get to list your questions alongside those of your students. When the students' and your questions have been written down, ask their help in determining the big ideas of the unit, and once students come up with acceptable approximations, you can write them on the evolving lesson plan.

Many teachers have fallen into the habit of writing specific objectives on the board and even having students copy these objectives into their notebooks. We find that it is more effective to focus on what we have called *big ideas*, what the students will be learning. The big ideas can emerge from the students themselves as a result of the questions that are generated about the topic. Big ideas can guide your selection of specific objectives and concrete activities. Big ideas are not simply topics; they specify the essentials of the new ideas or concepts that students are learning. When you write big ideas in the format of *We will learn that* ..., *We will learn how* ... or *We will learn why* ... (instead of *We will learn about* ...), it gives both teachers and students a clear and specific view of where they are headed during the unit. **Figure 5.5** shows questions posed by students for our unit on renewable energy and how those questions were transformed into big ideas. These big-idea statements can be used during and at the end of each lesson or unit to check for concept attainment.

FIGURE 5.5: **Questions generated by students and corresponding big-idea statements**

Questions we have (these are generated by students, perhaps with the guidance of the teacher)	**Big ideas we will learn** (these statements are created by students with the help of the teacher)
How many renewable-energy sources are there?	We will learn that there are X number (to be filled out after information is gathered) of renewable-energy sources.
What are the sources of renewable energy?	We will learn what the sources for renewable energy are called.
How long ago did we start using renewable energy?	We will learn how long ago we started using renewable energy.
In what way is renewable energy better or worse than non-renewable?	We will learn why renewable energy is better or worse to use than non-renewable energy.
What is renewable energy used for?	We will learn what renewable energy is used for.
How will not having renewable energy affect me and future generations?	We will learn how renewable energy affects our lives.

To help students plan their own learning in an efficient and meaningful way, you can ask them to determine if there are any questions that they think are easier or more basic than others. For example, in **Figure 5.5**, the first two big ideas form the building blocks that everyone can use in researching the additional big ideas. So we would begin by giving students a few minutes to find out, in small groups, the answers to the first two questions. In fact, it is not unusual for a student to jump up and call out the answer to these simpler questions even before other students have had a chance to think about them. Then you can discuss the best ways to research each remaining question, and small groups can be created to research each question over the next couple of days or week.

Having a sequence of questions that go from concrete to more abstract is recommended. In fact, it is advisable to sequence objectives and questions about the topic in such a way that you move from aspects of the big idea that can be learned experientially because they are relatively concrete to aspects of the big idea that are more abstract and, as a result, require more language competence. As a general rule of thumb, whenever a new topic, lesson or unit begins, it is a good idea to begin with the concrete and move to the more abstract. This makes learning the new concepts, and the language linked to those concepts, easier.

During this time, you can refer to any language posters or charts that had been created, encourage students to use the charts as resources for their work, and add new language to them that emerges during discussions and presentations. This is also an opportunity to add bilingual labels to posters and charts, when appropriate (Principles 4 and 5). This and other forms of scaffolding described in the preview-phase section make abstract concepts more accessible. Remember that much small-group or pair work can be carried out in students' more proficient or home language; but, whatever product they prepare or plan, presentation to the whole class should always be in the language of instruction.

This is also a time when you can introduce and teach general learning skills. For example, taking notes during an oral presentation or from a text, making diagrams on the board to guide the organisation of information that students are gathering for presentations to other students, or keeping a learning log or journal about their investigations to reflect on their own learning (Principle 6). Students can also be guided to use online searches and to find additional reading material about the topic in the library, thereby reinforcing their research skills (Principle 3).

After students have met in small groups and returned to the whole group with information about the question they chose or were assigned, each group can share their findings with the rest of the class. The following strategies are some ways of sharing small-group work with the whole class:

- Each group presents its findings orally, preferably accompanied by slides so that both oral and writing skills are developed. Make sure you set time limits and, for lower-proficiency students, give guidelines, phrases and words they can use when presenting information.

- Each group makes a poster showing its findings, and then students walk around to view the posters and discuss and ask questions of the students who made the posters. Posters can be produced in two languages. However, we encourage students to present orally in the language of instruction. Groups decide if they have anything to add to either their own poster or to others' posters.

• Jigsaw: Each group member is assigned a different question. Group members then join with members of other groups assigned the same question and gather information together. Students then return to their original groups and share information they have acquired from others.

When all the information gathered by groups has been shared and noted, a whole-class discussion pulls everything together. The teacher or students can jot down, either on the board, flip chart or on a smart board, a summary of their findings. This is a perfect opportunity to teach, model and practise summarising skills; this is also an opportunity for you to observe what students have learned and to note your observations in your anecdotal records as part of your assessment of the lesson (Principle 6). During the lesson, you can look out for opportunities to teach or reinforce general learning skills, such as note-taking.

The next step in the unit plan is to read a text on renewable energy. Up to this point in the unit, students will have done some reading on their own. However, having all students read a common text provides you with an opportunity to guide and steer the discussion in a more restricted way to ensure that students understand the big ideas set out at the beginning of the unit. Students will read the text that you have chosen and will then discuss what they have learned from it, adding any additional information they gathered from earlier sections of the unit. **Additional Resources 5.4** lists some websites that provide texts on renewable energy. In a classroom at a dual-language school, you could give some of the students a text in one language and others a text of the same genre in another language. This would give the discussion a more interesting and complex quality and would address the last cross-linguistic objective we had set for ourselves.

Next, the groups are given a chance to change anything in their findings in light of the whole-class discussions and the readings they have done. Under your guidance, if the class feels that enough information has been obtained and the big ideas have been mastered, the focused-learning phase of the lesson is complete. In the unit-planning template

5.4   ADDITIONAL RESOURCES

Sources for texts on renewable energy

This is a small sample of many magazines about energy that are available on the web. For other languages, write *renewable energy webzines* in translate.google.com and enter in a search engine.

For younger students:

www.childrensuniversity.manchester.ac.uk/interactives/science/energy/renewable/

www.energykids.eu/what-is-renewable-energy

www.fplsafetyworld.com/?ver=kkblue&utilid=fplforkids&id=16183

www.alliantenergykids.com/energyandtheenvironment/renewableenergy/

www.eschooltoday.com/energy/renewable-energy/what-is-renewable-energy.html

www.eia.gov/kids/energy.cfm?page=renewable_home-basics

www.ducksters.com/science/environment/renewable_energy.php

http://climatekids.nasa.gov/

For older students:

www.realpower.lansdownepublishing.com/ruk-42.html

www.renewableenergyfocus.com/

www.renewableenergymagazine.com/

www.renewableenergyworld.com/magazine/renewable-energy-world.html

www.renewableenergymagazine.com/articles-Europe-Europe/tag/europe/

www.supersmartenergy.com/

www.energetica-india.net/

www.homepower.com/

in **Figure 5.6**, we have included assessment as the last step for this focused phase; assessment is discussed in **Chapter 7**, where we provide ideas and suggestions for this unit. Once you have a good sense of how well students have understood the big idea and concepts linked to it, you can reword the big ideas on the board to the past tense to indicate what has been learned and check off each objective in your lesson plan. For example, with respect to the big idea '*We will learn what renewable energy is used for*', you write: '*We learned that solar energy is renewable and it can be used to produce hot water and electricity.*'

FIGURE 5.6: Unit-planning template: *Focused-learning* phase

Focused-learning phase

Sample teaching activities:	**Grouping arrangements:**
1. Elicit questions and write them down.	1. Pairs
2. Turn questions into big ideas.	2. Whole class
3. Determine which questions can be answered quickly; get answers.	3. Whole class
4. Discuss how we can get answers to the rest of the questions.	4. Small groups
5. Small groups choose or are assigned questions to research.	5. Groups and whole class
6. Groups return with findings and share with the rest of the classroom.	6. Groups and whole class
7. Summarise.	7. Whole class
8. Read text.	8. Individual, pairs and whole class
9. See if any groups need to change the information they reported on.	9. Small groups
10. Quick assessment to see if concepts are understood correctly by checking the big ideas.	10. Individual and whole class
11. Change the big-idea statements from future to past tense.	11. Individual, small groups or whole class

Assessment: *(To be described in Chapter 7)*

In concluding our discussion of the focused-instruction phase, we want to emphasise how important it is to maintain a balanced instructional approach. By incorporating the various strategies and activities described in the previous sections, we have attempted to maintain a balance in five aspects of instruction – see **Table 5.1**.

TABLE 5.1

Creating a balance in five aspects of instruction

1. A balance between introducing concepts in a specific subject area and the language that is needed for learning about those concepts: We have done this by building a loop where language related to the concepts about to be taught is introduced in a concrete way that then leads to discovery and learning about the concepts; this, in turn, leads to reinforcing and expanding the language needed to learn more about the concepts.

2. A balance between teacher-constructed and student-constructed learning: We have done this by making students owners of their own learning while encouraging CLIL teachers to guide them through the learning process.

3. A balance between controlled and free language use by students: We have allowed free usage of language but counterbalanced this with teacher feedback on form and structure of language and an expectation for appropriate language use.

4. We have struck a balance between giving students sources of information (like texts and websites) and letting them find information and choose texts on their own.

5. We have also balanced the use of the non-instructional language and the language of instruction by encouraging students a) to see similarities and differences between their two languages, and b) to use their more proficient language to process the information and the concepts they are learning but to create final products (such as oral reports, written material, posters, and so on) in the language of instruction. Also, use of the more proficient language must be balanced with the need to support students in their acquisition of the less proficient language – especially when students' home language is the majority language, because that language can come to dominate classroom usage if teachers are not careful.

EXTENSION PHASE

When you are satisfied that your students have had enough experience with the new concepts and they have mastered the big ideas that you started the unit with, you can move into the extension phase. Even if you have engaged the students in relatively authentic and real-life activities during the focused-learning phase, the new concepts are still only part of a single topic in an isolated domain of the curriculum unless you take steps to show how they are related to the rest of the curriculum. This is the phase when what was learned gets connected to as many subject areas as you have time for (See **Table 5.2** for suggestions on making connections to other subjects in the curriculum). Now it's time to take the newly learned concepts outside the subject area in which they were presented so that students can expand their range of knowledge and skills in the concepts just learned.

Some of the activities listed in the preview phase can be used here as well; for example, you can make a solar oven and bake something in it as a culmination of the unit. This activity could make connections to Art (drawing the plans for making the solar oven), Language Arts (writing the instructions on how to make a solar oven, or the recipe for the product made in the oven), Geometry (calculating the angle at which the oven should be tilted so as to get the maximum sun power), Family and Consumer Science (making bread, cake or cookies), Geography (finding out what months in which parts of the world a solar oven would work best), and so on. In this step of planning the unit, it is important to co-ordinate with the teacher(s) who specialise in each content area that you want to connect with. Those teachers will be able to help you apply CLIL strategies to incorporate one or two content objectives from their content areas. From the examples above, the Language Arts teacher can give the Science teacher who is teaching the unit on renewable energy some ideas about appropriate objectives from the Language Arts curriculum relating to genres.

TABLE 5.2

Examples of connections that can be made with other subject areas from our renewable-energy unit

The following are only a few examples of what can be done in different subject areas on the topic of renewable energy to connect with the unit taught in Science class. The examples cover different grade levels and are not specific to any educational context. They can be adapted to fit the needs of specific classrooms or groups of students.

Arts:

Investigate or make green products that have an artistic element. For example, solar bags and totes, eco-friendly fashion, household goods made with solar panels.

Produce crafts made with recycled or re-used goods. This would be most appropriate for FL programmes where most students have not attained a high level of proficiency in the additional language.

Biology:

Research the effects on the environment from non-renewable-energy sources.

Analyse what happens in biomass energy production.

Chemistry:

Study the meaning of *chemical footprint*.

Investigate the concept of chemical hazard from non-renewable energy.

Drama:

Produce a play based on the story written in the Language Arts class.

(Continued over page)

Government:

Investigate local, provincial and national laws regarding renewable energy.

Compare the laws in your country with those of neighbouring countries.

History:

Research the birth and growth of solar panels.

Write a biography of a famous person in the field of renewable energy.

Language Arts:

Students write a story about the world after all the non-renewable-energy sources have been depleted.

Turn the story into a play.

Literature:

Compare different countries' folktales about the sun, wind and water.

Find poems about the sun, wind and water.

Mathematics:

Calculate or investigate various types of statistics regarding renewable-energy use.

Media:

Search for advertisements for renewable energy and analyse them.

Find or create advertising jingles for renewable-energy use or products.

Music:

Look up and learn the 'Reduce, Reuse, Recycle' song and act it out (for younger students).

Perform the jingle created to advertise renewable energy (in Media class).

Physics:

Study the circular motion of wind turbines.

Study the role of magnetism in generating electrical power.

Psychology:

Investigate attitudes toward setting up wind generators close to people's homes.

The extension phase also gives you a last chance, before you end the unit, to make sure that your secondary objectives were addressed. For example, now is the time to make cross-linguistic connections between what was learned in one language to the other language; cross-cultural links can also be made now.

Extension-phase activities

For our sample unit that focused on Science, we have decided to extend it into Mathematics and Geography. This could be done by comparing how the countries represented by students in your classroom use renewable-energy sources. Specifically, you could investigate what percentage of each of the five sources of renewable energy contributes to the total production and use of energy in each country. With this goal in mind, you could ask the students to rank the countries according to the percentage of renewable energy they produce from each source and to investigate and form hypotheses as to why there are differences among countries. **Figure 5.7** shows the extension-phase section of the unit-planning tool.

FIGURE 5.7: Unit-planning template: *Extension* **phase**

Extension phase	
Sample teaching activities:	**Grouping arrangements:**
1. List the countries represented in the class. If all one country, pick countries on the basis of another relevant criterion. Mark countries on the map.	1. Whole class
2. Divide students into groups by country or by energy source.	2. Small groups
3. Students investigate via websites, texts, contacting embassies or consulates, universities.	3. Small groups
	4. Small groups and whole class
4. Groups return with findings and share.	
5. Likely for conflicting information to be found. Discuss.	5. Whole class
6. Discuss why sources of renewable energy are used differently in different regions or countries.	6. Groups and whole class
Assessment: *(To be described in Chapter 7)*	

Relating what has been learned in the classroom to students' lives outside school is also of utmost importance, and it is the next and last step of this unit. Making connections between what is learned in the classroom and in the community in which your students live is discussed in detail in **Chapter 6**.

Next we turn our attention to the materials that you need to complete the activities listed in the three phases of the unit plan.

MATERIALS

That the quality of instruction is of fundamental importance to successful bilingual education is indisputable (Mehisto, 2012). However, we cannot deny that good materials make the life of any teacher significantly easier and their work more successful. It is, therefore, critical that you start by choosing materials that support your objectives, topics, big ideas and classroom activities, rather than the other way around. We have seen schools where the choice of how to teach and what to teach are dictated by the materials that are available. CLIL teachers often mention that there is a lack of good materials for them to draw on (Infante, Benvenuto & Lastrucci, 2009). Indeed, lack of good materials in multiple languages is a challenge in new CLIL programmes and for new CLIL teachers. You may need to develop some of your own materials over time as you create and modify lesson plans over the years.

Depending on the type of CLIL programme, materials may be needed in both languages of instruction. Short texts about various aspects of renewable energy can be found on the web. We listed some websites that have texts on renewable energy in **Additional Resources 5.4**. Sometimes materials in one language may be difficult to obtain and it may take years before a solid collection is available at the school. Translated versions of books or shorter texts can be produced by the school; however, they must meet certain criteria to ensure that the translation really reflects the quality of the original in all respects. **Table 5.3** is a checklist that can be used to assess the quality of books in languages other than the mainstream language. In one school we worked in – Dhahran Ahliyah Schools in Saudi Arabia – there was a large enough population of students that they were able to establish their own publishing house and produce not only student texts but also professional reading material for teachers as well. This is a luxury that few schools enjoy. Student-produced materials that meet criteria for high-quality texts or books (see **Checklist 4.3** in **Chapter 4** for evaluating CLIL materials) can also be a useful resource for a school over time.

TABLE 5.3

Checking for quality of books in languages other than the mainstream (adapted from Cloud, Genesee & Hamayan, 2009)

In translated books:

☐ The translation represents the original justly.

☐ The language contains no errors of any sort.

☐ The language is not too formal.

☐ The language is not artificial sounding.

☐ The cultural context is authentic to the story.

☐ Words or phrases in the illustrations are in the appropriate language.

☐ Photographs or illustrations are embedded in a cultural context that is appropriate for the story so that there is a good fit of pictures to text.

In monolingual books:

☐ The quality of the type is adequate (especially with non-roman alphabet scripts).

☐ The print quality is adequate; the colours, images and words are sharp and well defined.

☐ The binding can withstand classroom use.

☐ The content is compatible with the school's curriculum.

In addition, in bilingual books:

☐ The status of the two languages is equally represented (one language does not take precedence).

    • The two languages are printed in the same size and quality font.

    • The writing in the illustrations is in both languages.

    • The names of the characters are appropriate to both languages.

    • The directionality of the book is appropriate to both languages, even if one language goes from left to right and the other goes from right to left.

☐ One culture does not take precedence over the other; the language other than mainstream is not nested in the dominant culture, as in, for example a story titled *Mr McGillicutty se va a McDonald's*, where the language is translated from English but there is no effort to ground the story in one of the appropriate cultural contexts of Spanish.

Clearly, the main texts that provide information about the concepts in a lesson or unit are important; but so too are support materials that help make the additional language visible and comprehensible. Visual aids have been shown to facilitate listening and reading comprehension significantly, especially for students with relatively low levels of proficiency in a language of instruction that they are still learning (Abraham, 2007; Lee, 2014) These are the visuals, realia and other materials that we depend on to convey the meaning of new language, both content obligatory and content compatible. These are the materials that help make the preview-phase activities successful in preparing students for learning new abstract concepts through a language that they are still learning.

In the section of the unit-planning template in **Figure 5.8** that shows the materials needed for a lesson, we chose simply to list the types of materials we would use rather than specific texts or books, since the actual materials will vary a great deal depending on grade level and students' ages.

FIGURE 5.8: Unit-planning template: *Materials*

Materials:

Preview:

- Pictures: sun, waterfall, river, geothermal, logs, biomass, wind, wind turbines, solar panels, solar water heaters, lightbulb, TV, radiator, plug, hot water, farm animals, food cooking, water boiling, shower

- 5- to 10-minute video

- Pictures: logs burning, wood-burning fireplace, nuclear plant, coal, running water, waterfall, plants, animals, sun

Focused learning:

- List of possible websites for students to consult

- Text

Extension:

- World map

- Possible sources of information for countries

SUMMARY

In this chapter, we have described a sample unit using our three-phase planning tool that 1) familiarises students with the language that they will need for the subject-area concepts they are about to learn, 2) engages students through activities and investigation to learn the new concepts, and 3) makes connections with other subject areas, across languages and cultures. Most of the instruction we have talked about in this chapter takes place inside the school. In the next chapter, we explore the importance of making connections with the students' families and the communities in which they live.

6   Coordination and integration: The way we work together

We hope that it has become clear from our discussions of key issues in CLIL and from our descriptions of a CLIL unit that it is practically impossible to integrate content and language instruction effectively without some coordination with fellow teachers. Efficient and smooth coordination with other teachers is also imperative when you use common themes across different content areas. This is true in the higher grades where teachers specialise in specific subject areas, but even in lower grade levels where one teacher is responsible for most of the content areas. Coordination with specialist teachers, such as Arts, Music and Physical Education, is also essential. In this chapter, we discuss how staff within the school can coordinate with each other most efficiently.

We also discuss a type of coordination that goes beyond the physical confines of the school – coordination with students' families and communities and with society in general. This is an important component in the unit because it makes concepts that students have just learned less abstract and more relevant to their daily lives. In addition, it allows students to become active participants in society and gives them the opportunity to be actively engaged in social issues. Involving students in some type of social or community project is the last step in our sample unit. We suggest extension activities in our sample unit-planning tool as we have done in the previous chapter for other parts of the unit.

Before we discuss coordination among adults in CLIL programmes, we want to reiterate and elaborate an important feature of CLIL that that we have alluded to in other chapters – students working with each other and with their teacher.

COORDINATION INVOLVING STUDENTS

Much CLIL instruction takes place in student- and activity-centred classrooms, which by definition means that students are working together either in small groups, in pairs or putting together parts of a task that they have completed separately. When groups are formed to complete an activity, cooperative learning strategies are often used in CLIL classrooms to ensure smooth completion of tasks at the same time that language use is promoted (Himmele & Himmele, 2011). All this requires that students work together collegially, in a way that shows mutual respect. Although things such as mutual respect and collaboration are not typically on the list of objectives, let alone part of the curriculum, they are part of teachers' unwritten responsibilities as educators of future generations of adults. Mehisto (2012) lists positive interdependence, interaction among students, individual and group accountability, interpersonal and small-group skills, and group-processing skills as key characteristics of effective CLIL instruction. It behoves teachers to keep these aspects of personal growth and development in mind as they monitor students when they are working together independently. The following checklist can be used to monitor these aspects of the CLIL classroom.

6.1	CHECKLIST: ASSESSING HOW WELL STUDENTS ARE WORKING WITH ONE ANOTHER		
You can focus on one student or a group of students working together *Students:*			
work with all members of the group not just their close friends		Y	N
share materials willingly		Y	N
listen to others and consider others' points of view		Y	N
respect the roles assigned to them		Y	N
follow the rules set out for them		Y	N
complete their responsibilities		Y	N
seem comfortable contributing ideas		Y	N
explain things with patience to group members who do not understand		Y	N
respond appropriately and respectfully to any language used by group members		Y	N
help each other with language difficulties		Y	N

Because promoting students' development of the additional language is a critical part of CLIL classrooms, teachers must be cognisant of the way they put working groups together. Groups consisting of different levels of language proficiency are effective for enabling students with lower levels to reach a step or two beyond their level when communicating with their more proficient peers. Remember that if students share a common mother tongue or a more proficient language than the language of instruction, they will likely be communicating with one another in that language while completing the task. As we have said many times, by no means should this be discouraged except in contexts where majority-language students are learning a minority or a foreign language. Nevertheless, students will be expected to present the final product, whether orally or in writing, in the language of instruction. If these working groups are managed well, with different students having different roles, lower-proficiency students will gain opportunities to practise and use the additional language. Students with higher levels of proficiency will also benefit from heterogeneous groupings by providing language models for classmates and supporting them as they raise the bar for language use (Kagan, 1994).

Another aspect of coordination that is worthy of attention is collaboration between teacher and students. In **Chapter 5**, we discussed the importance of teachers learning along with their students and becoming members of the learning community that is created within the classroom. We suggested that one way of accomplishing this is for teachers to join the students in posing real questions about the topic that is under study and investigating it alongside their students. This not only gives teachers insight into what it means to be a learner in that particular activity but it also makes it clear to students that everyone is a learner no matter what age they are or what role they play in the classroom. However, learning along with students does not diminish the teacher's very important role as guide throughout the unit. Nor should it take away her control of the lesson. It does bring the teacher closer to what students are experiencing during the lesson. In Anne Haas Dyson's words (1986), it frees you to *dance with the children*.

Staying free to *dance with the students* also allows you to assess them continuously from a closer vantage point. Learning alongside students makes it easier to observe the learning process more clearly and gather information about each student's achievements, progress and any challenges they may be facing. How to do this is discussed in detail in **Chapter 7**.

Next we look at coordination within the school, first among staff who are involved in the CLIL programme and then with staff in other parts of the school.

COORDINATION AMONG CLIL STAFF

For CLIL instruction to be most effective, all teachers must coordinate their teaching and bring it into alignment with one another. Since all teachers are working on language and content all the time, a CLIL approach requires that language and content teachers at the same grade level take into account how each is building on the other's lessons and how each can help the other expand learning.

Two primary goals are accomplished by teachers coordinating with one another. First, you ensure that the language and content objectives that are set for each unit make sense. Teachers who are more skilled in a subject area other than language can suggest content objectives that are appropriate for a given lesson or unit. Similarly, language teachers, whether they are Language Arts or second-/foreign-language teachers, can make sure that the language objectives are suitable for understanding concepts in a given lesson. Second, teachers can help each other by suggesting teaching strategies and activities that fit in a particular lesson. Teachers who specialise in teaching the additional language can support content-area teachers by giving them guidance regarding how to respond to students' use of the non-instructional language, how to address cross-cultural issues, and how to reinforce newly acquired language. Conversely, subject-area specialists can suggest activities and strategies that they know to be most effective for getting concepts across.

Of course, if a single teacher is teaching all subject areas, including additional-language development, this coordination can be accomplished easily and smoothly. However, in most schools, especially above 3rd or 4th grade, different teachers are responsible for different areas of the curriculum. Coordination is more challenging when different teachers are involved and, therefore, it is even more important to create the right environment and the most straightforward communication system within the school to make it happen.

6.1 PERSONAL PERSPECTIVE
The critical role of leadership in a one-way content-based immersion programme

Lyle French, Director of Teaching and Learning,
Avenues – The World School, São Paulo, Brazil

I've been working in immersion education for over 17 years and have attended my fair share of pedagogical meetings. Although we sit, talk about students, plan school strategies etc., we tend to work in language silos. We may be fortunate enough to have integrated curricula that are planning for success across languages, but in most cases teachers are planning and teaching in seclusion. Isolation seems to be a side effect of becoming a teacher. In an immersion school, we are aiming not only for fluency in each language but also academic abilities in each. In order for us to take more advantage of transfer, we need to plan and share more to make this happen.

When I was the pedagogical director at *Escola Beit Yaacov* in São Paulo, I began leading our collaborative, grade-level meetings differently. Rather than each teacher (first language and second language) sharing what they were doing and talking about students, we started to look at how we could tackle the same learning outcome and plan for transfer. This was mostly done through reading and writing in English and Portuguese in our school. During the process, I began to transfer leadership roles to the teachers to empower them to run the project and to develop a shared vision. As Lindholm-Leary (2005) observed, even a very successful program may collapse if it relies on a single person for leadership.

The results were astounding! Not only did we get better performance in both languages, most noticeably in L1 due to transfer, we also had much better, long-lasting collaboration between the two teachers. This turned into a school-wide initiative that changed the way all looked at language and indeed teaching in immersion!

If school leadership is multifaceted, school leadership needs to be much more sophisticated and provide more administrative support to foster a focus on real partnership that will improve student output.

Challenges

Coordination among teachers is challenging for many reasons. The most commonly cited hurdle for teachers working together is lack of time. Teachers usually do not have the time to sit down with colleagues on a regular basis to plan coordinated instruction. This requires knowledgeable and strong administrative support; administrators who understand CLIL and the importance of teacher collaboration will build time into the school schedule for teachers to meet and work together.

Another more subtle factor that can impede teacher collaboration occurs when teachers feel that they need to protect their areas of specialisation; this is especially common in the higher grades. When teachers identify themselves as specialists in a specific area of the curriculum, such as Science, they often feel compelled to protect their territory and might even resent having an 'outsider' enter their field of expertise to teach some of it. Or they may feel that someone who is not a specialist in their area cannot do justice to it as they can. These are all barriers to cooperation among all teachers in CLIL programmes that can stand in the way of smooth coordination among CLIL teachers.

6.1   RESEARCH NOTE

Professional boundaries and communication problems

Many studies have shown that subjective biases, narrow professional attitudes, and strict adherence to discipline-specific practices often result in a lack of perspective-taking and a breakdown in communication among educators (see, for example, Elias & Dilworth, 2003; Gutkin & Nemeth, 1997). Even the use of acronyms that are known in one specialised field and not others (TPR, for example in second-language circles) can lead to a collapse of collaboration among teachers (Hamayan, Marler, Sanchez-Lopez & Damico, 2007).

Effective interaction can occur when disciplinary boundaries defining teacher specialisations are loosened. Open collaboration among teachers calls for an understanding of the basic principles of CLIL, a shared language that is used to talk about issues relating to instruction, the freedom to ask questions, and effective communication skills. Conversations about these issues coupled with teachers' reflections on their own attitudes, beliefs and experiences can help open pathways to collaboration and make communication smoother. Checklist 6.2 can be useful in starting this conversation as well as for providing teachers with a tool that they can use to reflect on the efficiency of their own collaboration with other teachers.

6.2 CHECKLIST: ASSESSING THE EFFECTIVENESS OF COMMUNICATION DURING COLLABORATION AMONG TEACHERS
(adapted from Hamayan, Marler, Sanchez-Lopez & Damico, 2007)

This checklist can be used individually and/or together with your collaborating teacher(s)

Clear and congruent principles		
I have a clear understanding of CLIL principles that our teaching is based on.	Y	N
I agree with the principles that we adhere to.	Y	N

A shared language		
There are very few terms that we use repeatedly that are not clear to me.	Y	N
Whenever someone uses a vague or unknown word, I ask for clarification immediately.	Y	N
If needed, we have a glossary of terms and acronyms that I can refer to for clarification.	Y	N

Respectful questioning		
I feel comfortable asking for clarification from any of my partner teachers.	Y	N
I feel respected by all the teachers with whom I collaborate.	Y	N
I know whom to go to for questions about issues that I do not feel expert in.	Y	N
I feel comfortable answering questions that others ask of me.	Y	N

Effective interpersonal and communication skills		
I can communicate clearly about topics that other teachers are not familiar with.	Y	N
I rarely misunderstand something that a partner teacher has said.	Y	N
If a communication breakdown occurs, we are generally able to repair it quickly.	Y	N
When a miscommunication escalates into an emotional argument, we are generally able to step back and start over.	Y	N

Strategies for coordination

A good starting point for working together is for partner teachers to observe each other's classrooms once or twice a semester. The language teacher and the content teacher combine information from these observations that can serve as context for setting objectives and generally determining the activities that will make up a lesson or unit. Setting up these observations is no easy task, not only because of the time element but also because of the more awkward issue of how comfortable some teachers feel about being observed by a colleague. As we mentioned in the previous section, reflection and candid conversations can go a long way to easing the process for all teachers involved.

6.2   PERSONAL PERSPECTIVE
Building a collaborative model in Shanghai

Jon Nordmeyer, WIDA International Program Director,
University of Wisconsin-Madison, Madison, Wisconsin, USA

As coordinators of the EAL (English as an additional language) program at Shanghai American School, we recognized the need to transform our program in order to better serve English language learners. Increasing cultural and linguistic diversity required all classes to provide access to grade-level content while facilitating academic language development. Shifting away from a more traditional self-contained EAL classroom towards an integrated, collaborative model was both exciting and challenging.

While some teachers were anxious about a change in roles, or reluctant to shift away from working exclusively in pull-out EAL classes, most welcomed the opportunity to develop new ways of serving students and new strategies for working with colleagues. We took several deliberate steps to manage the change process to better serve students while honoring the complex shift in professional culture.

First, we redefined the new role of the EAL teacher as collaborator rather than isolated language specialist. As an EAL department, we honestly assessed concerns and hopes for this new role: both to surface possible roadblocks and build bridges with the department. With our K-12 administration, *(continued on page 172)*

COLLABORATION

A menu for supporting ELLs

FREE!

EAL DEPARTMENT

Starters: Co-Planning

- **Finding materials** - For history or science, the EAL teacher can locate a short story, non-fiction text or image related to a particular topic, then write up a guide sheet with vocabulary list and comprehension/inference questions
- **Creating materials-** For social studies or language arts, the EAL teacher can create graphic organizers and other scaffolding materials
- **Language objectives** - When doing long-term planning for a unit, the EAL teacher may be able to suggest a specific language focus area
- **Pre-reading** - The EAL teacher can preview a chapter or text to compile a vocabulary list, to highlight any potential language challenges, and plan teaser/sponge questions to access prior knowledge relevant to the text
- **Assessments-** plan for a variety of assessments or suggest alternative performance assessments accessible to ELLs
- **Task analysis-** Mainstream teacher gives a lesson plan (or the instructions for an assignment) to EAL teacher, who does a task analysis. It's one way to flag "hard to see" difficulties and determine which supports might need to be created.

Main dishes: Co-Teaching

- **Small group work** - While class is working on projects or research in pair or small groups, teachers divide the groups so each teacher consults with half the students (perfect for debate)
- **Consultant** - While groups are working on a project, they can visit a "mini writing center" in one area of your class to get feedback on their text. Or one teacher sits in the hall, and students come out one by one to re-tell a plot or historical event, or to practice a speech.
- **Vocabulary expert-** while students are working/reading, both teachers circulate and respond to raised hands by giving "instant / impromptu" vocabulary lessons

Just Desserts: Co-Assessing

- **Co-assessing presentations** - Two teachers use the same rubric to evaluate oral presentations. Can focus on separate criteria or double up and moderate scores
- **Co-assessing writing-** Two teachers use the same rubric to evaluate a writing sample OR EAL teacher can assess language (spelling, grammar, mechanics) and the other can evaluate content (organization, ideas, evidence).
- **Writing Process Check-in** - require students to come to the Writing Center to have their thesis statement checked before they can continue with their essay or research project
- **Co-creating assessments-** creating a mix of assessments over the course of a unit/semester that are beyond paper & pencil (ie- one oral presentation, a written work, in-class writing, at-home writing, speeches, etc.)
- **Co-writing rubrics-** make a rubric, create "models" that meet different levels of the rubric

What's cooking?

Side Dishes: On the spot collaboration

While one teacher is lecturing/explaining...
...the other teacher can be taking notes on the board/LCD

While one teacher is giving instructions orally...
...the other teacher can be modeling instructions or writing them on the board

While one teacher is handing out papers...
...the other teacher can be clarifying feedback or giving a new task

While one teacher is facilitating a silent activity...
...the other teacher can be reading aloud with a small group in another space

Adapted from Murawski & Dieker (2004)

Source: Mulazzi F. and Nordmeyer, J. (2012). www.infoagepub.com

we integrated this new job description into our school's portfolio-based evaluation system for EAL teachers. We also identified existing expectations for mainstream teachers, which supported the new collaborative approach. For example, all teachers were expected to differentiate instruction; an EAL teacher could help identify English proficiency levels and co-plan differentiated lessons.

Next, we created a menu (see page 172) to define possible co-teaching, co-planning and co-assessing activities. Since initiating a new collaborative approach relied on a coalition of willing volunteers, this tool allowed colleagues to literally order off the menu. It also provided skeptical or reluctant EAL teachers with concrete examples of how they could engage with mainstream colleagues.

Finally, we communicated the shift in program to students, parents and colleagues. Throughout the year, we shared new collaborative strategies, gathered feedback on the transition, and co-ordinated with our leadership team to support the change process.

Working together has become significantly easier with the use of technology that is readily available, and this has certainly made coordination among teachers more realistic. You can set up communication groups using email and mobile-phone texting or chat. However, even the best-functioning distribution lists and virtual groups cannot replace face-to-face communication. Time needs to be set aside when the two or three teachers who need to coordinate their lessons can meet together during school time, with no interruptions. Getting together during recess in the teachers' lounge would not qualify as an appropriate venue for coordination.

Regardless of whether coordination is taking place online or face-to-face, a schedule for communication has to be set up and adhered to strictly. If Friday afternoon is a good time for teachers to send messages to one another regarding their lessons, activities or questions, then that particular time must be respected. Taking Adela to the nurse's office or dealing with the fight that Françoise and Jeanine had in the hallway that Friday afternoon cannot replace that time. Also, regardless of the form of communication, whether it is online or in person, having a common structure helps focus conversation about key issues. The conversation can be organised around the unit- or lesson-planning tool that you use and around a set of questions such as:

- What has been covered so far?
- What content-related language (compatible and obligatory) was taught?
- Any special difficulties that students seemed to encounter?
- Where does the unit or lesson go from here?
- What suggestions does each teacher have for the other(s)?

Coordination across grade levels

Coordination among teachers in an effective CLIL programme is not limited to only language and content teachers at the same grade level; it includes coordination across grade levels. Coordinating across grade levels ensures that students' language development is continuous and that the receiving teacher at the next grade level builds on the language that was acquired the previous year. Whereas grade-specific coordination needs to happen on a weekly basis, cross-grade coordination is typically done once a year, either at the end of the school year or before the school year starts. However, it is helpful to have cross-grade discussions between trimesters or semesters so that teachers can gauge the appropriateness of the sequencing of language objectives from grade to grade. This is critical at the lower grade levels where language is developing at a fast rate. Receiving teachers need to know what to expect from children who will be entering their classroom the following year. Similarly, teachers at the lower grades need to know of any gaps in children's language the following year so that they can pay more attention to those particular aspects of academic language. In **Chapter 7**, you will find reporting strategies that are helpful in conveying information about students to next-year teachers.

Another type of coordination is also needed in schools where the CLIL programme is offered to only one part of the student population: coordination between the CLIL programme and the rest of the school. We discuss this in the next section.

COORDINATION BETWEEN THE CLIL PROGRAMME AND THE REST OF THE SCHOOL

In some schools, the CLIL programme is offered to only some students. Regardless of the educational context, ensuring that the CLIL programme is an integral part of the everyday work of the entire school is essential. When the CLIL programme is offered to only one section of the student population, it is important for it to be well integrated into the rest of the school rather than being seen as a separate programme that functions independently. Even when the CLIL programme and CLIL teachers are physically part of the rest of the school, the absence of collaboration and the lack of interest from teachers at the same school are challenges that CLIL teachers mention (Infante, Benvenuto & Lastrucci, 2009).

For some educational contexts, specifically where the CLIL programme is offered to students who are seen as coming from a minority group or with a minority language that is not highly regarded by the mainstream, integration is critical. Here are some examples of situations from each of the educational contexts where the CLIL programme is only one part of the rest of the school:

IMM: In a few schools, one or two classrooms out of the total at each grade level offer immersion in an additional language; the rest of the students follow a monolingual programme of instruction.

ILS: Only students who come with a language other than the mainstream language are given instruction through CLIL. In some schools the CLIL programme aims for high levels of proficiency in the students' home language as well as the main language of instruction (DL-CLIL) whereas other schools simply aim for developing proficiency in the main language of instruction without paying much heed to the students' home language (ML-CLIL). If the school has non-ILS students, these students would not be taught using CLIL strategies. In the recent past, and perhaps still, it was common to see programmes for ILS physically separated from the rest of the school – in classes that were held in one wing of the school building or relegated to mobile units on the playground. Not only is this arrangement unproductive for students; it is also insensitive to their basic educational needs to be integrated with their peers. Any kind of segregation, whether physical or intangible, hampers collegiality among staff. The distance between staff is often more pronounced when the students who are receiving CLIL instruction are seen as a low-status minority and when their home language is not valued.

FL: CLIL strategies may be used with only one content area; for example, the Italian teacher coordinates her lessons with the Music or Arts teacher. Or only one of the FL teachers integrates additional-language instruction with a content area using CLIL strategies. The rest of the curriculum is taught monolingually, and the other FL classes do not use CLIL strategies. Teachers who are not collaborating with the FL teacher do not have an immediate need to coordinate with the teachers who are currently involved in integrated instruction. However, it may be beneficial for future collaborations to at least feature the successes of the integrated model so as to attract other teachers to this type of instruction and to stimulate interest and support in a CLIL approach to FL instruction.

INT: In INT schools with partial CLIL programmes, only students who come with a language other than the main language of instruction are taught using CLIL strategies, which is typically ML-CLIL. Or only students who opt for it are given instruction in an additional language through CLIL, typically in the host-country language. As with ILS programmes, integration is critical if the students and the language(s) they come with are seen as low status in order to enhance the value attached to those students, their languages and their cultures.

Regardless of the educational context, CLIL staff and students must have equal access to any and all resources the school has to offer. This includes materials, copying privileges, free-time opportunities, technology, extracurricular programmes, time and space at school-wide events, and so on. It is important that non-CLIL staff, in any educational context, understand the basic premises on which CLIL instruction is based. In fact, many CLIL strategies and almost every CLIL principle can benefit mainstream students who are learning in a monolingual environment through their home language. Moreover, it is important for all staff in a school where CLIL is offered only to some students to see the positive results of CLIL. Informational meetings and events showcasing students' accomplishments can be held on a regular basis once or twice a year. DL-CLIL programmes have the added value of showing students' skills in two languages, an advantage that few people would discount. Understanding the structure of the CLIL programme and creating a positive attitude toward it can have significant benefits for CLIL teachers. Non-CLIL staff are more likely to respect the time that CLIL teachers spend coordinating with one another when they know that it is essential for the success of the programme.

COORDINATION OUTSIDE OF SCHOOL

Linking lessons and big ideas that students are learning in the classroom with what goes on in their homes and communities is an essential part of CLIL. Linkages with home and community enhance students' experiences in school and in the classroom. These linkages are bi-directional: families and community members contribute to the learning process, and, in turn, students can make a contribution to the well-being of the community. Let us first look at what students' families and communities can contribute to the programme.

How can students' families and their communities contribute to the learning process?

At a very concrete level, students' families and the community that the school serves can provide strong support to the school. This support can take the form of financial assistance to help the school attain various resources they need – from material help such as opening a new building for the school (see **Personal Perspective 6.3** by Alain Weber in this chapter) to professional help such as making the curriculum culturally appropriate for a particular student population (see Personal Perspective by Nicole Bruskewitz in **Chapter 1**). Community members can also lobby on behalf of the programme with local legislators or board members to pass laws and establish policies that improve the quality of education. This aspect of community support is vital in schools that serve minorities such as immigrants, refugees or disadvantaged families.

6.3 **PERSONAL PERSPECTIVE**

Building links with the business community to support CLIL

Alain Weber, Former Head, Lycée Français de Chicago, Chicago, IL, USA

After more than 50 years teaching and heading bilingual schools, some conclusions emerge. In regard to graduates finding a job nowadays, and given that there is now global competition for jobs, elementary and secondary schools must now not only prepare their students for university entrance but also give each graduate an edge, a unique feature to facilitate employment. For any employer or entrepreneur, finding talent has always been a priority, but now talent must be linked to global effectiveness.

Given these observations, the edge a school can provide is the ability to speak several languages, with the background to enable each graduate to work, function and enjoy life in different cultures and countries. In the three schools I have headed in San Francisco (French American), Indianapolis (International School) and Chicago (Lycée Français), the parents and the community at large wanted that advantage for their students and they saw dual language education as the way to achieve it.

In Indianapolis, for example, the civic and business leaders understood the importance of bilingual competence in the global market place and got together to support the creation of the International School of Indiana. In 1994, the school started with a two-track immersion Pre-K to grade 12 school (Spanish American and French American) with the goal of graduating bilingual if not trilingual students. The business community helped by advocating, putting company and personal resources behind the project, and leading an incredibly successful capital campaign. They helped build the school. After 22 years, ISI is doing well and its graduates work and live in the US and abroad.

In Chicago, more recently, the parent community helped grow and affirm the Lycée. Through their personal contacts and by lobbying corporations and businesses, they raised funds to move the Lycée from a rental facility to its own state-of-the-art campus. This fall, the new school opened and welcomed close to 730 students.

Beyond raising funds, these parents and community leaders became extraordinary advocates for dual language education … Many enrolled their children as they believed in the bilingual, bi-literate edge. As CEOs, they also looked to the future – at employing our graduates who had the background and ability to work in diverse international work environments.

Communities where the additional language is spoken can also fill an important need – they can provide authentic contexts for additional-language use. In programmes where the additional language is a second language, that is, it is used by the mainstream community, there are typically many opportunities for authentic language use. This would be the case for IMM programmes such as in Quebec where both English and French are commonly used languages in many communities. In ILS and INT programmes where the additional language is the language of the mainstream, or host country, opportunities for authentic language use are also abundant. However, in many ILS contexts, and even in some IMM programmes where the additional language is a minority language, we find that the mainstream community is reluctant to take advantage of the rich language that is used locally. For example, in some English–Spanish IMM schools in the US, students are given the option to travel to Spain for exposure to Spanish rather than setting up exchange programmes in their own towns and cities where there are vibrant Spanish-speaking neighbourhoods. In FL programmes with no easily identifiable community of native speakers of the additional language, schools often arrange for exchanges or study programmes with countries where that language is spoken (see Luz Helena Aljure and Edith Ceferino's Personal Perspective).

6.4 PERSONAL PERSPECTIVE
Enriching students' language and cultural knowledge through home-stay abroad

Luz Helena Aljure and Edith Ceferino, Research Centers Coordinator and Elementary School Head, Gimnasio Campestre, Colombia

As a Colombian bilingual school, Gimnasio Campestre conceives language learning from an enrichment perspective, a form of bilingual education that seeks to develop additive bilingualism, thus enriching the students' cultural, social and personal growth. A competence-based curriculum approach to English and Spanish, the students' home language, that accents language development across all subjects has been established since 2007 under the Common Underlying Proficiency Model precepts of Cummins (1984 and 2000), involving more cognitively demanding tasks such as literacy, content learning, critical thinking, creativity, metacognition and problem-solving in both languages. Still, we found that the students' cultural knowledge was not increasing at the same pace as the cognitive side. In 2008, the school started a cultural immersion program in Canada. Since then, our 11–13-year-old students do a 3-month home-stay in a community in eastern Canada so that they gain a different cultural perspective while developing an understanding and appreciation of different idiomatic expressions, accents and behaviors in English. During the 3 months in Canada, our fifth 5th graders attend classes in regular public schools and participate in excursions, sports and other cultural activities that have helped them successfully achieve a genuine cultural immersion as well as the use of English in real settings.

The home-stay program has been very successful and has helped round out our program because it is embedded in a bilingual policy that provides a comprehensive and complete understanding of second language acquisition. In other words, it works as a powerful and effective strategy when attached to a vision; otherwise it turns into a nice tour abroad with totally different results.

For almost 70 years, internationalism and interculturalism have been part of the framework in which Gimnasio Campestre's community participates in globalization, assumes cultural diversity and promotes democratic and civic ideals. The language and cultural immersion program in Canada, a strong bilingual curriculum design, inspired teachers to work together to support a vision that encourages the pursuit of autonomy, open-mindedness, adaptability and, of course, English fluency.

At a more academic level, each student's family is a source of cultural, linguistic and experiential wealth. Regardless of whether students are all members of the mainstream culture, or come from different countries and have different religions or language backgrounds, each one of them comes to school with what Luis Moll calls funds of knowledge (Gonzalez, Moll & Amanti, 2005). When these funds of knowledge become part of the everyday functioning of the classroom and school, an important link is created between students' home lives and their life in the school. Students become aware that they are not entering a different world when they set foot in the school building. They become aware that their two worlds – home and school – are part of one broad experience. What is learned at home becomes the building block for what is learned at school, and what is learned at school can be used at home and in the community. In this manner, what students learn at home enriches and forms the basis for what they learn at school, and vice versa.

Family and community can be brought into the everyday working of the school and classroom in many ways. James Banks' approach (Banks, 2013) to multicultural education is helpful in thinking about ways of bringing community and home issues into the classroom as well as taking issues that have been raised in the classroom to improve the community. While Banks' model focuses primarily on issues of prejudice and discrimination, we use it for organising ways of integrating what is learned at school, and at home and in the community, more broadly. Banks suggests a four-stage framework for integration: the contributions approach, the additive approach, the transformation approach and the social action approach. We discuss the first three in this section and leave the fourth to a later section about how students can contribute to the community.

The contributions approach

In this, the simplest, most superficial and most frequently used way of including home cultures, students are introduced to heroes/heroines, important people, folktales from their heritage as discrete lessons. In its least effective format, these aspects of a group or culture are 'celebrated' on a specific day, typically by the whole school. You might call it *the taco-day* approach to Mexican culture, or *tango-day* for Argentina. Sometimes these discrete lessons about a specific famous person or a holiday are inserted into a lesson in a timely fashion. This is the easiest way to include a small aspect of some students' community in the curriculum. The goal is to expand all students' knowledge about a specific group in the school at the same time as affirming that group's contribution to the world. However, it is a relatively superficial way of conveying knowledge rather than developing a deep understanding of a complex aspect of a group of people or of a country.

Since these kinds of discrete aspects of students' home cultures are typically dealt with as separate lessons or events throughout the school, this approach may lead to students seeing them primarily as appendages to the 'real' curriculum. This approach tends to gloss over important information about the context in which these individuals achieved their fame or the multi-layered meaning of a ritual or celebration. In fact, this approach may have the negative effect of encouraging stereotypes that shrink a complex issue down to an insubstantial detail or two. However, this approach has its value; if you are hesitant to begin with a more meaningful way of bringing students' cultures into the classroom, the contributions approach would be a good place to start, with a plan to go to the next step, the additive approach.

The additive approach

In this approach, content, topics or themes that are part of students' cultures and backgrounds are inserted into a lesson or unit, without changing the basic structure of the mainstream curriculum. For example, the writings of Ibn Sina (Avicenna) on geological formations can be brought in while studying Earth Sciences in a classroom with Arabic-speaking students. In a school with many Mexican students, the works of Diego Rivera can be studied during Arts, or his influence on the labour movement can be the focus in a History class. This allows individual teachers to put content relevant to a particular community into the curriculum without restructuring it. As with the contributions approach, the additive approach is a sporadic treatment of an ongoing aspect of students' lives and remains at a superficial level. However, the additive approach could be useful as a preliminary step toward a more in-depth integration of a minority community's culture and contributions into the classroom and into the everyday functioning of the school.

Since both the contributions and the additive approaches result in a rather shallow treatment of complex issues, usually in too short a time, you must ensure that students at least get a perspective from an authentic source. In addition to reading material written by someone who can present the depth and breadth of the cultural context of the particular concept or event you wish to integrate, it is essential that multiple perspectives are discussed in class. This is particularly critical for History texts, which, as many people have pointed out, are usually written by those who won the battle. As James Banks points out, a unit on 'The Westward Movement' –about the movement of European Americans from the eastern to the western part of the United States – can just as well be called 'The Invasion from the East' when described from the perspective of the Oglala Sioux. Thus, it is important when incorporating features of other cultures into the curriculum to ensure that cross-cultural perspectives are also presented.

Participation of family and community in the school or classroom:

To ensure that students hear a first-person perspective about topics and issues in the curriculum, family and community members can be invited to come to school or participate in the class to talk about their experiences or to showcase their skills. Do not feel compelled to restrict your guest list to only highly educated or high-status professions. A parent who owns a grocery store in the neighbourhood can explain, in real-life ways, how profit is calculated (Mathematics), how shipping distance of produce affects business (Environmental Studies, Biology, Economics), how customers' purchasing habits have changed over the years (History, Sociology), how displaying fruits and vegetables can affect sales (Psychology, Marketing, Art, Music), what nutritional value different vegetables and fruit have (Health, Biology), and so on.

Another benefit of bringing families and community members into the classroom or school is that students see that their parents' values, customs, skills and ways of doing things are valued. This is particularly important for students who have a minority status within the school or the community in which they live; for example, Arabic-speaking students in mainstream schools in England (ILS), Navaho students in dual-language schools in New Mexico, USA (ILS), or Serbian students in an international school in Vienna (INT). Many of these students do not enjoy prestige status among their peers and, as a result, many feel embarrassed by their home culture. It is critical for administrators and teachers to show explicitly that these minority families' ways are enriching and just as valuable as those of the mainstream. Many of these minority students have had rich, albeit sometimes difficult, experiences as a result of their travels and having left their home country to settle in an unfamiliar environment.

Family members whose home language differs from the languages of instruction can be invited to teach simple greetings in their language. In multilingual classrooms, greetings in all the languages represented can be written down on a poster. Any of these activities can be extended to reinforce concepts that the students have been learning. Comparisons of the linguistic and cultural significance of different greetings can be made in Language Arts or Social Studies. In classrooms for younger children, a parent can teach a song in his or her language as part of a Music class. A family member can tell a children's story or folktale from their home country when students study different types of narratives; if the parent does not speak the language of the majority group, the story could be translated by their children or other students who are proficient in the language of instruction.

To go beyond the superficial, however, it is necessary to change the way that school functions, the way that classrooms are run and the way that the curriculum is set up. This can be achieved by what Banks calls the transformation approach.

The transformation approach

In the third level of Banks' integration model, the fundamental goals, structure and perspectives of the curriculum begin to change. Many aspects of the curriculum are examined from different perspectives, beginning with the various cultures represented in the CLIL programme and moving to additional cultural groups with different sets of norms, values and perspectives. Students are encouraged to develop divergent views and to look critically at single-perspective representations of the world around them. In a lesson on the water cycle, for example, you can examine how the cycle affects urban vs rural communities and relate that to school location, how farmers are affected as opposed to city-dwellers. Students can explore extreme events during the water cycle, such as hurricanes or volcanic eruptions, which they or their parents experienced in their home country, and so on.

When this approach to multiculturalism becomes part of the curriculum, students, teachers and administrators will begin to pose questions rather than give quick answers during discussions of different norms and values. If parents of a certain cultural group consistently arrive late to events and meetings, try to figure out why rather than jump to the conclusion that they do not care about their child's education or that they lack respect for other people's schedules. If students say they understand something and you discover that they really do not, figure out what value they hold that is making them say yes rather than no; is it possible that they would be showing disrespect to you, the authority figure, by admitting they did not understand? Are they embarrassed to show what they perceive as failure in front of you and their peers?

CLIL programmes lend themselves well to this level of multicultural education due to the fact that other languages and cultures are an inherent aspect of CLIL. This approach to including cross/multicultural education in the curriculum can be beneficial for all students in any kind of school, even homogeneous monolingual non-CLIL contexts.

Adopting this approach to exploring and reflecting on norms and values can help reveal aspects of one's own culture and give everyone a better sense of who they are and why they do the things the way they do. These are all outcomes that are invaluable in an increasingly interconnected global world. For schools where only one part of the student population is in a CLIL programme, the CLIL programme can be a model for the rest of the school.

How can students contribute to their community?

So far, our discussion of learning and teaching has been restricted to the classroom or the school. In **Chapter 4**, we talked about making connections among different academic subject areas, and in **Chapter 5** we showed ways of doing that in our unit on renewable energy. We also mentioned making connections between the students' two languages. In this chapter, we have looked at bringing the community and family into the classroom to make cross-cultural connections and bring the outside world into the classroom. Now it is time to take the classroom into the world, keeping in mind that one of our responsibilities as educators is to guide students to become ethical participants in their community. Pauline Gibbons reminds us that children learn language so that they can learn about the world around them (Gibbons, 1993). We broaden that thought by saying that children learn language and content so that they can begin not only to understand but also, eventually, to act upon the world around them in responsible and ethical ways.

Extending school learning into the community in these ways also serves to reinforce newly learned concepts and to place these concepts in the context of students' daily lives. We often hear students, especially adolescents, complaining: 'Why do we have to study *logarithms*? When am I ever going to use *logarithms* (replace *logarithm* with a word from almost any part of the curriculum)?' When you extend your teaching one step further, students can apply what they learn to their community or family life.

Extending lessons into the community and the home not only reinforces what the students have learned in school, but actually contributes something to the community as well. To accomplish this, we turn to Banks' fourth approach to integration, the social action approach. Our premise is that students' families and communities can help strengthen the school by providing it with resources, funds of knowledge and experience, and advocacy. At the same time, students can help strengthen the community through what they are learning.

The social action approach

This final stage in Banks' integration model includes all the elements of the transformation approach but, in addition, has students making decisions and taking actions related to the topic or issue studied in the unit. Students investigate how a topic they are studying impacts their community or how it is practised or applied in their home, neighbourhood or community. They then find out what the community needs in order to improve what they already have or what they are doing. The outcome of the project is for students to take some action, come up with a product or procedure that would fill a need in the community. The product could be as simple as a brochure that gives information on recycling or it could be establishing a children's story hour at the public library where students take turns reading books to children in their home languages.

In this approach, students learn how to participate in social change by looking critically at individual and communal customs, everyday events and socially established procedures or ways of doing things at home or in the community. In addition to critical analysis, students learn how to make decisions and, because most of the activities in this phase of the unit are completed in small groups, they learn to work in groups, to consider different views and to reach consensus.

Extending activities into the community

Extension into the home or the community typically entails a concrete project, parts of which are implemented in small groups. The culmination of these activities is often an outcome or a product that benefits the community. **Table 6.1** lists examples of projects that can be done in tandem with a unit on renewable energy. Some projects may take all year to complete or, at least, they last beyond the end of the unit with which the project started. For example, using our unit on renewable energy and gearing it toward upper-secondary grade levels, we could have a project that would take several months if not the whole year. It could be the only extension into the community that students will have that year as it is broad and could be completed in depth. Choosing a community-focused project of this scope of ours would require a coordinated decision among many teachers. As the project moves forward, students will need the support of various content-area teachers. It is better that projects for younger students are of shorter duration and, of course, simpler to complete.

TABLE 6.1

Examples of extension projects

Examples of projects for extension into the home/community	Content area(s) involved
Measure electricity consumption at home and assess how consumption can be reduced (turn off used lights, use fireplace instead of electrical heater, and so on).	Maths, Science
Develop a brochure that can be placed in the public library, municipal and community centres; it would list ways that homes and businesses can reduce their consumption of non-renewable energy sources.	Language Arts
Put on a play about renewable energy, waste, recycling, and present it to the community (enter 'play scripts renewable energy school children' into a browser and you will find several sources of play scripts).	Theatre, Language Arts
Identify children and adult books on renewable energy in the public library and set up a display. If there are not enough books, see how funding can be obtained to purchase books.	Language Arts, Arts, Librarian
Arrange with public officials in charge of the local park, the municipality esplanade or the town square to set up a bicycle that generates electricity to make lights or music go on. Have a brief brochure available.	Science

Activities for extending the unit on renewable energy into the community:

In **Chapter 5**, we ended the last part of the lesson with students investigating the use of different sources of renewable energy in students' home countries. To extend this unit into the community, students will build a solar oven and donate it to a local community-based organisation that offers food as one of its services to needy community members. We begin this last step in the extension phase by reviewing whether any of the student groups acquired information about the use of solar ovens. We then expand our knowledge of solar ovens. First, in small groups, students are asked to find information about solar ovens and, in particular, if they are used anywhere nearby – locally or further afield, such as in other regions of the country. The information that the various working groups gather is then displayed using a graphic organiser; see **Figure 6.1** for an example.

FIGURE 6.1: Information gathered on solar ovens

Pictures	Kinds	How it works	Where it's used	Materials & tools for building	Missing information
	Fixed Can rotate by hand Rotates with the sun	Pot sits on adjustable concave reflector disc Disc concentrates heat from sun on the pot. Pot heats up and cooks food!	Neighbour Dept. Envrnt Protect. has model Formosa province	15x15 mm square steel pipe 15 mm round pipe Polished aluminium/ stainless steel sheet metal Rivets, nuts & bolts Electric grinder Electric welder Electric drill Rivet tool	How does it compare to regular oven? How much does it cost? How are we going to get the money?!

Next, invite a local expert on solar ovens to give a talk and show what is involved in building such an oven. Make sure to show your expert the graphic organiser so that he or she sees what information has already been gathered and discussed, and, just as importantly, the additional information that students feel they need to build one. If no such person can be found, a video can be shown instead. At the end of the presentation – either in person or via the video –students fill in more information in the graphic organiser and cross out questions that have been answered. Then you assign each group to one of the next tasks to be completed:

a) Make a list of the various local organisations that provide some kind of service to the community and that also offer food services; for example, the state school, a senior citizens home, a community centre, a public childcare centre, and so on. Students enlist the help of the Social Studies, Civics or Sociology teacher. This is a good step for bringing in families who are familiar with their neighbourhood and community centres.

b) Calculate how much it costs to bake a cake in the solar oven as compared with a gas or wood oven. If possible, find out the chemical footprint of each type of oven. The Science, Mathematics and Economics teachers can assist with this step.

c) Find where to get the materials necessary to build an oven and an estimate of the cost. The Arts teacher can help this group as well as the next one.

d) Develop a plan for making the oven.

When these tasks are completed, students report back to the class, and Groups B, C, and D begin to write descriptions or results of their investigations for a brochure that they will use for informational and fund-raising purposes. Group A will put together the whole brochure. The Language Arts teacher can monitor and assist during this phase of the project.

Next, students examine the list of community organisations that were identified earlier and consider the pros and cons of donating a solar oven to each of them. Parents can be invited to participate in these discussions and share their knowledge of the various organisations. An organisation is chosen, and the next step is to inform its administrators of the project. The teacher and a few representative members of the class can visit the centre, explain the project to them and develop a plan for building the oven. Funding needs to be discussed with both the receiving organisation and parents as well as with other community members, and so on. The oven is built and is first shown at a school-wide event, perhaps with representatives of the receiving organisation, after which it is taken to its new home and presented by the whole class to its new owners.

Figure 6.2 shows the community extension activity on the unit-planning template we have been using.

FIGURE 6.2: Unit-planning template: community extension

Extension into family/community	
Sample teaching activities:	**Grouping arrangements:**
1. Find out if any information on solar ovens showed up in the previous investigation.	1. Small groups
2. Start collecting more information on solar ovens.	2. Small groups
3. Display information collected by everyone on a graphic organiser.	3. Whole class
4. Invite an expert to give a presentation on solar ovens.	4. Whole class
5. a) Make a list of local organisations and service centres in the community that offer food. b) Calculate how much is saved by using solar oven. c) Find where to get materials to build oven. d) Make plan for building oven.	5. Small group for each task, with help from Social Studies or Civics teacher (A), Science, Maths or Economics teacher (B), Arts teacher (C and D)
6. Groups B, C and D each write a section for the brochure. Group A puts it together.	6. Groups and whole class with help from the Language Arts teacher
7. Discuss pros and cons of offering a solar oven to each of the organisations identified.	7. Whole class
8. Choose an organisation to donate an oven to.	8. Whole class with input from parents
9. Approach the organisation and offer project, develop timeline, and so on.	9. Teacher with select students
10. Raise funds to cover costs.	10. Whole class with the help of a parent committee
11. Build oven.	11. Groups under supervision of adult who knows solar ovens
12. Show oven to school, then present to organisation.	12. Whole class

Assessment: *(To be described in Chapter 7)*

This completes the part of the unit that is primarily instructional. In **Chapter 7**, we discuss different types of assessment that can be useful in CLIL classrooms.

7   Assessment in CLIL classrooms

In this chapter, we discuss the much-dreaded topic of assessment. Many teachers hate assessment because they see it as an imposition on their time and teaching. This is probably because, when assessment is discussed, it is usually about tests and testing and about deciding who passes and who fails. We need not fear assessment. After all, our daily lives outside work are based on hundreds of little assessments. We constantly assess the situation around us to make the myriad day-to-day decisions we need to make – from the minute we wake up in the morning and have to decide what to wear and what materials to take to work, to when we are leaving work and have to decide whether to eat at home and, if we decide to eat at home, whether there is enough food to make supper, and so on. Assessment is about collecting information and making informed decisions using that information.

Assessment is a very broad topic; we cannot discuss everything there is to know about it. Our focus is on classroom teachers and practical ways in which they can design assessment to guide instruction and improve learning. We do not consider assessment that is the primary responsibility of people outside the classroom – for example, testing conducted by district officials to place students in particular programmes or by educational specialists who assess students with special needs. We focus on assessment of language skills but also talk about how to assess acquisition of academic knowledge when students' proficiency in the additional language is limited.

We start by talking about the goals of assessment, then the qualities of effective assessment and the unique features of assessment in CLIL contexts. We then go on to discuss alternative assessment tools – why and how each is useful, how each can be particularly useful in CLIL classrooms – and we give tips on how to use each effectively in CLIL classrooms.

GETTING STARTED: IDENTIFYING YOUR GOALS FOR ASSESSMENT

Assessment in a CLIL programme can serve a variety of goals. Therefore, the first step when planning assessment is to carefully identify your goals – the reasons for doing assessment. Once you have made those decisions, you can then decide what, when and how you will assess. We discuss the assessment goals listed in **Table 7.1** one at a time and then describe a number of alternative forms of assessment – how they can be useful for different goals of assessment.

TABLE 7.1

Goals of assessment

☐   To demonstrate to others that students are learning as expected.

☐   To monitor student progress in order to plan appropriate and effective instruction.

☐   To understand students' learning styles, learning strategies, interests, attitudes, motivations, and relevant background factors that might affect their learning so that you can individualise instruction and meet individual student's needs.

☐   To engage students in self-assessment so that they take active responsibility for their own learning.

A common and important goal of assessment is **to demonstrate to others that students are learning as expected**. This is more generally referred to as **accountability**. Teachers are accountable to parents for the progress their children are making in school and to administrators and other educators about students' achievement with respect to school or district standards or objectives. While accountability is important in all educational programmes, it is especially important in CLIL programmes. There may be people in the community at large or even in the school who are sceptical about this approach to education. CLIL teachers need to demonstrate that their students attain the same high levels of achievement that are expected of all students, despite the fact that they are learning at least some subject areas in an additional language. You, along with school administrators, must collect the assessment results you need to demonstrate that your students are achieving as expected so that everyone supports the programme (Principle 8).

Another very important goal of assessment is **to monitor student progress in order to plan appropriate instruction and modify curriculum, if necessary** (Principle 6). You can assess what incoming students know, and can do, at the beginning of the school year so that you can take account of their starting-level skills and knowledge when planning instruction for the coming year. This is particularly important in CLIL programmes where students may already have some competence in the additional language but are not fully competent or, conversely, they may not have any competence in the language. If possible, it is also important to assess students' home language skills, especially in domains related to reading and writing. Students who have some competence in reading and writing in the home language have already acquired important foundational skills that they can use to learn to read and write in the additional language. The teacher who teaches in the additional language does not need to start from the beginning with these students.

7.1 SPECIAL NOTE

Identifying students who are likely to have reading or language-learning difficulties

Identifying students who might be at risk for reading or language-learning difficulties is important. Because it can be difficult to know how to interpret the performance of students who are learning an additional language during the early stages of development, assessing them in their home language can provide a more valid measure of their abilities. If you wait to assess students when they have advanced in their acquisition of the additional language, their difficulties may have become entrenched and difficult to remedy. Assessing them in their stronger first language allows you to estimate their chances of risk earlier and, therefore, to provide additional support earlier. Students who have an underlying reading or language impairment will demonstrate difficulty in both languages. More details about identifying students, in dual-language programmes, with language and/ or reading difficulties can be found in Chapter 3 in Hamayan, Genesee & Cloud, 2013; Erdos, Genesee, Savage & Haigh, 2014; and Genesee, Savage, Erdos & Haigh, 2013.

Assessing students' competence in the home language is also critical in order to identify and support students with language-learning needs so that they can be as competent as possible (Principle 7).

You will also want **to monitor your students' performance continuously while you are teaching** so that you can tailor your instruction as you proceed in order to improve students' learning. Of course, you also usually have to conduct assessments at the end of major instructional units in order to plan follow-up instruction that will extend learning further (Principle 6). Assessments at the end of the school year are useful if they are shared with teachers who will teach the same students in the next grade so that they can plan appropriate and individualised instruction that better reflects students' existing competencies. Including a note to share assessment results in your annual plan reminds you to collect, record and share student information with next year's teachers or students themselves. Without such a plan, these important activities may not take place or they may not be done in a way that is most useful to others.

Assessment is not just about how much students have learned. It is also about getting **to know your students so that you can plan instruction that will interest, motivate and engage them** (Principle 3). Certain assessment tools are especially useful for providing information that helps you to understand students' learning styles and strategies, their interests, attitudes, motivation and other relevant background factors, past or current, that might impinge on classroom learning. While this is true for all classroom teachers, it is especially true for CLIL teachers working with students from diverse linguistic and cultural backgrounds whose competence in the language of instruction is varied.

Yet another goal of assessment is **to engage students in self-assessment** so that they can take active responsibility for their own learning (Principle 3). Many approaches to assessment treat students as objects of assessment, giving them no active role in assessing their own progress and accomplishments. We view students as active learners who can take a significant role in shaping their own learning. Engaging students in CLIL classrooms in self-assessment is particularly important because they are learning an additional language that is really important – for their educational success, for their social well-being if their home language is a minority language in the community in which they live, and for their long-term personal and professional lives. Students who are participating in CLIL programmes that aim for advanced levels of bilingualism have a vested interested in taking charge of their own learning since they clearly see the additional language as a lifelong asset. Engaging CLIL students as active partners with teachers in assessment gives them the opportunity to do this. For this to happen, learning objectives and criteria for assessment of those objectives must be evident and clear to students; otherwise, they cannot assess their own progress properly.

Student self-assessment in CLIL programmes is particularly important and useful because it allows you to identify their language needs outside the classroom. For example, students in IMM classrooms where the additional language is used in the community (e.g. Russian-speaking students in Estonia in an Estonian–Russian IMM programme) can monitor their ability to use the additional language for social purposes outside school, when they are interacting with their peers who are native speakers of that language. Likewise, students in ILS contexts who speak a minority language at home need to use the additional language outside the classroom; self-assessment that focuses on out-of-school use of the majority language indicates to the teacher whether the students need additional support using that language in social situations. Self-assessment with minority-language students in ILS contexts can also tell you how much and in what contexts they are using the minority language – are they using it simply for playing with their friends or are they also using it to read, write and in other ways? This can indicate whether the teacher needs to enrich their experiences with that language so that they develop a full range of competencies in it. In the case of students in FL programmes, self-assessment can tell you whether they have opportunities to use the language outside school; if they do, you may be able to supplement activities they carry out in class to reflect the additional practice they have had outside school. Finally, all of the above can apply to sub-groups of students in INT schools since they have such diverse backgrounds. When students share insights with their teacher about their language needs outside school, the teacher can then include content-compatible language objectives that can extend their language skills so they are useful outside the classroom. Conversely, you can devise classroom activities that build on their language experiences outside school to supplement and enhance students' opportunities to practise the language.

Effective assessment

Effective classroom-based assessment in CLIL classrooms has five important qualities that apply to any type of classroom. These are the focus of discussion in the section that follows, after which we focus on distinctive features of assessment in CLIL classrooms.

TABLE 7.2

General qualities of effective assessment

Effective instruction is:

a. linked to instructional objectives and methods
b. designed to optimise student performance
c. based on expectations that are clearly defined and communicated to students
d. continuous, and
e. planned.

To begin, effective assessment in any classroom should be **closely linked to instructional objectives and activities** (Principle 6). This is critical if the results of classroom-based assessments are to be used to improve the curriculum and teaching and, ultimately, student learning. Assessment that is aligned with learning objectives does not just tell you what students have or have not learned; it can also tell you whether the objectives were reasonable and whether instruction has been well planned to achieve those objectives. One of the great failings of standardised testing, and testing sponsored by outside agencies, is that it is not useful for these purposes because the content of the tests often does not reflect what you are trying to teach and how you teach. This is why using a unit/lesson-planning tool, discussed in **Chapter 4**, is so important.

Effective assessment also aims to **optimise student performance** so that you get an accurate picture of what students can actually do. Student performance is optimised when: (1) assessment tasks are developmentally appropriate, interesting, and authentic, (2) the methods and expectations about assessment are culturally appropriate, (3) learning expectations are clear and evident to students and (4) learning objectives and assessment methods are fair, and are seen to be fair. To ensure that assessments provide an accurate picture of students' competencies, they must reflect learners' levels of cognitive ability; they must be engaging; and, therefore, they must be interesting and authentic. These qualities, of course, emerge from the principles of CLIL that we talked about in **Chapter 2**.

Ensuring cultural sensitivity is very important in CLIL classrooms with students from different language and cultural backgrounds, especially when students are new to the school and may not yet have adjusted to the culture of the school and the community around them. Some immigrant and indigenous-language students in ILS contexts, for example, often have norms about how to behave in school that differ radically from the norms that typically govern Euro-American schools – they may be reluctant to raise their hands to show what they know or to look at the teacher when responding to questions; girls from some families might be particularly hesitant in these situations. In these cases, it is not because they are not engaged or have not been learning; rather, for them, these ways of behaving in school violate important norms in their home culture. See **Table 7.3** for a list of ways in which cultural variation can be important in a CLIL classroom.

TABLE 7.3

Cultural differences to consider when designing assessment

Wait time: some second-language learners require longer wait times than others

Individual or group response: some students prefer to respond to teachers' questions or calls for displays of knowledge as part of the entire group; they are reluctant to give individual responses because they think it is inappropriate. Some students also prefer to work with their fellow students to formulate a response to a teacher's questions. This is frowned on in many Euro-American schools but is highly valued and preferred by others.

Feedback: whereas some students like to receive individual and public praise from the teacher, others are deeply embarrassed by such praise; they do not expect public or explicit praise from the teacher.

Eye contact: in contrast to some students from the Anglo-American culture, who are taught to look directly at adults when being spoken to, children from many cultures are taught that direct eye contact with adults is inappropriate and is a sign of impertinence.

Guessing: some students will not give the answer to a question unless they are certain that they are accurate; others are generally comfortable with guessing.

Question-and-answer format: be sure your students understand and have had prior experience with the question and/or answer format that you are using; for example, do they understand what to do with multiple-choice questions that are presented with blank bubbles?

Volunteering: some students are uncomfortable showing what they know by volunteering a response or initiating interaction with the teacher – such behaviour is seen as bragging and showing off. Choral or group responding can be used to circumvent this preference.

If assessment is to provide meaningful and useful feedback to teachers and students alike, the **expected outcomes should have been clearly presented to students** beforehand, along with the criteria for judging the quality of successful performance. In short, from the students' point of view, assessment should not be a guessing game. If the performance criteria have been made clear to students and the methods of assessment are fair, then you can interpret assessment results in meaningful ways that lead to useful follow-up instruction, revisions to instructional plans, or even changes in the curriculum. This means that you should be sure to tell students what they are expected to learn in language they can understand; your instructional activities should be aligned with those objectives in ways that are evident to students; and you must remind students why they are doing what they are doing so that it makes sense to them.

Effective assessment is also continuous (see **Table 7.4**). A great deal of useful classroom assessment goes on during day-to-day instruction. It is fully integrated, virtually invisible during classroom activities, and does not take valuable time away from teaching; we talk about ways to do this later. This is particularly important for IMM, ILS and INT contexts that aim for high levels of bilingual proficiency because students spend a great deal of their day learning through the additional language. Assessment at the end of instructional units, and especially at the end of the school year, is more formal and systematic since it is often shared with parents and is used to make decisions about individual students.

TABLE 7.4

Assessment is continuous

Assessment in CLIL classrooms occurs:

- at the beginning of each school year and at the beginning of a unit, so that teachers can identify skills and background knowledge that are relevant to their instructional plans; to identify students who might need additional support with language or reading (see Hamayan, Genesee & Cloud, 2013, Chapter 3, pp. 104–108); to assess students' background knowledge with respect to the topic, and so on.

- during day-to-day instruction so that teachers can monitor student performance on a continuous basis and modify instructional plans to maximise learning.

- at critical points during the year – at the end of a unit or semester – so that teachers can take stock of students' cumulative learning and evaluate the effectiveness of their plans.

- at the end of the year to be shared with next year's teachers so that they can plan. their instruction and/or with school administrators and parents.

Finally, assessment is **planned** along with instruction to ensure that ample time is provided to design and conduct appropriate assessment. A number of the assessment tools or activities we talk about, such as dialogue journals and conferencing, have instructional value and, thus, can serve instructional as well as assessment goals at the same time.

Unique aspects of assessment in CLIL classrooms

There are a number of ways in which assessment in CLIL classrooms differs from other classrooms (see **Table 7.5**). Most of these differences are associated with the assessment of language proficiency.

TABLE 7.5

Distinctive features of assessment in CLIL classrooms

1. Assessment must distinguish between students' language proficiency and their academic achievement.

2. Assessment must monitor students' proficiency in language for both academic and social purposes.

3. Assessment must assess students' socio-cultural competence with respect to language use and social interaction in the target language.

4. Assessment must be culturally appropriate.

5. Assessment should consider students' competence in the home language.

First of all, CLIL teachers must be able to distinguish between students' language proficiency and their competence in the subject matter being taught, at least during the early stages of second-language acquisition. Students who are being educated through their first language already have considerable proficiency in the language of instruction when they begin school, although even these students continue to develop their language skills for academic purposes in school. In contrast, students who are learning through an additional language initially usually lack the full range of language skills they need to express fluently and completely what academic knowledge and skills they have acquired. This means that you must be able to assess academic achievement during the initial stages of learning using methods that require only basic skills in the additional language. This is true for students from both minority-language and majority-language backgrounds if they are in CLIL programmes that teach significant portions of the curriculum through the additional language; it is not such an important issue for students in FL programmes since the emphasis there is on language, and mastery of content is of secondary importance. **Table 7.6** describes some strategies that you can use to assess students' conceptual development when they have limited proficiency in the additional language to express what they have learned.

TABLE 7.6

Assessing content knowledge when students have low proficiency in the additional language

- Students can demonstrate knowledge or understanding of new material by drawing pictures that represent what they have learned; for example, they might draw pictures identifying the members of their family, the westward migration of early European explorers, or the phases of the water cycle.

- Students can demonstrate their understanding of categories, rank order and other relational knowledge by manipulating objects that vary with respect to certain physical attributes that have been reviewed in a Science unit – for example, students are given a set of objects that vary in weight, length, volume, and so on, and are asked to cluster, order or compare them.

- Students act out their knowledge; for example, they might express certain emotions or reactions to evocative verbal cues, or as a group they could represent the relationship of the planets in the solar system.

- Students can demonstrate knowledge by pointing to sets of pictures that go together; for example, foods taken from the oceans versus foods grown in soil; mammals and their habitats; historical events, peoples and places that go together in some way.

- Teachers may permit students to demonstrate what they have learned using their primary language even though instruction has taken place in the second language. This strategy is most useful during early stages of acquisition of the additional language when students' proficiency is very limited. Keep in mind that this strategy does not always optimise students' performance if they are not able to express what they have learned using their primary language because learning has taken place in the second language.

In CLIL contexts where two languages are being used for instruction, and teachers would be expected to know both languages at least to some minimum level of competence, here is a general strategy you can use to differentiate between what concepts students have learned and the language needed to express those concepts. This strategy is most useful when students are in the beginning grades of the programme and their competence in the additional language is very limited.

1. Give students instructions in both of their languages, accompanied by pictures that they could use as communication aids.

2. Let students use any of the strategies in **Table 7.6**.

3. Using a combination of what students say in both languages, and what they act out using the pictures you provided, assess what they know about the concepts being assessed.

4. Then reflect on how much students were able to express themselves using the target language – rather than the pictures or actions – in order to express what they knew. During follow-up instruction, pay special attention to those aspects of academic language linked to the target concepts that students were unable to use. This gives you opportunities to help students fill those gaps in their language.

As students progress in the programme, their proficiency in the additional language will advance. They will acquire more and more of the language associated with specific academic subjects. When teaching advanced-level CLIL students, it is important that you assess their proficiency in such specialised language skills in order to determine whether they are acquiring the academic language skills that are a critical aspect of those subjects. While this would be inappropriate in the beginning stages, it is entirely appropriate in later stages of learning. In a related vein, you must also be able to assess your students' academic language skills before they need them so that you can identify which specific skills they are currently lacking and then plan activities that promote acquisition of those skills.

A second difference in CLIL assessment is that teachers can assume that most majority-language students have already acquired, or will acquire, without instruction, the social language skills they need to interact with other students and adults in and outside school. However, this is not necessarily the case for students learning through the medium of an additional language. Students in CLIL programmes that aim for high levels of bilingual proficiency may have difficulty using the additional language during social interactions in and outside school with other second-language speakers, or with native speakers of that language, for strictly social purposes. Teachers in CLIL programmes must monitor their students' proficiency in the social uses of the additional language and they must identify those aspects of social discourse where students need support. Teachers can support CLIL students' acquisition of social language skills by including activities in class that engage students in the use of such skills. This would give students opportunities to learn and practise skills like turn-taking, how to ask for clarification, how to disagree and agree, and so on. These are not skills that they might require in the normal course of classroom activities with their teachers.

Third, and in a related vein, students in CLIL programmes who are learning content through the additional language also need to learn the socio-cultural norms associated with use of the additional language in and outside school. For example, if they are learning languages that distinguish between formal versus familiar forms of address ('*Tu*' and '*usted*' – you, in Spanish), they must learn to use each. Cultures vary in their norms about interrupting one another and students must learn when it is appropriate to interrupt and when it is not. You must be able to assess your students' socio-cultural competence with respect to use of the additional language so that you can identify gaps in their socio-cultural competence and provide opportunities for learning relevant norms and customs.

As well, CLIL teachers must be familiar with interactional and cultural norms of students in their classrooms and how they differ from the norms that govern the assessment setting. Let us consider an ILS context where immigrant or indigenous-language students are being taught and assessed through English. Some students are not accustomed to public and individual displays of knowledge; instead, they expect to respond in whole- or small-group formats along with their classmates. These students may also not be comfortable making direct eye contact with adults since this is disfavoured in their home culture. In contrast, these behaviours are favoured within Anglo-European cultures, especially among school children during class time. In collectivist societies, such as the Inuit and other indigenous-language groups in North America, individual displays of competence are generally considered inappropriate and rude because they are seen as boasting and come at the expense of one's peers. Students with these types of norms who are being assessed in a more Anglo-European assessment context may be seen as lacking competence when they hesitate to show what they know and they fail to look the teacher in the eye.

Cultural differences of this sort are especially difficult for students from minority backgrounds who have just joined a school that is dominated by another cultural group. Assessment of these students' language and academic competencies requires that CLIL teachers use alternative formats, formats that accommodate the culture of their new students – at least in the beginning – until they add the social norms of the additional language group to their own. Some cultural differences to think about when designing assessment for culturally diverse students are summarised in **Table 7.3**.

Finally, teachers working in CLIL classrooms must be prepared to work with and assess students' competence in their home languages in addition to the language of instruction. This should not be problematic in CLIL contexts that use two languages for teaching academic content – that is, IMM, DL-CLIL in ILS and INT contexts and FL contexts – because teachers working in these programmes, collectively, should be

---

7.2 SPECIAL NOTE

Assessing students who speak a language unfamiliar to the teacher

A good strategy for assessing reading abilities in a language that is unfamiliar to the teacher is to ask them to bring a book from home and to read from it. Alternatively, you can keep a stock of age-appropriate books in several languages that students in your class often speak. You ask each student to read whatever he or she can from the book using their finger to shadow their reading while you observe. Although you do not know if the child is reading correctly, you nevertheless get a sense of whether the child has grasped the basics of reading – how he holds the book, and whether he reads from left to right or vice versa depending on the language. You can also ask the child to write his own name and the name of the school to assess his writing skills. Older students can be asked to write a letter to a family member back home. In addition to observing how smoothly this simple writing task is completed, you can ask a community member or a university student to give a general assessment of how well the student writes.

---

competent in the two languages that are used for instruction and they should know how to access resources for assessing students in both languages. It is much more challenging in CLIL contexts that are teaching minority-language students through a majority language – ML-CLIL in ILS contexts and ML-CLIL in INT contexts; for example, in classrooms in France and Germany with children who speak Berber at home but are being taught in French or German. Here the difficulty is that teachers themselves, and even specialists in these schools, might not have competence in the minority languages and, as well, assessment tools in those languages might be difficult to obtain. At times, it is nevertheless important to try to ascertain the competence of minority students in the minority language. Alternative assessment tools discussed in the following section can be useful for this purpose. For a rudimentary assessment of literacy in a home language that is unfamiliar to the teacher, **Special Note 7.2** provides some tips.

ALTERNATIVE ASSESSMENT TOOLS

In this section, we discuss a variety of assessment tools that are useful in CLIL classrooms. The focus is on alternative forms of assessment or assessments that do not look like traditional tests; we talk about tests later in the chapter. These forms of assessment are particularly useful in CLIL classrooms because they allow you to do several things at the same time – to assess students' language development; to collect information about students' interests, learning styles and backgrounds so that you can plan differentiated or individualised instruction; and, in some cases, to provide students with opportunities to use the additional language in individualised ways. The tools we discuss are:

1. observation
2. portfolios
3. conferences
4. dialogue journals and learning logs.

7.1 **PERSONAL PERSPECTIVE**

Evaluator toolkit for CLIL teachers

Kathryn Lindholm-Leary, Professor, San Jose State University, San Jose, California, USA

For the past 30 years, I have worked with about 100 schools/districts in helping develop and improve dual language programs through research and evaluation. Most of this work began when there was federal funding in the US (Title VII or FLAP-Foreign Language Assistance Program grants) for the development, implementation and evaluation of new or existing dual language programmes. In my role as evaluator, I helped schools define a realistic set of expectations (goals and objectives) and measurement instruments (many times imposed by state requirements) and then set about the tasks of collecting, refining, analyzing and interpreting data that were collected using these new assessment tools. At some sites, there was little interest in the actual outcomes, while at other sites, teachers and school leaders were interested not only in the findings but also in using the data to improve their programme and student outcomes. It was at these schools that we usually witnessed the best school outcomes (high levels of bilingualism and academic achievement along with student, parent and teacher satisfaction).

Because of the interest we saw in teachers and school leaders in better understanding the research/evaluation process, Gary Hargett and I developed the Evaluator's Toolkit (www.cal.org/twi/EvalToolkit/index.htm), which provides step-by-step instructions for how to develop an evaluation at a school site. We have seen that, once they understand the research process, teachers and school leaders, as well as parents and even former dual-language graduates, conduct their own research for Master's theses, dissertations or other research projects or grants. In addition, we have asked students for feedback on some of the student surveys we developed and we received some helpful leads for how better to word items or for additional items to consider. Educators who have used this Toolkit have mentioned that they have a greater understanding of their student language and academic outcomes and are excited to be engaged in research at their school site.

1. Observation

We begin with a form of assessment that can guide instruction every minute of the school day – observation. Teachers continuously observe their students and classroom events informally and in various ways; based on what they observe, they redirect students and restructure activities to ensure optimal learning. To make observation a really useful classroom assessment tool, it is recommended that you focus in some way. For example, you may want to observe students systematically while they are engaged in a planned activity – such as cooperative learning or during an oral report on a science experiment, to see how they are learning the social conventions of the additional language. You may want to focus on the performance of an individual student, perhaps a student who has just arrived in your class, during a reading activity to assess his reading level. Or, you may want to observe how a new small-group activity you are trying out is working; in this case, you might move from group to group, observing their engagement in the activity – did it work the way you wanted?

There are several methods you can use to record your observations:

- anecdotal records
- checklists
- rubrics (or rating scales)
- teachers' journals.

Anecdotal records are brief notes that you can make about your observations of individual or groups of students, new activities or student interactions in classroom or other social contexts. Organise your notes around a list you created to direct your observations, since that list should reflect what you think is important to observe. Anecdotal records can be made on file cards, adhesive labels or in a notebook that is keep expressly for this purpose; you can have a file with notes about individual students, specific units of instruction, certain activities and so on. Recording your observations about your students, and the effectiveness of the activities you planned, is critical so that you can refer to them later and use them to inform future teaching. Anecdotal records can focus on anything you want; they are particularly useful for recording observations about individual students – their successes and difficulties, for example. A narrative report is simply a longer, more detailed description of a classroom event or of a student that you want to keep track of for later use. Without such records, teachers' recollections of student performance or the success of failure of particular activities can be forgotten or distorted because of memory overload or simply the passage of time.

Another method of recording your observations is to use **checklists**. Checklists are more focused than anecdotal records, although they can be used together. As their name implies, checklists are used to indicate whether student performance exhibits, or does not exhibit, certain features or whether certain things happened, or did not happen, during a classroom activity. Checklists can be used for assessing written assignments, oral presentations by students, student interactions during planned or unplanned activities, or anything you think is important. For example, to assess students' ability to use the narrative form in writing, you could use a checklist while you read each student's narrative to indicate whether students' written stories included information or references to the setting of the story, the principle and supporting characters in the story, the resolution of the conflict or problem that characterises their relationship, and so on. A checklist devised to assess a student's understanding of the life cycle of the butterfly during an oral presentation in Science would indicate whether the student had identified the main phases of its life cycle, whether main facts were presented accurately, and whether secondary facts were presented accurately and so on. In this latter example, the checklist identifies what knowledge the student has acquired about a topic in Science, whereas the former example identifies what understanding the student has acquired about a genre of language use. **Table 7.7** is a sample checklist that could be used to assess a whole class with respect to students' understanding of the main components of narratives. In this case, students might be asked to write a story, and orally present what they have created to the whole class. While they are making their individual presentations, you could check off which features of narrative each student includes in their story. Once all students have presented and have been assessed, your checklist gives you an idea of features they have mastered and those they need more help with – in this case, the concept of setting and the moral or lesson of the story.

TABLE 7.7
Sample checklist for assessing student understanding of narrative text

Check each of the features identified correctly by each student

	JY	HS	VS	NB	LF	JH	CS	JD	RF	TK	RP
Setting	✓							✓	✓	✓	✓
Principal character	✓	✓	✓	✓	✓		✓	✓		✓	✓
Secondary character	✓		✓			✓		✓		✓	
Conflict/problem	✓	✓		✓				✓	✓		✓
Resolution	✓	✓	✓	✓	✓	✓	✓	✓			
Moral/lesson	✓	✓						✓			

Checklists generally assess student performance or an activity in an all-or-none fashion and, thus, are not useful for assessing variations in the quality of students' language use or performance. This would call for rubrics (or rating scales).

Rubrics (or rating scales) are useful for describing variations in the quality of student performance along specific dimensions. Rubrics consist of descriptors that refer to specific aspects of performance. They can focus on the linguistic quality of students' performance or on the appropriateness or accuracy of the content of their answers. Rubrics that refer to the quality of language use can focus on discrete aspects of language use, such as organisation, sentence formation, style or mechanics; or on the overall quality of performance. The former is called an **analytic scale** and the latter a **holistic scale**. **Table 7.8** is an example of an analytic scale for assessing writing skills in a relatively advanced grade level. Analytic scales can be especially useful for planning instruction because they provide feedback about specific aspects of performance. Holistic scales can be useful in formulating grades for students and they allow you to use multiple sources of input to formulate the grade.

Teachers' journals are another useful way to record observations that you want to keep a record of for later use. The journal itself is simply a notebook, digital document file or written diary that is set aside for this purpose. You do not need to note down all observations since this would be overwhelming; your journals should be reserved for those aspects of your teaching or student learning that are important – such as a new set of materials you are trying out, the performance of a new student in class or of a student who is struggling, the outcomes of a field trip, and so on. Your journal can be organised ahead of time to reflect aspects of teaching and learning that you want to evaluate and keep track of – for example, group strategies, new materials and readings, assignments, performance of individual students and so on. You could set up headings in the journal that reflect your unit-planning entries: preview activities, intensive teaching activities, extension activities, and so on. Recording observations of a new unit can be particularly useful since you will probably want to revise it; having a written record of your impressions of aspects of it as they unfolded would be useful. Usually, entries in teachers' journals are simply impressions of the activities or aspects of instruction that you have just engaged in. While you may use abbreviations to make your notes, be sure that they are not so abbreviated that you cannot decipher them later on. To ensure some accuracy in your notes, try to make entries in your journal as soon after the event as possible.

TABLE 7.8 *Sample analytic rubric for writing assessment (from Cloud, Genesee & Hamayan, 2000)*

Student Name/date/class:

ORGANISATION:

5. Outstanding – very well organised; excellent use of opening and closing paragraphs; appropriate use of paragraphing; coherent, logical and well developed arguments/story line

4. Above average – well organised; effective introduction and ending; good paragraphing; coherent

3. Average – includes opening and closing paragraphs; main ideas/story line clear; good use of paragraphing

2. Below average – weak introduction and ending; somewhat incoherent; weak use of paragraphing

1. Unsatisfactory – no obvious organisation; disconnected ideas

SENTENCE STRUCTURE AND VARIETY:

5. Outstanding – effective and sophisticated use of varied sentence types; complex and accurate use of grammar; sentence structure and variety appropriate for purpose of writing

4. Above average – good variation in sentence types; good use of simple and complex grammar

3. Average – some variation in sentence type; sentence grammar generally accurate and appropriate; use of some complex sentence grammar

2. Below average – mainly simple sentence types; some major errors in sentence grammar

1. Unsatisfactory – incomplete sentences, many errors in sentence grammar leading to incoherence

CONTENT AND ORIGINALITY:

5. Outstanding – highly original ideas; outstanding details

4. Above Average – original ideas and interesting details

3. Average – good ideas; some supporting details

2. Ordinary – little originality or use of supporting details

1. Uninteresting – no originality or use of interesting details

VOCABULARY:

5. Outstanding – appropriate use of varied, sophisticated and colourful vocabulary

4. Above average – good use of varied, appropriate vocabulary

3. Average – appropriate use of appropriate vocabulary

2. Below average – use of simple, common vocabulary; little variation

1. Needs lots of development – repetitious use of simple vocabulary

MECHANICS:

4. Above average – consistent use of correct punctuation, capitalisation, spelling

3. Average – generally correct use of punctuation, capitalisation, spelling; some minor errors

2. Needs work – inconsistent use of correct punctuation, capitalisation, spelling

1. Unsatisfactory – frequent errors in capitalisation, punctuation, spelling

2. Portfolios

Educators are increasingly realising the advantages of assessing student achievement using more than one test, one written report or one oral presentation. Evaluations that are based on single instances of performance may not be reliable indicators of students' full abilities and, thus, they might provide invalid (inaccurate) assessments of what students can do. As an alternative to one-shot assessments, more and more teachers are using portfolios to collect a number of pieces of student work that can be used to provide an overall assessment. A **portfolio** is a purposeful collection of a student's work that documents their efforts, achievements and progress over time in given areas of learning, either language or subject matter, or both. Portfolios are useful in any educational context, but we believe they are particularly useful in CLIL contexts because they provide a picture of the full range of students' abilities and they provide teachers and students with opportunities to monitor learning together. For students who are learning a lot of content through an additional language, portfolios have the added advantage of capturing examples of their work in multiple areas of the curriculum. It can also be useful to share portfolios with parents to show them their children's progress in acquiring their new language or new academic skills and knowledge.

Students can have different kinds of portfolios – portfolios of work in progress, completed work or best work. With modern technology, it is possible to be creative in devising portfolios:

- Samples of speaking can be recorded on cassette tapes or smartphones for later playback.
- Conversational skills can be recorded on a smartphone or by video/audiotaping students interacting with one another.
- Samples of writing or talking can be transcribed using computers.

Portfolios can have a broad focus – samples of work from different areas of the curriculum – or a narrow focus – a portfolio of work in Science or Language Arts only. Portfolios with a narrow focus are desirable for assessment purposes because it is easier to assess work samples of a common sort. You can use rating scales or checklists of the type we have already described to assess each piece in a portfolio or the entire collection of work in a portfolio. You can also include students in assessing their own work in their portfolios using any of these techniques; portfolios then become useful forms of student self-assessment. In fact, portfolios are particularly useful when they are managed and reviewed jointly by teachers and students. Including students makes them active partners in assessment and enhances their sense of responsibility of their own learning. This in turn promotes students' autonomy (Principle 3).

3. Conferences

Portfolio **conferences** are another useful way for teachers and students to work together to assess the contents of portfolios. Portfolio conferences are semi-structured conversations between students and teachers about work in a student portfolio – for example, a student describes to the teacher strengths and weaknesses of a piece of work, how two pieces of work show progress, how a piece of work could be improved, or how the teacher could help the student make improvements. **Table 7.9** suggests some other questions that teachers might use during a portfolio conference.

Portfolio conferences can be done with a single student or with a small group of two or three students; including more than one student makes it easier for some students to talk about their own work. Portfolios also provide opportunities for students to practise their language skills in an authentic situation in a one-on-one or small-group situation with their teacher about schoolwork. If passed on to the students' next-year teachers, portfolios also provide invaluable documentation of students' developing proficiencies that assists teachers in higher grades with their instructional planning. Portfolios can also be shared with parents, who might otherwise not know how well their children are progressing.

TABLE 7.9

Teacher questions to guide portfolio conferences

☐ Why is this a good piece of work?

☐ What did you enjoy about doing this piece of work?

☐ What part of this work was the most difficult to do?

☐ What did you learn from doing this work?

☐ How is this work different/better than your earlier work?

☐ What did you learn from doing this work?

☐ How can you make this work better?

☐ How can I help you make this work better?

When teachers and students collaborate in assessing the work in a portfolio, a number of positive effects can result:

- Student involvement in and ownership of their own learning is enhanced.

- Students take an active and responsible role in monitoring their own progress.

- Students take pride in their work and enjoy their successes.

- Students come to understand what is required to do good work in school.

- Teachers gain insights about each student that can then be used to individualise instruction (Principle 6).

4. Dialogue journals and learning logs

Dialogue journals and learning logs are other ways of collecting information from students about their learning experiences. They are particularly useful because they are written conversations between students and teachers. Thus, they provide students with opportunities to practise writing in the additional language in authentic ways. They can be about anything students and/or teachers think is important – topics pertaining to schoolwork or even out-of-school activities. Generally speaking, students use separate books for journal writing and they are given regular times in class, or sometimes at home, to write in them. The real benefits of journals occur when they are routinely and frequently shared with teachers; that is, when they take the form of a dialogue between students and teachers. When students write about their classroom experiences, you gain information that is useful for individualising instruction. You can gain useful insights about your students' general likes/dislikes, hobbies and lives when they write about their school or out-of-school activities. Of course, journals also provide teachers with samples of students' writing skills and the strategies they use when writing.

STUDENT SELF-ASSESSMENT

There are multiple benefits to be gained from involving students in self-assessment:

- Students can assess their language proficiency at times when it is difficult for you to do the assessing – in subject-matter classes taught by other teachers, in the school yard or cafeteria when students are socialising with one another, and even out of school.

- Students gain a greater sense of responsibility for, and involvement in, their own learning and become more motivated to learn.

- Students come to understand learning objectives and the criteria or standards for assessing performance; as a result, they can focus their time and efforts effectively in the pursuit of those objectives.

- Students learn to identify their learning strengths and weaknesses and, thus, can better decide where and how to focus their energies.

- In learner-centred classrooms, teachers can use students' self-assessment to individualise instruction.

There are a variety of ways in which you can involve students in self-assessment; most of these have already been discussed in previous sections:

- portfolio conferences with teachers and other students

- portfolios with reflection questions that students respond to every time they add a piece of work to their portfolio such as 'Why did you include this work?', 'What do you like about this piece?', 'Does this piece need extra work? Why?'

- conferences with teachers and individual or small groups of students that focus on language or subject-matter skills

- dialogue journals and learning logs

- peer-assessment during oral presentations or read-aloud sessions.

TESTS

We have left the discussion of tests to the end of this section because we assume that most teachers are familiar with tests. However, there are some features of tests that are particularly important to consider when they are used in CLIL contexts. To begin, we must define tests to distinguish them from the alternative forms of assessment we have discussed so far. We use the following simple definition: a test is a method of examining the knowledge and abilities students have acquired using a standard or uniform method followed by the assignment of letter or number grade. In general, performance on tests is assessed as correct or incorrect, but it could also be evaluated using a rating scale or rubric that differentiates differences in the quality of students' responses. The primary use of tests is to grade and compare students on what they have learned using standardised criteria. Tests are not particularly useful for collecting information about students' learning styles, backgrounds or interests; nor are they useful for telling us about students' understanding of the concepts or skills we are trying to teach because they usually focus only on whether students got it right or not. Moreover, they only reveal information about what you test and nothing about broader aspects of students' knowledge and language ability. Particularly in regard to the job of classroom teachers, they do not tell you much about whether your instructional plans were appropriate or effective and need fine-tuning.

7.2 PERSONAL PERSPECTIVE
Assessment as a collaboration-building process

Margo Gottlieb, WIDA Co-founder and Lead Developer, Wisconsin Center for Education Research, University of Wisconsin-Madison, and Director, Assessment and Evaluation, Illinois Resource Center; Virginia Blais, EAL teacher, Taipei American School, Taiwan

The integration of language and content in assessment requires the creation of an alliance between English as an Additional Language (EAL) and mainstream teachers. This partnership is even more powerful when students and teachers also develop a common understanding of what is expected from the learner in both content and language learning. When this happens, students become the primary stakeholders and teachers take the role of primary supporters of assessment (Gottlieb, 2016). They (the teachers) can do this by guiding students in interpreting their own written work using a set of criteria.

Elementary school teachers at the Taipei American School (TAS) in Taiwan exemplify this coordination of instruction with assessment. TAS is a multilingual, multicultural American school in an international setting with approximately 2400 students. There is a heterogeneous mix of students in the elementary school, with an EAL student population of approximately 30%. We began by forming professional learning teams at each grade level, facilitated by the EAL teachers. Together, we identified academic language objectives across the content areas that contributed to students' entries in their Academic Language Portfolios. This enabled teachers to communicate the students' strengths and to plan next steps for language development with both students and their parents.

This collaborative team-building process between EAL and mainstream teachers was prompted by a mutual concern for students' academic language use in English Language Arts. It started by the second grade teachers comparing students' language in locally developed assessments with the written language students produced. We examined the academic language embedded in Language Arts standards to develop assessments across all content areas – expecting all students to use the language of Language Arts in all the content areas. We used tools from WIDA (a consortium of over 200 international schools and 38 US-based members) to understand features of academic language. These were expressed in standards-referenced performance terms. Additionally, the WIDA writing rubric was used to help demystify the criteria associated with language learning for both teachers and students.

Resulting from this ongoing professional learning, common assessments for all students have been built based on a thorough understanding of academic language development. The process has solidified collaboration between EAL and mainstream teachers around the critical role of language in content assessment and has led teachers to have more confidence in data used for local decision making.

Returning to the beginning of this chapter – where we discussed the reasons for, or goals of, assessment – you can see that tests have limited utility relative to that list. However, tests are an inescapable part of education – all students have to take tests at times. Tests can also be useful if they are well-constructed and if you need to provide numeric estimates of students' accomplishments that have been derived in a uniform fashion for all students. Authorities often require test results and parents also often expect grades on tests to tell them how well their children are doing relative to a standard that has been set. For these reasons, testing should be taken seriously. It is important that the tests you construct respect the qualities of good assessments that we discussed earlier – see **Table 7.2**.

We discuss alternative test formats that CLIL teachers can create on their own. We focus on language tests but also talk a bit about tests that teachers might devise to assess content knowledge and skills that are not linguistic in nature.

To begin, for classroom tests to be useful, they must be linked in meaningful ways to your language and/or content objectives – Quality (a) in **Table 7.2**. In the case of FL-CLIL contexts, the primary focus of testing will be on language learning, whereas in the other CLIL contexts we have discussed, tests could focus on either language, content or both. Classroom tests should also reflect, or be based on, the kinds of learning activities you have used to teach. This is particularly true for students in the lower grades insofar as their learning is often highly context dependent. Tests that require students to generalise what they have been taught in class to a new situation are another kind of ability. In fact, as learners advance in school, they should be able to generalise what they have learned in class under one set of conditions to new conditions – within reasonable limits; for example, if grade 7 CLIL students have learned to write a Science report in the additional language based on an experiment linked to the unit described in **Chapter 5** on alternative sources of energy, they should be able to write a report based on a different experiment. This is all part of ensuring that the goals of testing are clear to students. If students are asked to respond to tests that are unclear or unfamiliar to them, then you are really testing their ability to guess what you want rather than what they know and can do.

Test formats

When devising tests for CLIL classrooms, it is useful to distinguish between open-ended, limited-response and closed-ended test formats because these formats are more or less appropriate for students at different stages of language development. In **closed-ended tests**, students are provided with alternative responses, or answers, and they simply select the one that is most appropriate or right. A common form of closed-ended response task is multiple-choice. For example, a kindergarten teacher who is interested in assessing students' vocabulary skills might say a list of words (e.g. *'cookie horse sandwich shirt'*) and then ask students to select the word that refers to an animal. Students only have to recognise the correct answer; they do not have to produce an answer. Because response alternatives are provided by the teacher, this format does not lend itself to assessing student-generated or discourse-level skills; however, it is useful when students are in the very early stages of language development or are learning brand-new language skills.

Limited-response tests are like closed-ended formats except that they allow students more extended response choices; for example, the same kindergarten teacher might ask her students to say words that refer to animals, family members and so on. With limited-response tasks, it is possible to elicit language skills that represent somewhat more advanced or complex levels of language production than in a closed-ended task. By choosing the context carefully, teachers can focus on specific aspects of language; for example, teachers could assess students' knowledge of adjectives by selectively deleting all adjectives from a reading passage and asking students to fill the gaps with appropriate words. The shortcomings of this format are similar to those of closed-ended formats – they elicit very limited aspects of language production or content knowledge if the test is based on content objectives.

However, there are times when you want to assess students' comprehension skills without requiring that they be able to use the language productively. Here are a number of techniques that do not require verbal responses but that can be used to assess beginning-level comprehension skills:

- Students act out responses to questions – for example, students can respond non-verbally to verbal commands to move parts of their bodies or perform certain actions, such as sit, stand or turn around.

- Students can point out answers to questions – for example, to identify objects in the classroom that are different colours, shapes or sizes, or that are useful for standing on to reach high objects, for holding the door open, and so on.

- Young learners can draw answers to questions – for example, 'What are the planets in the solar system and what are their positions in the solar system?'

Closed-ended and limited-response test tasks are similarly useful for assessing content knowledge during early stages of language development when students' mastery of academic language is limited; this is equally true for young and older students. There are a number of techniques that you can use that permit students to express what they know in academic subjects, even though their proficiency in the second language is limited:

- Students can demonstrate knowledge or understanding of new material by drawing pictures that represent what they have learned; for example, they might draw pictures identifying the members of their family, the journey of a European explorer, or the phases of the water cycle.

- Students can demonstrate their understanding of categories, rank order and other relational knowledge by manipulating objects that vary with respect to certain physical attributes that have been reviewed in a Science unit – for example, students are given a set of objects that vary in weight, length, volume, and so on, and are asked to cluster, order or compare them.

- Students act out their knowledge; for example, they might express certain emotions or reactions to evocative verbal cues, or as a group they could represent the relationship of the planets in the solar system.

- Students can demonstrate knowledge by pointing to sets of pictures that go together; for example, foods taken from the oceans versus foods grown in soil; mammals and their habitats; historical events, peoples and places that go together in some way.

- Students can demonstrate what they have learned using their home language even though instruction has taken place in an additional language.

Open-ended response tests, as the name indicates, elicit responses that are not highly specified, although some restriction on how students should respond is usually involved. Writing an essay or a Science report or giving an oral book report are examples of assessment activities that call for open-ended responses. This response format resembles more closely the kinds of language skills that students are usually called on to use in their everyday uses of language in and outside school. Open-ended response tests are also common when testing mastery of content – since writing a summary of a historical event or making a short oral presentation to your fellow students of a historical event requires knowledge of the event, not just language skills. However, you must be careful to not let inaccurate language interfere with your assessment of content learning. For example, the student response: *In the chemical reactions, how atom is connected, they break and come out different material with different how they are* should get a full point for knowledge that during a chemical reaction bonds between atoms break and they form different substances with new properties. This response should also trigger more instructional attention to the past tense, pronouns, the term *characteristics* or *properties*, and so on.

Open-ended assessment formats are not only useful when devising tests; they can also be useful for more informal assessments as well. They are particularly suitable for assessing the language skills or content knowledge of students who have attained relatively advanced levels because they call for students to construct and organise responses, not simply to recognise the correct answer. There is clearly no absolute distinction between limited-response and open-ended response tasks; rather, tasks can vary from one extreme to the other. It is helpful to use checklists, rubrics or rating scales to evaluate responses to open-ended questions; in these cases, the rubric or checklist would be devised to reflect your objectives for that activity.

Tests should never be the only source of information for assigning grades or making decisions about individual students. Tests only give you an indication of what students know and can do at one point in time under specific conditions. If students are not feeling well or simply do not understand what the test requires, then their performance is not a valid indication of what they really know. More valid results require that you have information about students on more than one occasion and preferably under different assessment conditions. This is much more likely to give you a true indication of what they know.

SUMMARY

To illustrate how the various assessment tools we have discussed can be useful, we have completed the assessment sections of the unit-planning tool from **Chapter 5** on alternative sources of energy in Appendix 7.A.

Table 7.10 identifies the ways in which each type of tool can be used and the kinds of information that each can provide.

TABLE 7.10 **Assessment tools and their uses**

Tools / Uses	Observation	Portfolios	Conferences	Learning logs	Tests
Accountability		×			×
Plan and modify instruction	×	×	×	×	×
Individualise instruction	×	×	×	×	
Student self-assessment		×	×	×	

APPENDIX 7:A   ASSESSMENT ACTIVITIES FOR THE UNIT ON RENEWABLE ENERGY

Preview phase assessment activities:

Careful observation of students during preview activities.

Use checklist to identify which content-obligatory language skills (vocabulary, grammar) included in your lesson plan students in general have and which they do not have.

Anecdotal record at the end of the preview phase to summarise overall impression of students' readiness for unit with respect to language, background knowledge and interest – these impressions will be used to modify your original focused-phase plans to better reflect students' readiness for the unit.

Focused-learning phase assessment activities:

Portfolio of work samples at different stages of a unit; students' reflections on each piece of work in response to 'guided questions': why piece was chosen, what student likes about it; what needs more work.

Entries to be made in writing to reveal writing skills.

Students meet with teacher in small groups (for efficiency) to discuss portfolios with teacher at mid and end points of unit.

Extension phase assessment activities:

Learning logs: students keep learning logs of their work during this phase; students can do this in writing or use audio-recordings.

Students are given prior 'training' in using learning logs so that they clearly understand your expectations and reasons for their keeping logs.

You can also ask students to make entries in logs based on out-of-school activities related to the unit of study.

Assessment at end of unit:

Assignment of final 'grades' will take into account each student's progress during the unit along with an assignment at the end of the unit.

The actual 'grade' assigned to each student (e.g. letter, number or other) will depend on the school's policy.

The proportion of the final grade assigned to work during the unit will be based largely on the conference in which students discuss work in their portfolio on renewable energy, held earlier.

A proportion of the final grade will also be based on an end-of-unit assignment – each student is given the choice to do either a written or an oral summary on renewable energy; there will be two components to the assignment: What is renewable energy, where does it come from, and what are its advantages and disadvantages? And why is it important for the community to invest in renewable energy?

Each part of the written/oral assignment will be graded using a rubric designed to reflect each part (to be determined) and this will be combined with the grade from the portfolio conference to come up with a final grade with comments.

8   Summing up

We sum up our book in three ways – by providing a detailed checklist that can be used to determine whether your school conforms to the eight key principles we set out in Chapter 2. Understanding these principles – and referring to them during programme planning, instructional planning and professional development – will insure that your decisions result in policies that promote CLIL and in practices that support students.

We have also included in this chapter the entire completed unit-planning template that we used in Chapters 4 to 7 to explicate how to plan and put CLIL into action. Planning is critical for the success of CLIL because you are aiming for value-added education – you are aiming to accomplish all of the goals of sound monolingual education as well as the goals of education that values linguistic and cultural diversity. Since CLIL programmes aim for more than traditional education, every minute counts and nothing can be left to chance. We used the unit-planning tool we introduced in Chapter 4 to help you succeed in planning effective CLIL, no matter what context you are working in: IMM, ILS, FL or INT.

Finally, we end our book with commentaries from students from around the world who have actually participated in each of the types of CLIL contexts we have talked about. In the final analysis, it is students' voices that validate what we have tried to achieve in writing this book.

THE 8 KEY PRINCIPLES OF CLIL: A CHECKLIST FOR IMPLEMENTATION

PRINCIPLE 1: Additional-language instruction is more effective when integrated with content instruction

☐ Students use the additional language while engaged in day-to-day classroom activities.

☐ The teacher uses the additional language to teach some or all of the curriculum.

☐ Students are expected to use the additional language for communication during periods when that language is the language of instruction.

☐ Students use the additional language with the teachers who are proficient in that language outside class as well as in class.

☐ When using the additional language to teach new content, the teacher provides linguistic and non-linguistic scaffolding to make sure that students can understand what is being taught.

☐ Activities are structured so that students have lots of opportunities to use the additional language with one another and with the teacher.

☐ Teachers also use scaffolding to help students express themselves using the additional language.

☐ Professional-development activities have been planned that expand teachers' knowledge of CLIL and their ability to integrate language and content knowledge effectively.

PRINCIPLE 2: Explicit and systematic language instruction is important

☐ Content-obligatory language skills, including vocabulary, grammar and useful phrases for specific subjects, are taught during the preview phase of teaching to prepare students for instruction of new content using those language skills.

☐ Teachers note recurrent errors in students' use of the additional language during content instruction and they plan explicit instruction to address students' most important difficulties. Direct instruction is provided both during Language Arts and also during content classes where those language skills are relevant.

☐ Teachers identify their students' future content-obligatory language skills and find opportunities during Language Arts or during classes where content is being taught to teach those language skills.

☐ When planning units of instruction, teachers identify content-specific and general academic language skills that students will need and include them in their learning objectives.

☐ Teachers ask students to identify areas of language they need support with during student–teacher conferences and in their journals and learning logs. Gaps that a number of students identify in their logs are then included in unit and lesson plans so that they can be taught explicitly.

☐ Teachers identify the language skills that students have difficulty with during interactions with one another and with the teacher; these are included in lesson plans under content-compatible language objectives and are taught explicitly when possible.

PRINCIPLE 3: Student engagement is the engine of learning

☐ Teachers individualise instruction to motivate and engage students.

☐ Teachers plan activities and projects that afford students lots of opportunities to actively use the additional language in collaboration with other students, through field work or through online and library searches.

☐ Classroom activities are planned that are cognitively engaging and require exploration and critical thinking about topics, not simply memorising facts and procedures.

☐ Students are given opportunities to determine how and what they are doing during a lesson.

☐ Students are offered choices in learning activities in order to motivate them and stimulate language use for personal interests while, at the same time, supporting curricular objectives.

☐ Student self-assessment activities are planned that motivate students to become autonomous and responsible learners.

PRINCIPLE 4: Both languages should have equally high status

☐ Teachers reflect on their attitudes and values toward each language to ensure that they value both.

☐ Teachers use each language equally and, in some cases, favour use of the minority language in order to indicate the value of that language to their students.

(Continued over page)

☐ Teachers use activities linked to the cultures of both languages when planning instruction to make sure that the cultures of both instructional languages are equally represented.

☐ Both languages of instruction are equally visible in classroom and in hallway displays, announcements over the PA system and to parents; other languages spoken by students in the class are also given a prominent role in classroom and hallway displays.

☐ Administrative and support personnel in the school actively value both instructional languages and the linguistic diversity of the students; they demonstrate the value of linguistic and cultural diversity in their day-to-day interactions with students and parents.

☐ Books and other materials in the library and elsewhere in the school are available in both languages of instruction and in widely spoken third languages.

☐ Teachers are offered professional-development options related to culturally sensitive teaching.

PRINCIPLE 5: The first language is a tool for additional-language learning

☐ Teachers are familiar with the characteristics of the languages of instruction, even in the language they themselves do not teach.

☐ Teachers include explicit cross-linguistic objectives in their unit plans.

☐ Teachers assess students' competence in reading and writing in both languages at school entry and at the beginning of each grade in order to obtain a complete picture of their literacy skills. Resources are available to do this in both languages of instruction for teachers who are monolingual.

☐ Teachers differentiate instruction in reading and writing according to students' existing competencies in each language and they draw on students' competencies in students' home language to support development of the additional language.

☐ Together, teachers responsible for teaching in each language plan instruction that emphasises skills that are unique to each language while reinforcing those that are shared.

☐ Sometimes, students are allowed to use the home language to express themselves or problem-solve with support from more proficient students who model how to use the additional language.

☐ In their self-assessments, students are encouraged to reflect on their competencies in each language and to identify areas of strengths and weakness in each.

PRINCIPLE 6: **Classroom-based assessment is critical for programme success**

☐ Teachers are familiar with and competent using alternative forms of assessment to serve alternative goals.

☐ Teachers include assessment activities in their unit plans along with the goals of each.

☐ Teachers use results from their assessment activities to modify and plan future instruction and to individualise instruction.

☐ Teachers engage students in self-assessment in order to encourage autonomy and responsibility for learning.

☐ Assessment is included in professional-development activities, which are planned in collaboration with teachers.

☐ Teachers use alternative assessment types to provide students with additional opportunities to use and practise the additional language.

PRINCIPLE 7: **All children can become bilingual**

☐ The school has an official policy of non-discrimination towards students with learning challenges.

☐ Instructional, administrative and support personnel in the school believe that all children can become bilingual.

☐ Instructional, administrative and support personnel in the school believe that children from minority backgrounds should be supported to maintain and develop their home language while becoming proficient in the mainstream language of instruction.

☐ Professional development is available to school personnel who need or want up-to-date information about dual-language development and children with disabilities.

☐ The school has an up-to-date and approved policy on how to identify students with common learning challenges, such as language, reading and learning impairment, and accepted procedures for providing additional support for them. All educational personnel in the school are familiar with the policy.

(Continued over page)

☐ The school administration/district guarantees that students with learning challenges and parents have access to the same range of diagnostic and support services that are available to students with learning challenges in mainstream education.

☐ Instructional and specialist support staff know how to identify and support students with special learning needs; or they know how to seek competent assistance for these purposes.

☐ As part of their routine planning, teachers know how to differentiate instruction for students with learning difficulties that do not require clinical support.

PRINCIPLE 8: Strong leadership is critical for successful dual-language teaching

☐ School administrators understand the principles of effective CLIL and are familiar with best practices for instruction in CLIL classrooms.

☐ The head of school makes provisions in the school schedule for teachers to work together collaboratively on programme development and instructional planning.

☐ The head of school collaborates with instructional and other educational personnel in the school to plan appropriate professional-development activities.

☐ The head of school and other administrative personnel support and actively express support for linguistic and cultural diversity within the school and to members of the broader community.

☐ The school, under the leadership of the head of school, has developed a mission statement or similar document that guides the co-development of all programmes in the school and has the support of all school personnel. The school's mission statement is reviewed and re-affirmed each year by all school personnel.

☐ The head of school understands the human, financial and material needs of the CLIL programme and takes an active role in fulfilling those needs.

COMPLETE CLIL UNIT-PLANNING FORM: RENEWABLE SOURCES OF ENERGY

Topic: Renewable energy

Big ideas:

(These can be identified by the teacher prior to beginning the unit; however, final big ideas will be an amalgamation of your initial ideas and big ideas that emerge from students' questions during the focused-learning phase.)

- We will learn that some sources of energy are renewable while others are not.

- We will learn which sources are renewable and how they function.

- We will learn why renewable sources of energy are becoming more important instead of or in addition to non-renewable sources.

Time frame:

2–3 weeks (this time frame was determined rather arbitrarily for this example; it will depend on how much this unit is extended into other subject areas and who teaches what part of the lesson).

Content objectives:

To describe the differences between renewable and non-renewable sources of energy.

To list five types of renewable energy: hydropower, wind power, solar energy, geothermal energy and bio energy.

To explain in general terms how any two of these types of energy function.

To give three reasons why we need to use renewable energy.

Content-obligatory language objectives:

To write or say the names of the five types of renewable energy using words such as *provide*, *system*, *result*, *use*.

To define, give examples or show what *renewable* means.

To use appropriately the phrase *X does Y by Z-ing* (e.g. wind produces energy by turning a propeller), or *X does Y in order to Z* (e.g. solar panels convert the sun's power in order to produce electricity).

To use appropriately the phrase *X does Y, therefore...* (e.g. coal contaminates the air; therefore we should use it for producing energy as little as possible) or *because X, we can Y* (e.g. because renewable-energy sources never run out we can use them for a long time) ...

Content-compatible language objectives:

To demonstrate what *light bulb*, *wind* and *waste* mean.

To define, give examples or show what energy is.

To use the future tense appropriately.

To use "because" in a sentence appropriately.

(Continued over page)

Cross-linguistic objectives:

To see if there are cognates for important words in the texts we read.

To compare the use of the negative affix *non-* in English with the way negatives are formed in the other language.

To compare how questions are formed in the two languages.

To compare where adverbs are placed in the two languages.

To compare the text used in class with a similar text of the same genre in the other language (younger students can compare concrete aspects, such as length and use of expressions, while older students can compare the tone of the piece and the way words are used to convey social values and attitudes).

Cross-cultural objectives:

To compare the level of renewable-energy use in our country to that of its neighbours and other countries around the world.

To compare the symbolic meaning that the sun, water and earth have in different communities as evidenced in myths, legends, sayings.

For older students – to analyse the reasons for differences in the levels of renewable-energy use in different countries.

General learning skills objectives:

Choose any of the skills listed in the section on general learning skills in Chapter 4 that can be brought out during the lesson; e.g. how to scan a text for key ideas; how to keep track of key ideas brought up in discussion groups.

Background knowledge needed:

Awareness of the fact that we use different sources of energy.

Awareness of what energy is used for.

Assessment:

Brainstorming and developing a KWL chart that we add to as the lesson proceeds (described in greater detail in Chapter 7).

Teacher observations with anecdotal records of what students know and do not know about the language related to the topic and the topic itself.

Entries in journals, learning logs.

Preview phase

Sample teaching activities:	Grouping arrangements:
1. Distribute energy pictures.	1. Individual or pairs
2. Students guess topic.	2. Whole class
3. Students form groups that belong together and produce a label for their group.	3. Small groups
4. Call out label for group.	4. Groups
5. Write a text describing activity or, for older students and more advanced students, what we learned.	5. Whole class
6. Build a semantic web as lesson unfolds.	6. Whole class
7. Watch video.	7. Whole class
8. Groups can reorganise as a result of what they saw on the video if they wish.	8. Groups
9. Show pictures for renewable and non-renewable energy. For students with low proficiency in the language of instruction, show examples of *new* and *renew*.	9. Whole class
10. Elicit topic and write down on an evolving lesson-plan chart.	10. Small groups and whole class

Assessment:

• Careful observation of students during preview activities.

• Use checklist to identify which of the content-obligatory language skills (vocabulary, grammar) included in your lesson plan students in general have and which they do not have.

• Anecdotal record at the end of the preview phase to summarise overall impression of students' readiness for unit with respect to language, background knowledge and interest – these impressions will be used to modify your original focused-phase plans to better reflect students' readiness for the unit.

(Continued over page)

Focused-learning phase

Sample teaching activities:	Grouping arrangements:
1. Elicit questions and write them down.	1. Pairs
2. Turn questions into big ideas.	2. Whole class
3. Determine which questions can be answered quickly; get answers.	3. Whole class
4. Discuss how we can get answers to the rest of the questions.	4. Small groups
5. Small groups choose or are assigned questions to research.	5. Groups and whole class
6. Groups return with findings and share with the rest of the class.	6. Groups and whole class
7. Summarise.	7. Whole class
8. Read text.	8. Individual, pairs and whole class
9. See if any groups need to change the information they reported on.	9. Small groups
10. Quick assessment to see if concepts are understood correctly by checking the big ideas.	10. Individual and whole class
11. Change the big-idea statements from future to past tense.	11. Individual, small group or whole class

Assessment:

Portfolio of work samples at different stages of unit; students' reflections on each piece of work in response to 'guided questions': why piece was chosen, what student likes about it; what needs more work. Entries to be made in writing to reveal writing skills; students meet with teacher in small groups (for efficiency) to discuss portfolios with teacher at mid and end points of unit.

Extension phase	
Sample teaching activities:	**Grouping arrangements:**
1. List the countries represented in the class. If all one country, pick countries on the basis of another relevant criterion. Mark countries on the map.	1. Whole class
2. Divide students into groups by country or by energy source.	2. Small groups
3. Students investigate via websites, texts, contacting embassies or consulates, universities.	3. Small groups
4. Groups return with findings and share.	4. Small groups and whole class
5. Likely for conflicting information to be found. Discuss.	5. Whole class
6. Discuss why sources of renewable energy are used differently in different regions or countries.	6. Groups and whole class

Assessment:

Learning logs: students keep learning logs of their work during this phase; students can do this in writing or use audio-recordings; students are given prior 'training' in using learning logs so that they clearly understand your expectations and reasons for their keeping logs; encourage students to make entries in logs based on out-of-school activities related to the unit of study.

Extension into family/community

Sample teaching activities:

1. Find out if any information on solar ovens showed up in the previous investigation.

2. Start collecting more information on solar ovens.

3. Display collective information on a graphic organiser.

4. Invite an expert to give a presentation on solar ovens.

5. Group A. Make a list of local organisations and service centres in the community that offer food. Group B. Calculate how much is saved by using solar oven. Group C. Find where to get materials to build oven. Group D. Make plan for building oven.

6. Groups B, C and D each write a section for the brochure. Group A puts it together.

7. Discuss pros and cons of offering a solar oven to each of the organisations identified.

8. Choose an organisation.

9. Approach the organisation and offer project, develop timeline and so on.

10. Raise funds to cover costs.

11. Build oven.

12. Show oven to school, then present to organisation.

Grouping arrangements:

1. Small groups.

2. Small groups.

3. Whole class.

4. Whole class.

5. Small group for each task, with help from Social Studies or Civics teacher (A), Science, Maths or Economics teacher (B), Arts teacher (C and D).

6. Groups and whole class with help from the Language Arts teacher.

7. Whole class.

8. Whole class with input from parents.

9. Teacher with select students.

10. Whole class with the help of a parent committee.

11. Groups under supervision of adult who knows solar ovens.

12. Whole class.

Materials

Preview:

- Pictures: sun, waterfall, river, geothermal, logs, biomass, wind, wind turbines, solar panels, solar water heaters, lightbulb, TV, radiator, plug, hot water, farm animals, food cooking, water boiling, shower

- 5- to 10-minute video

- Pictures: logs burning, wood-burning fireplace, nuclear plant, coal, running water, waterfall, plants, animals, sun

Focused learning:

- List of possible website for students to consult

- Text

Extension:

- World map

- Possible sources of information for countries

Assessment at end of unit:

- Assignment of final 'grades' will take into account each student's progress during the unit along with an assignment at the end of the unit.

- The actual 'grade' assigned to each student (e.g. letter, number or other) will depend on the school's policy

- The proportion of the final grade assigned to work during the unit will be based largely on the conference in which students discuss work in their portfolio on renewable energy, held earlier.

- A proportion of the final grade will also be based on an end-of-unit assignment – each student is given the choice to do either a written or an oral summary on renewable energy; there will be two components to the assignment: What is renewable energy, where does it come from and what are its advantages and disadvantages? And why is it important for the community to invest in renewable energy?

- Each part of the written/oral assignment will be graded using a rubric designed to reflect each part (to be determined) and this will be combined with the grade from the portfolio conference to come up with a final grade with comments.

LAST WORDS: FROM CLIL STUDENTS

Graduate: Nāwahīokalaniʻōpuʻu School, Hawaii

I luna o kēia paepae ʻana wau e ʻimi ana i ka holomua ma ka ʻoihana pāpaho hoʻokahi i mālama ʻia ma ka ʻōlelo a kuanaʻike Hawaiʻi piha a puni ka honua, ʻo ʻŌiwi TV hoʻi. Inā ʻaʻohe kumu, ʻaʻohe kahua a ʻaʻohe oʻu ʻike no koʻu kuleana he Hawaiʻi. No laila, ʻauhea ʻoukou "o ke keiki kēia, ola nā iwi o Nāwahī!'

[I seek progress for us working for ʻŌiwi TV, our sole Hawaiian language media outlet. Without the guidance of my teachers, who are indeed my family, there is no foundation for me and no means for me to realise my responsibilities as a Native Hawaiian. So, I say to you, 'Here is another child, one through whom the bones of Nāwahī shall live.'] – ʻIwalani

Grade 9 student: Dhahran Ahliyyah Schools, Kingdom of Saudi Arabia

Being in a bilingual school can be frustrating sometimes. You have to be aware of 2 different grammar systems. You have to know the right use of the punctuation marks, which is different in each language. However, I can clearly see the positive side of the school, and my school's goals. When we learn in two languages in the same time, it is easier to get introduced to new languages, and I've personally experienced that, as I am currently learning Korean. Other than languages, general learning and understanding of new things becomes much easier. Also, it is just better to know more than one language. In conclusion, I am very satisfiend with the idea of being in a bilingual school, and I competely understand the goal behind it.

Grade 6 student: Katoh Elementary School, Japan

I think the world is like a room and each country is like a plug that needs to be connected. The immersion programme helps me become bilingual so that I can communicate with different people and make these connections. I think I'm lucky to be one of these people. – Honori

Grade 12 student: Gyoshu High School, Japan

One of the benefits of being a bilingual student is that it has increased my future options. As a student trying to find solutions to local and global societal issues, the option to continue my university studies abroad provides me the opportunity to pursue an education that I feel will best enable me to meet this challenge. – Fumiko

Grade 9 student: Dhahran Ahliyyah Schools, Kingdom of Saudi Arabia

Being a dual language has helped me a lot in the past few years. Being a dual language gives me the advantage to communicate with people easier inside and outside the Arab world. In addition it gives me the opportunity to understand the thing that is in front of me in all aspects.

Meanwhile having this chance to be a dual language has helped me understand the world that I am in. In conclusion, what I can say is being in a dual language program is very beneficial in both ways: knowing the deep meaning of the world and communicating with people more effectively.

Grade 4 student: Immersion School in São Paulo, Brazil

It is good to learn English in an immersion school, because people outside of Brazil speak English, watch movies and read books all in English and also Sign on road are in English too. In School I speak English in Music, P.E, Arts, Social studies and Science classes. This is all good if you want to study in an university in the United States.

Grade 4 student: Immersion School in São Paulo, Brazil

Here in school we learn 3 languages and this is called an immersion school. If we learn English it will give us more opportunities to work in other countries. In school we learn English with Science, Social studies, Language arts, P.E and Music. Learning these things are fun and will help us in the future

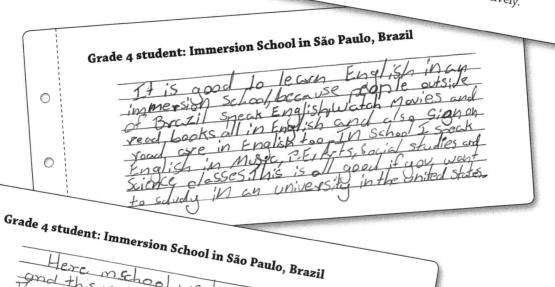

Grade 12 student: Nāwahīokalaniʻōpuʻu School, Hawaii

Makemake wau i ka hele ʻana i ke Kula ʻO Nāwahīokalaniʻōpuʻu ʻoiai makemake wau i ka pilina ma waena o ka poʻe. Loaʻa mau nā kumu e kōkua mai iā mākou haumāna. He pōmaikaʻi ka hiki ke ʻōlelo i ka ʻōlelo makuahine. Ma ka lohe mua ʻana o koʻu kupuna wahine iaʻu e ʻōlelo Hawaiʻi ana me koʻu ʻanakala, ua uē ʻo ia i ka nani o ka ʻōlelo Hawaiʻi.

[I like going to Nāwahīokalaniʻōpuʻu School because I appreciate the closeness of the people. There are always teachers to help us students. Being able to speak the mother tongue is a blessing. When my grandmother first heard me speaking Hawaiian with my uncle, she cried because speaking Hawaiian is so beautiful.]

– Kaʻōnohi

Grade 2 student: The Bilingual School of Monza, Italy

A casa parlo turco, ma anche italiano e inglese. Sento lo spagnolo nel mio cervello, il turco e l'italiano nel mio cuore, l'inglese nella pancia e il francese nelle mie mani. Quando gioco, parlo in italiano in Italia, e turco quando sono in Turchia. Quando sogno, sogni in turco e in italiano. Anche quando sono triste, parlo in turco e in italiano

At home I speak Turkish, as well as some Italian and English. I feel Spanish in my brain, Turkish and Italian in my heart, English in my tummy and French in my hands. When I play, I use Italian in Italy, but Turkish when I am playing in Turkey. When I dream, I dream in Turkish and Italian. Also when I am upset, I speak in Turkish and Italian. – Aylin

Grade 3 student: The Bilingual School of Monza, Italy

Il tronco è l'italiano e le foglie sono l'inglese perché il tronco ha bisogno delle foglie e le foglie hanno bisogno del tronco per vivere. L'italiano aiuta l'inglese e viceversa.

The body of the tree represents the Italian and the leaves represent the English language. This is because the log needs the leaves and the leaves need the log to survive. So, Italian helps English and vice versa. – Matilda

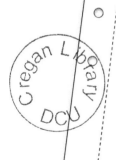

Students learning in Catalan in a school in Catalonia that uses CLIL strategies with immigrant students; these students were asked to respond to specific questions about learning Catalan and other languages; a gloss in English follows their responses.

Student X:

4. In school, do you like learning things in Catalan? Why?

Si. Perquè a l'escola i al carrer parla català aprenc sobre la biologia, valors, matemàtiques i puc llegir molt més llibres en Caltan

Yes, because at school and in the street everything is in Catalan. I learn about Biology, Maths, and everything else I can read about in Catalan.

5. What other languages would you like to learn?

Anglès pq vull anar a America i aixi els entendre.

English because I want to go to the USA and that's what they speak there.

Student Y:

4. In school, do you like learning things in Catalan? Why?

Si. Puc entendre coses que no sabia i que m'expliquen a l'escola, llegir, mirar la TV.

I like learning about things I didn't know and that are explained at school, when I read and watch TV.

5. What other languages would you like to learn?

Francès. Perquè un dia vull anar a França

French, beause one day I want to go to France.

References

Abraham, L. B. (2007). Second-language reading comprehension and vocabulary learning with multimedia. *Hispania*, 90, 98–108.

Anstrom, K., DiCerbo, P., Butler, F., Katz, A., Millet, J. & Rivera, C. (2010). *A review of the literature on academic English: Implications for K-12 English language learners*. Arlington, VA: The George Washington University Center for Equity and Excellence in Education. Retrieved from www.ceee.gwu.edu.

August, D. & Shanahan, T. (eds). (2006). *Developing literacy in second language learners. Report of the national literacy panel on minority-language children and youth*. Mahwah, NJ: Lawrence Erlbaum.

Aydemir, A., Chen, W. H. & Corak, M. (2008). Intergenerational education mobility among the children of Canadian immigrants. Institute for the Study of Labor (IZA) Discussion Paper 3759. Retrieved from http://ftp.iza.org/dp3759.pdf.

Banerjee, A. (2010). Teaching science using guided inquiry as the central theme: A professional development model for high school science teachers. *Science Educator*, 19, 1–9.

Banks, J. (2013). Approaches to multicultural curriculum reform. In J. Banks & C. Banks (eds), *Multicultural education: Issues and perspectives* (8th ed.) (pp. 181–200). New York, NY: Wiley & Sons.

Bialystok, E. (2015). Bilingualism and the development of executive function: The role of attention. *Child Development Perspectives*, 9, 117–21. doi://http://doi.dx.org/10.1111/cdep.12116.

Bialystok, E., Craik, F. I. M., Klein, R. & Viswanathan, M. (2004). Bilingualism, aging, and cognitive control: Evidence from the Simon task. *Psychology and Aging*, 19, 290–303. doi://http://dx.doi.org/10.1037/0882-7974.19.2.290.

Björklund, S. (1998). Immersion in Finland in the 1990s: A state of development and expansion. In J. Cenoz & F. Genesee (eds), *Beyond bilingualism: Multilingualism and multilingual education* (pp. 85–102). Clevedon: Multilingual Matters.

Bostwick, M. (2001). English immersion in a Japanese school. In D. Christian & F. Genesee (eds), *Bilingual education* (pp. 125–38). Alexandria, VA: TESOL.

Bruner, J. S. (1961). The act of discovery. *Harvard Educational Review*, 31, 21–32.

Bruck, M. (1978). The suitability of early French immersion programs for the language disabled child. *Canadian Journal of Education*, 3, 51–72.

Bruck, M. (1982). Language disabled children: Performance in an additive bilingual education program. *Applied Psycholinguistics*, 3, 45–60.

Callahan, R. M. & Gándara, P. C. (eds) (2014). *The bilingual advantage: Language, literacy and the US labor market*. Bristol: Multilingual Matters.

Carder, M. (2007). *Bilingualism in international schools: A model for enriching language education*. Clevedon: Multilingual Matters.

Clark, C. M. (1995). *Thoughtful teaching*. New York, NY: Teachers College.

Cloud, N., Genesee, F. & Hamayan, E. (2000). *Dual language instruction: A handbook for enriched education*. Boston: Heinle, Cengage Learning.

Cloud, N., Genesee, F. & Hamayan, E. (2009). *Literacy instruction for English language learners*. Portsmouth, NH: Heinemann.

Collins, L. & White, J. (2012). Closing the gap: Intensity and proficiency. In C. Muñoz (ed.), *Intensive exposure in second language learning* (pp. 45–65). Bristol: Multilingual Matters.

Collins, B. A., O'Connor, E. E., Suárez-Orozco, C., Nieto-Castañon, A. & Toppelberg, C. O. (2014). Dual language profiles of Latino children of immigrants: Stability and change over the early school years. *Applied Psycholinguistics*, 35(3), 581–620. doi:10.1017/S0142716412000513.

Coyle, D. (1999). Theory and planning for effective classrooms: supporting students in content and language integrated learning contexts. In J. Masih (ed.), *Learning through a foreign language*. London: CILT.

Coyle, D. (2008). CLIL – A pedagogical approach. In N. Van Deusen-Scholl & N. Hornberger (eds), *Encyclopedia of language and education* (pp. 97–111). New York, NY: Springer.

Crandall, J., with Stein, H. & Nelson, J. (2012). What kinds of knowledge and skills do general education teachers, English as a second language teachers, bilingual teachers, and support staff need to implement an effective program for English language learners? In E. Hamayan & R. Freeman Field (eds), *English language learners at school: A guide for administrators* (2nd ed.) (pp. 9–17). Philadelphia, PA: Caslon.

Crystal, D. (1997). *English as a global language*. Cambridge: Cambridge University Press.

Cummins, J. (1984). *Bilingualism and special education*. Clevedon: Multilingual Matters.

Cummins, J. (2000). *Language, power and pedagogy: Bilingual children in the crossfire*. Tonawanda, NY: Multilingual Matters.

Cummins, J. (2007). Rethinking monolingual instructional strategies in multilingual classrooms. *Canadian Journal of Applied Linguistics*, 10(2), 221–40.

Cummins, J. (2012). How long does it take for an English language learner to become proficient in a second language? In E. Hamayan & R. Freeman Field (eds), *English language learners at school: A guide for administrators* (2nd ed.) (pp. 37–9). Philadelphia, PA: Caslon.

Curtain, H. & Dahlberg, C. A. (2016). *Languages and learners: Making the match: World language instruction in K-8 classrooms and beyond*. Boston, MA: Pearson.

Dewey, J. (1933). *How we think: A restatement of the relation of reflective thinking to the educative process*. New York, NY: D. C. Heath.

de Jong, E. J. (2013) *Foundations for multilingualism in education: From principles to practice*. Philadelphia, PA: Caslon.

de Jong, E. (2014). Program design and two-way immersion programs. *Journal of Immersion and Content-Based Language Education*, 2(2), 241–56.

Dweck, C. (2006). *Mindset: The new psychology of success*. New York, NY: Random House.

Dyson, A. H. (1986). Staying free to dance with the children: The dangers of sanctifying activities in the Language Arts curriculum. *English Education*, 18, 135–46.

Echevarria, J., Vogt, E. & Short, D. (2013). *Making content comprehensible for English language learners: The SIOP model* (4th edition). New Saddle, NJ: Pearson.

Edwards, H., Wesche, M., Krashen, S., Clement, R. & Kruidenier, B. (1984). Second-language acquisition through subject matter learning: A study of sheltered Psychology classes at the University of Ottawa. *The Canadian Modern Language Review, 41*, 268–82.

Elias, M. J. & Dilworth, J. E. (2003). Ecological/developmental theory, context-based best practice and school-based action research: Cornerstones of school psychology training and policy. *Journal of School Psychology, 41*, 293–7.

Erdos, C., Genesee, F., Savage, R. & Haigh, C. (2014). Predicting risk for oral and written language learning difficulties in students educated in a second language. *Applied Psycholinguistics, 35*, 371–98. doi:10.1017/S0142716412000422.

Fogarty, R. (1991). Ten ways to integrate curriculum. *Educational Leadership, 49*(2), 61–5. Retrieved from www.ascd.org/ASCD/pdf/journals/ed_lead/el_199110_fogarty.pdf.

Fortune, T. W., Tedick, D. J. & Walker, C. L. (2008). Integrated language and content teaching: Insights from the immersion classroom. In T. W. Fortune & D. J. Tedick (eds), *Pathways to multilingualism: Evolving perspectives on immersion education* (pp. 71–96). Clevedon: Multilingual Matters.

Gallagher, E. (2008). *Equal rights to the curriculum: Many languages, one message.* Clevedon: Multilingual Matters.

García, O. (2009). *Bilingual education in the 21st century: A global perspective.* Malden, MA and Oxford: Blackwell/Wiley.

García, O., with Makar, C., Starcevic, M. & Terry, A. (2011). Translanguaging of Latino kindergarteners. In K. Potowski & J. Rothman (eds), *Bilingual youth: Spanish in English speaking societies* (pp. 33–55). Amsterdam: John Benjamins.

García, O. & Wei, L. (eds) (2014). *Translanguaging: Language, bilingualism and education.* New York, NY: Palgrave Macmillan.

Gaudet, S. & Clement, R. (2005). Identity maintenance and loss: A concurrent process among Fransaskois. *Canadian Journal of Behavioral Science, 37*(2), 110–22.

Genesee, F. (1976). The role of intelligence in second language learning. *Language Learning, 26*, 267-280.

Genesee, F. (1987). *Learning through two languages: Studies of immersion and bilingual education.* Cambridge, MA: Newbury House.

Genesee, F. (2002). Portrait of the bilingual child. In V. Cook (Ed.), *Portraits of the Second Language User.* Clevedon, Eng.: Multilingual Matters, 170–196.

Genesee, F. (2004). What do we know about bilingual education for majority language students? In T. K. Bhatia & W. Ritchie (eds), *Handbook of bilingualism and multiculturalism* (pp. 547–76). Malden, MA: Blackwell.

Genesee, F. (2007). French immersion and at-risk students: A review of research findings. *Canadian Modern Language Review, 63*, 655–88.

Genesee, F. (2008). Dual language in the global village. In T. W. Fortune & D. J. Tedick (eds), *Pathways to multilingualism: Evolving perspectives on immersion education* (pp. 22–45). Clevedon: Multilingual Matters.

Genesee, F. (2014). Is early second language learning really better? *Babylonia, 1*, 26–30.

Genesee, F. (2015). Myths about early childhood bilingualism. *Canadian Psychology, 56*(1), 6–15.

Genesee, F. & Fortune, T. (2014). Bilingual education and at-risk students. *Journal of Immersion and Content-Based Language Education*, 2(2), 165–80.

Genesee, F. & Geva, E. (2006). Cross-linguistic relationships in working memory, phonological processes, and oral language. In D. August & T. Shanahan (eds), *Developing literacy in second language learners. Report of the national literacy panel on minority-language children and youth* (pp. 175–84). Mahwah, NJ: Lawrence Erlbaum.

Genesee, F. & Lindholm-Leary, K. (2012). The education of English language learners. In K. Harris, S. Graham & T. Urdan, et al. (eds), *APA handbook of educational psychology* (Vol. III) (pp. 499–526). Washington, DC: APA Books.

Genesee, F. & Lindholm-Leary, K. (2013). Two case studies of content-based language education. *Journal of Immersion and Content-Based Language Education*, 1(1), 3–33.

Genesee, F., Lindholm-Leary, K., Saunders, W. & Christian, D. (2006). *Educating English language learners: A synthesis of research evidence*. New York, NY: Cambridge University Press.

Genesee, F., Savage, R., Erdos, E. & Haigh, C. (2013). Identification of reading difficulties in students schooled in a second language. In V. M. Gathercole (ed.), *Solutions for the assessment of bilinguals* (pp. 10–35). Clevedon: Multilingual Matters.

Gibbons, P. (1993). *Learning to learn in a second language*. Portsmouth, NH: Heinemann.

Gibbons, P. (2002). *Scaffolding language, scaffolding learning: Teaching second language learners in the mainstream classroom*. Portsmouth, NH: Heinemann.

Gonzalez, N., Moll, L. C. & Amanti, G. (2005). *Funds of knowledge: Theorizing practices in households, communities and classrooms*. Mahwah, NJ: Lawrence Erlbaum.

Goodlad, J. (1984). *A place called school*. New York, NY: McGraw-Hill.

Gottlieb, M. (2016). *Assessing English language learners: Bridges to equity. Connecting academic language proficiency to student achievement* (2nd ed.). Thousand Oaks, CA: Corwin.

Gullifer, J. W., Kroll, J. F. & Dussias, P. E. (2013). When language switching has no apparent cost: Lexical access in sentence context. *Frontiers in Psychology*, 4, 1–3. doi:10.3389/fpsyg.2013.00278.

Guthrie, J. T., Wigfield, A. & Perencevich, K. C. (eds). (2004). *Motivating reading comprehension: Concept-oriented reading instruction*. Mahwah, NJ: Lawrence Erlbaum.

Gutkin, T. B. & Nemeth, C. (1997). Selected factors impacting decision in prereferral intervention and other school-based teams: Exploring the intersection between school and social psychology. *Journal of School Psychology*, 35, 195–216.

Hamayan, E., Genesee, F. & Cloud, N. (2013). *Dual language instruction from A to Z: Practical guidance for teachers and administrators*. Portsmouth, NH: Heinemann.

Hamayan, E., Marler, B., Sanchez-Lopez, C. & Damico, J. (2007). *Special education considerations for English language learners: Delivering a continuum of services* (2nd ed.). Philadelphia, PA: Caslon.

Hattie, J. (2009). *Visible learning: A synthesis of over 800 meta-analyses relating to achievement*. London: Routledge.

Hawley, D. B. (2015). Stop, start, continue: Conceptual understanding meets applied problem solving. *Edutopia, December*. Retrieved from www.edutopia.org/blog/stop-start-continue-conceptual-meets-applied-david-hawley.

Hélot, C. (2006). Bridging the gap between prestigious bilingualism and the bilingualism of minorities: Towards an integrated perspective of multilingualism in the

French education context. In M. O'Laoire (ed.), *Multilingualism in educational settings* (pp. 49–72). Tübingen, Germany: Stauffenburg Verlag.

Hélot, C. & Young, A. (2006). Imagining multilingual education in France: A language and cultural awareness project at primary level. In O. Garcia, T. Skutnabb-Kangas & M. E. Torres Guzman (eds), *Imagining multilingual schools: Languages in education and globalization* (pp. 69–90). Clevedon: Multilingual Matters.

Hilliard, J. & Hamayan, E. (2012). How do we plan for language development? In E. Hamayan & R. Freeman Field (eds), *English language learners at school: A guide for administrators* (2nd ed.) (pp. 121–23). Philadelphia, PA: Caslon.

Himmele, P. & Himmele, W. (2011). *Total participation techniques: Making every student an active learner*. Alexandria, VA: ASCD.

Hmelo-Silver, C. (2004). Problem based learning: What and how do students learn. *Educational Psychology Review, 16*, 235–66.

Hole, S. & McEntee, G. (1999). Reflection is at the heart of practice. *Educational Leadership. 56*(8), 34–7.

Hornberger, N. & Link, H. (2012). Translanguaging and transnational literacies in multilingual classrooms: A bilingual lens. *International Journal of Bilingual Education and Bilingualism, 15*(3), 261–78.

Infante, D., Benvenuto, G. & Lastrucci E. (2009). The effects of CLIL from the perspective of experienced teachers. In D. Marsh, P. Mehisto, D. Wolff, R. Aliaga, T. Asikainen, M. J. Frigols-Martin, S. Hughes & G. Langé (eds), *CLIL practice: Perspectives from the field* (pp. 156–63). Jyväskylä, Finland: University of Jyväskylä.

International School Magazine. Retrieved from www.is-mag.co.uk/.

Jacobs, K & Cross, A. (2001). The seventh generation of Kahnawà:ke: Phoenix or dinosaur. In D. Christian & F. Genesee (eds), *Bilingual education* (pp. 109–21). Alexandria, VA: TESOL.

Jimenez, R., Garcia, G. E. & Pearson, P. D. (1996). The reading strategies of bilingual Latina/o students who are successful English readers: Opportunities and obstacles. *Reading Research Quarterly, 31*(1), 90–112.

Joaristi, L., Lizasoain, L., Lukas, J. F. & Santiago, K. (2009). Trilingualism (Spanish, English and Basque) in the educational system of the Basque country. *International Journal of Multilingualism, 6*, 105–26.

Kagan, S. (1994). *Cooperative learning.* San Clemente, CA: Kagan Publishing.

Kay-Raining Bird, E., Cleave, P. L., Trudeau, N., Thordardottir, E., Sutton, A. & Thorpe, A. (2005). The language abilities of bilingual children with Down syndrome. *American Journal of Speech-language Pathology, 14*, 187–99.

Kirschner, P. A., Sweller, J. & Clark, R. E. (2006). Why minimal guidance during instruction does not work: An analysis of the failure of constructivist, discovery, problem-based, experiential, and inquiry-based teaching, *Educational Psychologist, 41*, 75–86.

Kovács, A. & Mehler, J. (2009). Cognitive gains in 7-month-old bilingual infants. *Proceedings of the National Academy of Sciences, 106*, 6556–60.

Kroll, J. F. (2008). Juggling two languages in one mind. *Psychological Science Agenda.* Retrieved from www.apa.org/science/about/psa/2008/01/kroll.aspx.

Lambert, W. E. & Tucker, G. R. (1972). *The bilingual education of children: The St. Lambert experiment.* Rowley, MA: Newbury House.

Lee, H. (2014). Inquiry-based teaching in second and foreign language pedagogy. *Journal of Language Teaching and Research*, 5, 1236–44.

Lindholm-Leary, K J. (2001). *Dual language education*. Avon: Multilingual Matters.

Lindholm-Leary, K. J. (2005). Review of research and best practices on effective features of dual language education programs. Washington, DC: Center for Applied Linguistics. Retrieved from www.lindholm-leary.com/resources/review_research.pdf.

Lindholm-Leary, K. (2012). Success and challenges in dual language education. *Theory into Practice*, 51(4), 256–62. doi:10.1080/00405841.2012.726053.

Lindholm-Leary, K. J. & Borsato, G. (2006). Academic achievement. In F. Genesee, K. Lindholm-Leary, W. Saunders & D. Christian (eds), *Educating English language learners* (pp. 176–222). New York, NY: Cambridge University Press.

Lindholm-Leary, K. & Genesee, F. (2014). Student outcomes in one-way, two-way and indigenous language immersion programs. *Journal of Immersion and Content-Based Language Education*, 2(2), 196–209.

Lindholm-Leary, K. & Hargett, G. (2006). Evaluator's toolkit for dual language programs. Sacramento, CA: California Department of Education. Retrieved from: www.cal.org/twi/EvalToolkit/index.htm.

Lindholm-Leary, K. J. & Howard, E. (2008). Language and academic achievement in two-way immersion programmes. In T. Fortune & D. Tedick (eds), *Pathways to bilingualism: Evolving perspectives on immersion education* (pp. 177–200). Clevedon: Multilingual Matters.

Lyster, R. (1998). Negotiation of form, recasts, and explicit correction in relation to error types and learner repair in immersion classrooms. *Language Learning*, 48, 183–218.

Lyster, R. (2004). Differential effects of prompts and recasts in form-focused instruction. *Studies in Second Language Acquisition*, 26, 399–432.

Lyster, R. (2007). *Learning and teaching languages through content: A counterbalanced approach*. Amsterdam: John Benjamins.

Lyster, R., Collins, L. & Ballinger, S. (2009). Linking languages through a bilingual read-aloud project. *Language Awareness*, 18, 366–83.

Marinova-Todd, S. & Mirenda, P. (2016). Language and communication abilities of bilingual children with ASD. In J. Patterson & B. L. Rodriguez (eds), *Multilingual perspectives on child language disorders*. Bristol: Multilingual Matters.

Marshall, J. C. & Horton, R. M. (2011). The relationship of teacher-facilitated, inquiry based instruction to student higher-order thinking. *School Science and Mathematics*, 111, 93–101.

Mehisto, P. (2008). CLIL counterweights: Recognising and decreasing disjuncture in CLIL. *International CLIL Research Journal*, 1, 93–119.

Mehisto, P. (2012). *Excellence in bilingual education: A guide for school principals*. Cambridge: Cambridge University Press.

Mehisto, P. (2012). Criteria for producing CLIL learning material. *Encuentro*, 21, 15–33.

Mehisto, P. (2015). Conclusion: Forces, mechanisms and counterweights. In P. Mehisto & F. Genesee (eds), *Building bilingual education systems: Forces, mechanisms and counterweights* (pp. 269–88). Cambridge: Cambridge University Press.

Mehisto, P. & Asser, H. (2007). Stakeholder perspectives: CLIL programme management in Estonia. *International Journal of Bilingual Education and Bilingualism*, 10(5), 683–701.

Mehisto, P. & Genesee, F. (eds) (2015). *Building bilingual education systems: Forces, mechanisms, and counterweights*. Cambridge: Cambridge University Press.

Mehisto, P., Marsh, D. & Frigols, M. J. (2008). *Uncovering CLIL: Content and language integrated learning in bilingual and multilingual education*. Oxford: Macmillan.

Met, M. (1999, January). Content-based instruction: Defining terms, making decisions. *NFLC reports. Washington, DC: The national foreign language center*. Retrieved from www.carla.umn.edu/cobaltt/modules/principles/decisions.html.

Meyer, O. (2010). Towards quality-CLIL: successful planning and teaching strategies. *Pulso, 33*, 11–29. Retrieved from http://dspace.uah.es/dspace/bitstream/handle/10017/7204/Towards_Meyer_PULSO_2010.pdf?sequence=1&isAllowed=y.

Montecel, M. R. & Cortez, D. J. (2002). Successful bilingual education programs: Development and the dissemination of criteria to identify promising and exemplary practices in bilingual education at the national level. *Bilingual Research Journal, 26*, 1–21.

Mulazzi, F. & Nordmeyer J. (2012). Collaboration as professional learning, in Andrea Honigsfeld & Maria G. Dove, (eds), *Co-teaching and other collaborative practices in the EFL/ESL classroom: Rationale, research, reflections and recommendations*. Charlotte, NC: Information Age Publishing.

Muñoz, C. (ed.). (2012). *Intensive exposure in second language learning*. Bristol: Multilingual Matters.

Muñoz, C. & Singleton, D. (2011). A critical review of age-related research on L2 ultimate attainment. *Language Teaching, 44*(1), 1–35.

Myers, M. L. (2009). Achievement of children identified with special needs in two-way Spanish immersion programs. (Unpublished PhD dissertation). Faculty of Graduate School of Education and Human Development, George Washington University, Washington, DC.

Ogle, D. M. (1986). K-W-L: A teaching model that develops active reading of expository text. *Reading Teacher 39*, 564–70.

Organization for Economic Co-operation and Development. (2010). *PISA 2009 results: Learning to learn: Student engagement, strategies and practices (Volume III)*. Paris, France: PISA, OECD Publishing. doi: http://dx.doi.org/10.1787/9789264083943-en

Organization for Economic Co-operation and Development. (2013). World migration in figures. Retrieved from www.oecd.org/els/mig/World-Migration-in-Figures.pdf.

Ortlieb, E. T. & Lu, L. (2011). Improving teacher education through inquiry-based learning. *International Education Studies, 4*(3), 41–6. doi: 10.5539/ies.v4n3p41.

Osterman, K. F. & Kottamp, R. B. (2004). *Reflective practice for educators*. Thousand Oaks, CA: Corwin Press.

Paradis, J., Genesee, F. & Crago, M. (2011). *Dual language development and disorders: A handbook on bilingualism and second language learning* (2nd ed.). Baltimore, MD: Brookes.

Riches, C. & Genesee, F. (2006). Cross-linguistic and cross-modal aspects of literacy development. In F. Genesee, K. Lindholm-Leary, W. Saunders & D. Christian (eds), *Educating English language learners: A synthesis of research evidence* (pp. 64–108). New York, NY: Cambridge University Press.

Saunders, W. & Goldenberg, C. (2010). Research to guide English language development instruction. In *Improving education for English learners: Research-based approaches* (pp. 21–82). Sacramento, CA: California Department of Education.

Scarcella, R. (2003). *Accelerating academic English: A focus on the English learner.* Oakland, CA: Regents of the University of California.

Shoebottom, P. (2009). Academic success for non-native English speakers in English-medium international schools: The role of the secondary ESL department. Retrieved from http://esl.fis.edu/teachers/support/naldic.pdf.

Skutnabb-Kangas, T. (1988). Multilingualism and the education of minority children. In T. Skutnabb-Kangas & J. Cummins (eds), *Minority education: From shame to struggle* (pp. 9–44). Avon: Multilingual Matters.

Snow, C. E., Met, M. & Genesee, F. (1989). A conceptual framework for the integration of language and content in second/foreign language instruction. *TESOL Quarterly, 23,* 201–17.

Sparks, D. (2002). *Designing powerful professional development for teachers and principals.* Oxford, OH: National Staff Development Council.

Slaughter, H. (1997). Indigenous language immersion in Hawai'i: A case study of Kula Kaiapuni Hawai'i. In R. K. Johnson & M. Swain (eds), *Immersion education: International perspectives* (pp. 105–29). Cambridge: Cambridge University Press.

Stevens, F. (1983). Activities to promote learning and communication in the second language classroom. *TESOL Quarterly, 17,* 259–72.

Thompson, C. J. (2006). Preparation, practice, and performance: An empirical examination of the impact of standards based instruction on secondary students' math and science achievement. *Research in Education, 81*(1), 53–62.

Tompkins, J. & Orr, A. (2011). *Best practices and challenges in Mi'maq and Maliseet/Wolastoqi language immersion programs.* The Atlantic Aboriginal Economic Development Integrated Research Program. Atlantic Policy Congress and Saint Francis Xavier University.

UK Department of Education. (Jan. 2016). *Revised CGSE and equivalent results in England 2014–2015.* Retrieved from https://www.gov.uk/government/uploads/system/uploads/attachment_data/file/494073/SFR01_2016.pdf.

Usborne, E., Peck, J., Smith, D. & Taylor, D. M. (2011). Learning through an aboriginal language: The impact on students' English and aboriginal language skills. *Canadian Journal of Education, 34*(4), 200–215.

Valdés, G. (1997). The teaching of Spanish to bilingual Spanish-speaking students: Outstanding issues and unanswered questions. In M. C. Colombi & F. X. Alarcon (eds), *La ensñnanza del espanol a hispanohablantes: Praxis y teoria* (pp. 93–101). Boston, MA: Houghton Mifflin.

Van Lier, L. (1996). *Interaction in the language curriculum: Awareness, autonomy, and authenticity.* London: Longman.

Vygotsky, L. (1978). *Mind in society: The development of higher psychological processes* (pp. 79–91). Cambridge, MA: Harvard University Press.

Wilson, W. H. & Kamanā, K. (2011). Insights from indigenous language immersion in Hawai'i: The case of Nāwahī school. In D. J. Tedick, D. Christian & T. W. Fortune (eds), *Immersion education: Practices, policies and possibilities* (pp. 36–57). Clevedon: Multilingual Matters.

Index

academic language skills 36, 69, 71, 101–4, 120, 170, 173, 201, 215, 218, 225
additional language
    instruction 1, 2, 7, 17, 21, 27, 31–3, 36, 37, 40, 43–5, 48–51, 57, 58, 68–9, 79, 117, 174–5, 224, 226
    learning 1, 2, 4, 5, 31, 40, 117
Additional Resources 18, 46, 54, 92, 98, 104, 128, 138, 148, 152
Arabic 17, 75, 86–7, 137, 145, 181, 182
Arts 76–7
assessment
    classroom-based 24–6, 31, 46, 191–221, 227
    goals of 189, 191-6
    tests 191, 196, 213–18
    tools
        conferences vi, 204, 211, 213, 220, 225
        dialogue journals and learning logs 25, 134, 199, 204, 212–13, 230
        observation 25, 134, 151, 204–9, 220, 221, 230–1
        portfolios 25, 204, 210–11, 213, 215, 220, 221, 232

Banks, James 180–5
Basque 22, 59
big ideas 23, 115, 120, 122, 129, 130, 144, 147, 148–54, 158, 176, 229, 232
bilingualism 1, 2–5, 17, 18, 22, 28, 29, 43, 47, 49, 50, 69, 70, 88, 89, 94, 96–99, 106, 109, 112, 178, 195, 205
    additive 42–4, 62, 73, 178
    developmental education programmes 67
    cognitive benefits of 69
    myths around 46
    simultaneous 47–9, 85
Biology 38, 96, 155, 182, 238
Brazil 60, 167, 237
business community 176–7

Cambridge International Examinations 5, 15
Canada 2, 20, 33, 37, 42, 44, 49, 62, 64, 179
Checklists 107, 115, 120, 121, 164, 169, 224–8
Chinese 71, 137
CLIL (definition) 27
    context-sensitive vii
    dual-language (DL-CLIL) 8, 16, 32, 42, 66–73, 81, 82, 93, 116, 131, 174, 175, 203
    foreign-language 6, 76–78
    key principles of 29–54, 97, 222–28
    monolingual (ML-CLIL) 8, 16, 66, 73–6, 80, 82, 112, 117, 174, 175, 203
    objectives of
        primary 23, 100–6
        secondary
            cross-cultural viii, 21, 23, 67, 106, 110–11, 115, 116, 118, 122, 125, 130, 156, 166, 181, 184, 230
            cross-linguistic viii, 21, 23, 44, 72, 75, 92, 99, 106, 108–10
            general learning skills 21, 23, 99, 106, 108, 111–15, 117, 122, 125, 130, 150, 151, 230
    partial 19, 60, 81, 175
collaboration
    among students 120, 143, 164, 225
    among teachers 21, 51, 58, 85, 93, 117, 119, 167–9, 174, 175, 214, 215,
    between teachers and students 50, 77, 165, 227
Colombia 3, 10, 38–9, 178
community vii, 2, 4, 5, 8, 9, 10–17, 21, 24, 28, 41, 53, 59, 64, 66, 74, 81, 84, 87–90, 98, 109, 110, 111, 115, 116, 119, 121, 136, 145, 147, 157, 163, 165, 176–89, 194, 195, 197, 203, 221, 228, 234, 235
coordination 163–90

across grade levels 24, 173
among CLIL teachers 24, 72, 90, 106, 113, 163, 166, 168, 172
and technology 172
content-language 107
involving students 164, 165
outside school 24, 163, 176–89
strategies for 24, 170
   additive approach 181–3
   contributions approach 180–1
   transformation approach 183
within the school 173–5
cultures 3, 6, 71, 73, 112, 120, 136, 161, 175, 177, 180–3, 197, 202, 226

direct instruction 30, 36, 114, 143, 146, 224
Drama 58, 76–7, 155
dual language (DL) 8, 13, 20, 30, 31, 37, 41–7, 48, 49, 50, 51, 53, 54, 57, 66, 80, 81, 86, 94, 98–100, 112, 125–7, 151, 177, 182, 193, 204, 205, 227, 228, 237

Earth Sciences 181
Economics 182, 188, 189, 234
educational contexts 6–7, 17–20, 93, 106, 112–13, 135–6, 174
English 3–6, 8–9, 12–14, 16–19, 22, 27, 32, 34, 38, 41, 42, 44, 49, 52, 53, 56, 59, 62, 65–71, 75, 79–82, 87, 89, 104, 108, 110, 111, 113, 130, 135–8, 140, 141, 159, 167, 170, 172, 178, 179, 202, 214–15, 230, 238
as an additional language (EAL) 17, 81, 130, 135, 170, 172, 214–15
Estonian 22, 195
Europe 4, 8, 56, 92, 136, 152, 181, 200, 202, 218
European Common Market 56
explicit language instruction 31, 33–7, 55, 97, 111–12, 114, 132, 133, 182, 197, 224–6

4 Cs (content, cognition, communication, culture) 10, 39
Finnish 22
folktales 156, 180, 182
first language (L1) viii, 30, 31, 32, 43, 44, 45, 47, 49, 56, 57, 60–5, 69, 82, 88, 110, 167, 193, 199, 226
foreign language (FL) 4, 5, 6, 7, 13, 14, 16, 27, 55, 56, 58, 76, 77, 91, 165, 166, 204
formulaic language 145

French 5, 9, 14, 32, 34, 41, 44, 52, 53, 62, 71, 82, 88, 91, 110, 137, 145, 177, 178, 203, 238
functional language proficiency 7, 9, 14, 28, 32, 36, 49, 56, 62, 76, 97, 126

Gakuen, Katoh 19, 236
German 4, 12, 16, 52, 65, 81, 88, 145, 203

Hawaiian 22, 49, 236
heritage language 12, 17, 66–75, 89
History 15, 22, 36, 72, 79, 92, 94, 110, 126, 156, 181, 182

immersion (IMM) 5–9, 18–20, 22, 34, 36 42, 44, 49, 52–3, 58– 62, 67, 167, 174, 177, 179, 237
two-way immersion programmes (TWI) 67
immigrant students 11, 12, 13, 17, 18, 26, 27, 41, 44, 58, 59, 65, 66, 68, 70, 73, 74, 82, 94, 96, 97, 109, 176, 197, 202, 238
immigration 2, 74
indigenous languages 3, 6–7, 10, 11, 12, 17, 22, 38, 41, 42, 44, 65–76
indigenous-language students (ILS) 8, 11, 18, 27, 65–76, 82, 94, 96, 97, 109, 197, 202
instruction
activity-based 40, 143–4, 148
enquiry-based vii, 143, 147–8
language and content 17, 21, 31, 35, 37, 64, 83, 84, 85, 91, 106, 121, 145, 224
integration
across content areas 90–3
additive approach 180, 181–3
contributions approach 180–1
proactive 35
reactive 35
social action approach 180, 184, 185
transformation approach 180, 183–4
International Baccalaureate 5, 15, 19 137
internationalisation 1
international schools (INT) 4, 7, 15–17, 18, 27, 52–3, 58, 79, 81, 82, 136–7, 145, 177, 182, 215
Italian 7, 14–15, 76– 77, 80, 91, 111, 174, 238

Japanese 17, 19–20, 22, 32

K-12 6, 83, 170

Kazakh 4
Korean 136, 145

language allocation models 94–5, 121
Language Arts 27, 85, 91–3, 100, 105, 111, 146, 155, 156, 166, 182, 186, 188, 189, 210, 215, 224, 234
language status 31, 38, 41–4, 49, 74, 95, 96, 109, 110, 135, 136, 139, 159, 175, 225
language learning versus acquisition 6, 19, 25, 33, 37, 43, 52, 57, 68, 69, 73, 76, 78, 91, 92, 104, 154, 179, 193, 199, 200, 202
leadership
   teacher 17, 31, 167, 172, 228
   school 50, 51–3, 228
learning
   student-constructed 154
   teacher-constructed 154
lesson and unit planning viii, 21, 23, 37, 64, 75, 78, 100, 106, 113–23 125, 128–30, 133, 134, 138, 142, 148, 153, 158, 172, 196, 221, 225, 229, 231
literacy 8, 11, 19, 36, 45, 67, 69–72, 81, 89, 137, 178, 204, 226
Literature 19, 27, 58, 92, 156,

majority language 5, 6, 8, 12, 13, 16, 28, 41, 42, 44, 66–7, 69–75, 91, 98, 99, 109, 110, 135, 145, 195, 200, 203
   students 6, 18, 32, 42, 62, 64, 68, 75, 110, 139, 165, 200, 201
   teachers 72, 74, 91
Mathematics 1, 2, 10, 22, 24, 27, 35, 37, 56, 57, 58, 62, 71–3, 91, 92, 100, 103, 105, 113, 126, 156, 182, 188,
Media 77, 156
minority language 28, 178
   students 6, 8, 13, 32, 36, 42, 44, 51, 62, 64, 66–74, 76, 81, 98, 99, 109, 135, 136, 140, 174, 194, 195, 200, 203, 204
   teachers 72, 225
Mohawk 22
multiculturalism 18, 180, 183, 215
multilingualism 3–5, 53, 56, 80–1, 89, 98, 182, 215
Music 5, 15, 76–7, 91, 96, 126, 156, 163, 174, 182, 186

national language 3, 8, 11, 12, 16, 68, 72, 73, 96
Natural Science 79

Navaho 182
non-native languages 5, 18, 91, 112
North America 36, 52, 136, 202

oral language 13, 36, 57, 59, 66, 68, 69, 71, 74, 71

Personal Perspectives 10, 14, 19, 34, 38, 52, 60, 76, 80, 86, 88, 126, 136, 167, 170, 176, 178, 204, 214
Peruvian 12, 66
Physical Education 72, 96, 163
Physics 111, 156
policy-makers 2, 25, 29
Polish 12, 65
plurilingualism 88–9
prior knowledge 127, 131–4, 141, 147
Psychology 156, 182

qualifications, teacher 23, 116–19
Quebec 178
Quechua 12, 66

refugees 2, 70, 74, 176
Research Notes 2, 3, 9, 13, 32, 36, 40, 42, 45, 48, 51, 69, 87, 95, 109, 143, 147, 168
Russian 4, 22, 195

Saudi Arabia 86, 158, 237, 238
scaffolding viii, 19, 33, 62, 85, 88, 120, 126, 131–3, 143, 150, 224
Science 2, 10, 22, 23, 25, 27, 35–9, 52, 56, 57, 58, 62, 68, 71, 72, 73, 75, 86–7, 91, 92, 100, 101, 105, 108, 110, 126, 127, 140, 155, 156, 168, 181, 186, 188, 189, 200, 206, 207, 210, 216, 218, 234
secondary school 4, 9, 14, 15, 19, 34, 57, 60, 76, 85, 176, 185
second language (L2) vii–viii, 1, 4, 9, 14, 19, 20, 27, 37, 43, 56, 61, 62, 67, 77, 78, 86, 88, 104, 105, 167, 168, 179, 197, 199, 200, 201, 218
semantic web 134–5, 139, 142, 231
Serbian 182
Shanghai 170
Sikuani 11
social action *see* integration
Social Studies 79, 91, 100, 102, 182, 188, 189, 234
socio-economic status 33, 38, 40, 47, 49, 68
Sociology 182, 188
Spanish 11, 12, 14, 16, 22, 38, 44, 52, 53,

56, 59, 66, 67, 71, 75, 77, 80, 108, 110, 111, 126, 127, 135, 140, 141, 159, 177, 178, 202, 238
Special Notes 22, 30, 62, 90, 131, 138, 145, 193, 203
St. Lambert total immersion programme 9
student apathy 37
student engagement 31, 37, 39, 40, 45, 78, 89, 114, 144, 206, 225
students with academic learning difficulties 29, 47, 49, 68, 193, 228
Swedish 22

Taiwan 214
teacher journals 206, 208
tests
    closed-ended response 147, 216–18
    limited response 216–19
    open-ended response 218–19
Theatre 15, 186
third language (L3) viii, 2, 4, 79, 81, 138, 226

three-phase lesson planning 21, 84, 113, 125–8, 161
    preview phase 21, 23, 113–15, 123, 125–8, 130, 131, 132–5, 139–42, 143, 148, 150, 155, 160, 221, 224, 231
    focused-learning phase 113–15, 123, 125, 129, 131, 133, 134, 143, 146, 148, 153, 154, 221, 229, 232
    extension phase 23, 113–16, 119, 123, 125, 127, 128, 154, 156–7, 160, 163, 185–6, 188, 208, 221, 233
translanguaging viii, 11, 43, 89, 109
Turkish 12, 65, 238

UK 12, 13, 15, 65, 66
US (see also USA and United States) 12, 13, 15, 20, 42, 44, 53, 62, 66–8, 70, 109, 126, 170, 176–7, 178, 182, 204, 215, 238

Vietnamese 17, 82

Welsh 12, 66